DA
195
.W57   Wise, Terence.
Cop. 1   1066, year of
         destiny

DA
195   Wise, Terence.
.W57   1066, year of
cop. 1   destiny

DATE	BORROWER'S NAME	18.95
4-2-81		

4-2-81

626345

1066: Year of Destiny

1066: Year of Destiny

TERENCE WISE

OSPREY

First published in 1979 by Osprey Publishing Limited
12–14 Long Acre, London WC2E 9LP
A member company of the George Philip Group

British Library Cataloguing in Publication Data
Wise, Terence
1066, year of destiny.
1. Great Britain—History—Norman
period, 1066–1154
I. Title II. Ten sixty six, year of destiny
942.02′1   DA195 , W57 copy. 1
ISBN 0-85045-320-8

Designed by Bob Hook
Artwork by Richard Scollins
Filmset and printed by
BAS Printers Limited, Over Wallop, Hampshire

Contents

For my wife Shirley

INTRODUCTION

Over the years many books have been published on the subject of the battle of Hastings and the events leading up to it, for the year 1066 is dear to most English hearts. Generally speaking, these books fall into two main categories; academic works studded with extensive footnotes and quotations from primary sources, with discussion on the possible meaning behind those quotes, and plausible theories advanced to fill the gaps left by the contemporary historians; and those books, often by historians, which approach the subject from a storyteller's standpoint to produce an exciting and highly readable account of the events. And what a stirring tale 1066 can be, with all the basic ingredients of a masterpiece of fiction, culminating in the noble death of Harold at the battle of Hastings.

The academic works are vastly interesting to all those with an open and inquisitive mind, but they are not intended to be read straight through for pure enjoyment, rather they are meant to be dipped into to gain knowledge and provoke thought: they strive to throw new light on older or original works and are intended for reference and study during research. On the other hand, the storyteller's approach provides excellent reading, and the sequence of historic events makes the reader hurry through to the irrevocable drama at the end. But all too often this second type of book tells us only what we wish to hear – that William the Bastard was arrogant and brutal, and cheated Harold (and by implication all of us) of his Saxon birthright, whereas Harold was good and honest, and lost because he was so noble, and just plain unlucky, in the manner of so many literary innocents. The authors of these books also advance theories that seem plausible enough, but which all too often, when placed in the context of the period and studied more deeply, turn out to be utterly false, and have presumably been put forward only to convert the reader to the author's personal beliefs. One ends up distrusting everything written by these authors, some of whom are well known and highly regarded writers of historical works. How fiercely must men have felt nine centuries ago for their prejudices still to influence our thinking!

This particular book has two aims: to strike a posture somewhere between the academic textbooks and 'historical novels' mentioned above, so as to provide a readable but I hope unprejudiced account of the events of 1066, and to concentrate on the military aspects of that year, with first and last chapters which show the situation before and after the military campaigns of that fateful summer.

You will find my account of the events of 1066 often differs from the generally accepted views, yet all the theories used here to knit together the fragments of contemporary evidence are those accepted by most modern historians. If you enjoy reading this book and take a fresh and thoughtful look at the evidence presented here, I will have succeeded in my aim. If you then pursue the matter further via the works in my bibliography, perhaps there is hope for Truth after all.

Terence Wise
Doncaster   October 1978

1
The Reign
of Edward the
Confessor

On 5 January, 1066, Edward I of England died at Westminster Palace, the last king of the great Saxon house of Cerdic. His marriage in 1045 to Edith, daughter of the Earl Godwine of Wessex, had produced no children, and Harold Godwineson was quickly and apparently unanimously chosen as his successor by the *Witena gemot*, the king's council of earls, ecclesiastical magnates and other advisers. Contemporary chroniclers disagreed over the validity of Harold's accession to the throne and historians still argue about who that successor should really have been, which is perhaps appropriate, for Harold's rivals pressed their claims to the limit, with the momentous results which are the subject of this book.

The main problem at the death of Edward arose from the conditions which traditionally governed the selection of an English king: that he should be of the blood royal; that if the dying king was respected and named a successor, then that person be favourably considered, and that he should have the strength, both of character and position, to rule the kingdom justly and wisely. This ensured that, although only members of the royal house were eligible, the best man was chosen from amongst them. In January 1066 there was no one man who met all these requirements, but there were several who claimed at least one of them. This inevitably caused a number of rivals to come forward, all eager to gain control of such a rich kingdom.

That a variety of candidates should exist at all stems from the close link between England and Normandy at the end of the 10th century and the conquest of England (1013–16) by King Sven Forkbeard of Denmark and his son Knut. Therefore, it is necessary to go back to the turn of the century to understand fully the position in January 1066.

The main key to the succession problem was Emma, sister of Richard II, Duke of Normandy, who in 1002 became the second wife of Aethelred of England. England and Normandy were already linked commercially by a thriving trade between Rouen and London, and politically by the great Viking incursions of the 10th century, which had created a Scandinavian aristocracy in both Normandy and the Danelaw in England. The kings of England, faced with the problem of maintaining authority over their Scandinavian subjects, and continually threatened with invasion and perhaps conquest by the Danes, naturally sought the support of the Norman dukes, the closest and strongest of allies, and the mutual interests of the two dynasties had been recognized as early as 991, when a pact between them was ratified at Rouen under papal sponsorship. The marriage of Aethelred and Emma was therefore an important dynastic alliance, which both Aethelred and Richard of Normandy must have foreseen would have far-reaching consequences – which they both desired.

Emma had two sons by Aethelred, Edward (later Edward I of England) and Alfred, who were thus cousins of William the Bastard, grandson of Richard II of Normandy. And it was natural therefore that when in 1013 Sven Forkbeard launched his last great invasion of England, Aethelred, Emma and their two sons fled across the Channel to the court of Emma's brother for safety.

Aethelred returned to England in 1014 to fight his last and unavailing war against Sven's son, Knut, and he died early in 1016. The struggle was continued by his son of his first marriage, Edmund II (known as Ironside), and England was divided between Edmund (the south) and Knut (the Danelaw) until Edmund's murder in the same year. Knut was now King of all England, and took a number of steps to secure the throne and his line of succession. First, Edmund's brother Eadwig was murdered. Next Edmund's sons, Edmund and Edward, were sent abroad, possibly with the intention that they be murdered once out of the country. Edmund was a baby of but a few months and, possibly because of their extreme youth, both boys survived to live in exile at the court of the King of Hungary, where Edmund subsequently died. Edward (the Aethling) married a Hungarian princess and achieved a high position at the court.

To make absolutely sure of the succession, Knut then had Aethekweard, descended from Alfred the Great's elder brother and a member of the royal house, murdered, together with several prominent noblemen. And, finally, in 1017 he married Aethelred's widow Emma, despite the fact that he already had a common law wife named Aelfgifu, daughter of the former earl of Northumbria, and had had two sons by her. (The sons of Scandinavian nobles frequently took common law wives in their youth, and neither the wife's status nor that of any sons by her seems to have been affected by any later marriage entered into for purely political purposes.)

Emma's family belonged to the Viking aristocracy of Normandy, so Knut's marriage to her was a most astute move, for she was acceptable both to his Danish followers and to the English, whose queen she had been, while any sons he had by her would supplant Aethelred's sons, Edward and Alfred, who remained in exile in Normandy. This move was confirmed by Emma herself, who made one condition to the marriage – that any son she should have by Knut would be his lawful successor. The condition was probably made to ensure that Knut's sons by Aelfgifu did not gain the throne, but also had the effect of pushing her own sons by Aethelred farther back in the succession.

Knut died in 1035 and should have been succeeded by Hordaknut, his son by Emma, but Hordaknut was in Denmark, opposing a new northern leader, Magnus, who was threatening to take Norway out of Knut's 'empire'. England at once split into two factions, the shires south of the Thames under the leadership of the queen supporting Hordaknut, and the shires north of the Thames wanting to wait and see what happened in Scandinavia, with a regency in the meantime under Knut's son by Aelfgifu, Harald Harefoot.

It was at this point that Godwine came to the fore. Godwine had risen to power under Knut, married the sister of Knut's brother-in-law, and been granted the earldom of Wessex. He had become Knut's chief adviser in England, and now the queen looked to him for support. An emergency meeting of the *Witena gemot* was held at Oxford and it was decided that the kingdom should be temporarily partitioned, the queen to remain at Winchester with Hordaknut's housecarls, with Godwine in control of his own earldom and the whole of the south; and Harald Harefoot to control the rest of the realm. With a vast earldom and its accompanying riches at stake, Godwine appears to have played both sides, remaining with the queen in case Hordaknut was successful, yet perhaps already Harald Harefoot's man, for when, soon after the *Witenagemot* broke up, Harald sent a band of housecarls to Winchester to seize the royal treasure, Godwine avoided a confrontation. The passing of the treasure to Harald, without resistance from Godwine, did much to sway the waverers to Harald's cause.

In 1036 Aethelred's sons crossed the Channel to land on the south coast with a strong bodyguard of Norman mercenaries. Ostensibly they had come to visit their mother at Winchester, but may possibly have intended making an attempt on the crown while Knut's sons were at variance. Leaving Edward at Winchester, Alfred set out for London to meet Harald. He was met *en route* by Godwine, who escorted him to Guildford for an overnight stop and had Alfred's followers billeted in small groups about the town. Godwine then discreetly faded from the scene, and during the night Harald's men arrived to arrest Alfred and his men. Some managed to escape, but most were put in irons and afterwards sold as slaves or blinded, scalped, or had their hands and feet cut off. Some 600 other men were also put to death in Guildford, suggesting Alfred may already have gained some followers in England. Queen Emma at once shipped Edward back to Normandy, where the previous year William the Bastard had become duke (in name only) at the age of about seven. She was unable to save Alfred, however, and he was taken by ship to the Isle of Ely, where his eyes were torn out and he was left in the care of the monks. He died shortly afterwards.

Without Godwine's active support the queen was now powerless, and in 1037 Harald Harefoot became Harald I of England, Hordaknut being abandoned by the last of his supporters 'because he was too long in Denmark'.* Harald at once drove Emma from England and she found asylum in Flanders, where she died in 1052.

Harald Harefoot died in March 1040. Hordaknut arrived that summer with a fleet of sixty ships and was at once accepted as king. He ordered an enquiry into the death of his half-brother Alfred, at which Godwine was found innocent of complicity in the crime, but Godwine's gift to Hordaknut of a magnificent warship manned by a crew of eighty, each bearing a specially wrought battle-axe and wearing twelve ounces of gold in the form of bracelets, throws suspicion on the verdict.

Hordaknut's reign was brief and unpopular: he died in June 1042 of convulsions, at the age of only twenty-five, while attending a wedding feast.

Between them Knut and Aethelred had had four wives, and from these four separate unions has sprung seventeen known children. In 1042 there was only one male child surviving from these four families; Edward, son of Emma and Aethelred, still in exile at the Norman court. He was accepted at once by the *Witena gemot* and people of England, and crowned Edward I at Winchester on the first day of Easter 1043. He was then almost forty, and had been in exile for thirty years.

Edward could have had little or no expectation of becoming king of England, particularly after his abortive visit to that country in 1036, and he came to the throne a stranger to the kingdom and a complete foreigner by upbringing: he spoke Norman-French with more ease than his native tongue, and had

*Anglo-Saxon Chronicle

ideals, concepts, obligations and friendships which were all alien
to the English. Yet because of his parents and royal blood he
was welcomed as king by both the Saxon and Scandinavian
factions in England, and at the same time bore the goodwill of
Normandy. His father had forged the first dynastic link with
Normandy, and if ever an 11th-century king of England had a
chance to bring peace and prosperity to the realm it was
Edward. Yet his success was no mean feat; in the long run,
Edward survived his enemies and kept his kingdom intact by
diplomacy and compromise, and his reign was notable for its
peacefulness and longevity in an era when both were unusual.

But Edward was dependent on the support of his earls, and
chief among these was Godwine of Wessex, controller of the
richest and most heavily populated earldom. It was no surprise,
therefore, when in 1045 he married Godwine's daughter Edith,
even though Edward probably regarded Godwine as the
murderer of his brother.

Both sides benefited by the marriage, the king by the support
of Godwine and his sons, the Godwine family by the granting
of more lands: Swein, the eldest son, receiving an earldom
which included a sizeable portion of southern Mercia; Harold,
his second son, receiving the earldom of East Anglia; and
Beorn Estrithson, a nephew of Godwine, receiving an earldom
in the east midlands. The Godwine family now controlled the
whole of southern England as far north as Bristol and Oxford,
the Mercian shires of Oxford, Hereford and Gloucester, the
whole of East Anglia and probably the shires of Cambridge and
Huntingdon.

Nor should it have been any surprise to the English earls that
Edward should wish to maintain strong links with Normandy.
He owed much to the dukes of Normandy and, with the
constant possibility of an invasion from Denmark to re-
establish Scandinavian rule, it was natural he should turn, like
his father, to a closer alliance with Normandy as a common
defence against the northern threat. However, at this date
William of Normandy was still only a pawn in the power game
and in 1047 (at the age of nineteen or twenty) he was faced by
the revolt of his barons: it was to be another three years before

he could be sure of his dukedom. Although he must inevitably have felt committed to some extent to supporting Edward, he was too busy maintaining his own position to be able to do anything constructive at this time.

Therefore, in the first eight years of Edward's reign, his court remained much like those of his immediate predecessors, strongly Scandinavian in composition. Although he did introduce a number of Normans into the kingdom, as had his mother in 1003, few of them were men of the first rank. In fact almost all were his personal household officers and clerics, or fighting men, the latter employed on the terms which English kings had been giving to Scandinavians for almost half a century. Such men were the Norman Richard fitz Scrob, a housecarl who probably had lands granted to him in the west midlands as a reward for good service: the Frenchman Alfred, Edward's Marshal, who had estates in Herefordshire and Worcestershire: the Norman Osbern Pentecost, a soldier of fortune who built a castle in the Hereford marches, which he subsequently surrendered on going north to take service with Macbeth, king of the Scots: Ralph, a nephew of Edward, who had large estates in Herefordshire, Worcestershire and Gloucestershire, and was an earl before 1051: Odda, who was made Earl of Devon, Somerset, Dorset and Cornwall in 1051: the Breton Ralf of Gael, who settled in East Anglia: Robert fitz Wimarc, who may perhaps have been half Breton but was related to William and Edward and also had lands in East Anglia: and the brother of William's steward (William fitz Osbern), who became one of Edward's priest scribes and held part of the lands of the great church of Bosham, in Godwine's own earldom.

The situation was slightly different in the Church, for whilst Edward could not replace the English magnates, the benefices of the Church were largely in his gift and he granted important bishoprics to Normans: to his friend Robert, Abbot of Jumièges, the See of London in 1044, and to Ulf, a Norman priest in his household, the bishopric of Dorchester in 1049. But of the ten ecclesiastical offices which fell vacant between 1043 and 1051, seven were filled by Englishmen, and nowhere is there any real evidence of a build-up of royal or Norman favourites in key positions. Admittedly two Normans were earls and two others held the vital ecclesiastical posts of London and Canterbury, but Edward appears to have been surprisingly moderate in his appointment of Normans.

The Archbishop of Canterbury died in October 1050, and there seems to have been a struggle between Edward, who wished to appoint Robert of Jumièges, and Godwine, who tried to install a relative. At the *Witena gemot* held in March 1051, Godwine was overruled and Robert of Jumièges elected. The Norman already had considerable influence in the royal council and was a principal opponent of Godwine. His elevation caused much resentment amongst the Saxons, and the *Vita Edwardi Regis* tells us that the new archbishop 'began to provoke and oppose the earl with all his strength and might' and accused him of invading the lands of Canterbury.

Godwine might well have been guilty of such a charge, and would certainly have had a grudge against the new archbishop, but it would seem that greater events were already astir that caused Godwine to fear for his future. An article by T. J. Oleson suggests convincingly that sometime before the elevation of Robert of Jumièges, Edward had already decided to promise the succession to the Duke of Normandy, possibly openly – at the March *Witena gemot*. Such a move would not have been extraordinary. Edward's five-year-old marriage to Edith had not produced children and the king would naturally wish to ensure the succession. All his sympathies would lean towards his cousin William, who was by now achieving great stature in western Europe and attracting a number of leading magnates to his support. Normandy was England's natural ally against the northmen, and William could unite the two lands to prevent any likelihood of another Scandinavian conquest of England in the future. Edward may have been prejudiced in favour of William, but he may also have been choosing the best path for England.

Assuming that Edward had decided early in 1051 to promise the throne to William, the opportunity to convey this decision to Normandy occurred shortly afterwards, when Robert of

Jumièges set off for Rome to receive his archbishop's pallium, the symbol of the jurisdiction delegated to him by the Holy See, from the Pope: in fact one suspects that Edward's decision and the archbishop's appointment may well have been part of the same political manoeuvre.

The archbishop journeyed to Rome and back between mid-Lent and 27 June, 1051, passing through Normandy *en route*. If such a promise was conveyed to William at all, it is most likely to have been at this time, and this interpretation of the various chronicles is the one now accepted by most historians.

This makes the next incident most significant: the visit some time in July of Count Eustace II of Boulogne to his brother-in-law, King Edward. Florence of Worcester and the E version of the Anglo-Saxon Chronicle, the latter written at Canterbury and the best informed about affairs in the south-east, though pro-Godwine, both state that Eustace visited the king, at that time in Gloucester, then journeyed to Dover to embark for Normandy. We cannot now tell what transpired between Eustace and Edward, but it is not unreasonable to suppose that, if Edward had promised the throne to William, an embassy would have been sent to formally acknowledge such a dramatic development. Some historians go so far as to suggest that Edward may have pledged the important port and city of Dover to William as a sign of good faith, and certainly this does make more understandable the prominence given to Dover in Harold's oath to William in 1064.

His mission fulfilled, Eustace headed for Dover, and here we do know what happened. Seeking overnight accommodation for his men, Eustace seems to have adopted a rather arrogant attitude in the choosing of billets, and a fracas ensued in which at least seven and possibly as many as nineteen Normans were killed, together with about twenty townsmen. The people of Dover crowded into the streets and Eustace fled for his life, with only a few of his followers, returning to the king's court to seek Edward's protection. The remainder of Eustace's men appear to have occupied Dover 'castle', an Anglo-Saxon burh within the Iron Age earthworks on the cliff above the town.

If Edward had promised Dover, and if Eustace had occupied

the castle and tried to claim the town, or at least acted as if he owned the town – which he appears to have done – this would do much to explain the townspeople's reaction. It would also explain completely the reaction of the earl responsible for Dover – Godwine.

Edward is reported to have been furious with the action of the people of Dover, as well he might have been if Eustace had instructions to take over the port and town, and, without waiting to hear the townspeople's version of the incident – again an unreasonable stance for a king – he summoned Godwine to him and ordered the earl to carry out a harrying of Dover and Kent, a normal punishment of the time. Godwine refused, 'because it was abhorrent to him to injure the people of his own province' and, 'very indignant that such things should happen in his earldom', 'began to gather forces together over all his earldom, and Earl Swein, his son, over his, and Harold, his second son, over his earldom: and they all assembled in Gloucestershire at Longtree a great army and without number, all ready for war against the king, unless Eustace and his men were handed over to them, as well as the Frenchmen who were in the castle.'*

By refusing the king's order to harry Dover, Godwine had already laid himself open to a charge of rebellion. The assembly of his and his sons' forces in Gloucestershire was a direct threat to the crown, and could only be construed as an act of open rebellion. Was Godwine justified in creating such a crisis over a small incident, or was he himself infuriated at Edward's connivance with William or Normandy at the gift of one of his towns to the Normans, and seeking only to prevent Edward passing the succession – and Dover – to Normandy?

Godwine had been manoeuvring in English politics for over thirty years, and had been powerful under three kings before Edward – and survived each change of king. He had remained the most powerful earl in Edward's reign and was not the sort of man to risk all for the sake of Dover. But he might at last have been ready and willing to risk all in order to save his own earldom, and those of his sons, and to save England for the English.

*Anglo-Saxon Chronicle (D)

By 1 September Godwine and his two eldest sons had massed their forces near Tetbury in the Cotswolds: below them lay Gloucester, the king and Eustace. But Edward hastily summoned an emergency meeting of at least part of the *Witena gemot* on 8 September, this being attended by the Earl Leofric of Mercia and Earl Siward of Northumbria, accompanied by small forces. Both men supported the king and sent for reinforcements from their earldoms. These were joined by the troops of the Norman earl Ralph. At first it appeared there would be civil war, but then some of the king's party 'considered it would be great folly if they joined battle, because wellnigh all the noblest in England were present in those two companies, and they were convinced they would be leaving the country open to the invasion of our enemies, and be bringing utter ruin upon ourselves'.*

Hostages were exchanged and it was agreed a more complete *Witena gemot* should meet in London later that month to seek a peaceful settlement. This compromise spelled doom for Godwine's party, for in the breathing space thus obtained, the king summoned the national militia, which obliged all thegns and freemen to join the king's forces irrespective of the earldom in which they lived. Consequently, when the two parties assembled again at Southwark, many of Godwine's followers had been compelled to join the king, and those who remained with him were far from enthusiastic for his cause.

Godwine refused to face the king and *Witena gemot* without a promise of safe conduct, but each day saw his forces diminish as the king remained adamant that Godwine attend with no more than twelve followers, and that all the Wessex thegns should first come over to him. Finally Godwine was forced to flee to Bosham with his sons Swein, Tostig and Gyrth, and from there sailed to seek refuge in Flanders: his other sons, Harold and Leofwine, headed for Bristol, eluded a force sent in pursuit, survived a storm in the Bristol Channel, and found refuge in Ireland. No mention is made of Godwine's youngest son, Wulfnoth (born about 1045), and it is possible he was one of the hostages given at Gloucester, along with Godwine's grandson Hakon, bastard of Swein.

*Anglo-Saxon Chronicle (D)

Edward sent his queen, Godwine's daughter, to an abbey and strengthened the Norman element in his kingdom by appointments which included that of his chaplain William to the See of London at the expense of the English bishop-elect. He was at last free of Godwine's dominance, and wasted no time filling with his own men all those posts left vacant by the flight of the Godwine family.

In Normandy William had suppressed his barons, founded a strong ducal authority and was seeking a powerful alliance by marriage to Mathilde, daughter of the Count of Flanders and niece of Henri of France. But fresh troubles erupted in 1051 in the form of an ambitious neighbour, Geoffrey Martel of Anjou. Nevertheless, at some time during the winter of 1051–52, either William himself, or an embassy sent by him, arrived in England to confirm the Norman succession to the English throne. The D version of the Anglo-Saxon Chronicle and Florence of Worcester say that William himself made this visit, with a great retinue of Frenchmen, and there was an exchange of rich gifts. Although it is possible that William did visit England, it is difficult to see how he could afford to be absent from his duchy at such a crucial time in his life, though the crown of England was surely worth a quick trip, perhaps in early spring before the campaigning season started?

Historians are divided over whether it was William or only an embassy which visited Edward at this time, but the only important point is that such a visit was made, by someone of high position, and that he came to confirm Edward's promise, doubt perhaps having crept in owing to the rough handling of Eustace's embassy.

William of Poitiers, giving the Norman side of the story, confirms that Edward promised the throne to William in early 1051, in William's absence; that the promise was made with the assent of the great magnates of the kingdom, including the earls Godwine, Leofric and Siward; and that the son and grandson of Godwine (Wulfnoth and Hakon) were taken as hostages and sent to Normandy – probably with Robert of Jumièges. The implication is that Godwine was opposed to the nomination of William as heir, was overruled by the other members of the

Witena gemot, and compelled to give hostages to ensure he conformed to the decision. And those hostages were given to William, not Edward. If William of Poitiers is correct, then Edward's promise was made at the March 1051 *Witena gemot*, and this would do much to explain Godwine's dilemma and his uncharacteristic rebellion.

Edward's freedom from the Godwines was short-lived. In June 1052 Godwine sailed from Bruges with a small fleet and made a number of armed landings along the south coast of England to test the feelings of his former subjects. He found a wave of resentment sweeping the southern shires at the ascendancy of the Normans in Edward's court, and much support for his own cause in Kent, Surrey and Sussex. Meanwhile, Harold, with nine hired ships and a force of Irish–Scandinavian mercenaries, had landed at Porlock, burnt a royal manor there, and defeated the Devon and Somerset levies called out to oppose him, killing more than thirty thegns in the process.

Edward sent a fleet of forty ships under the Norman earls Ralph and Odda to sweep Godwine out of the Channel, but a storm enabled Godwine to escape and the fleet returned to London. Godwine and Harold now united their forces at the Isle of Wight and sailed eastwards along the coast, gaining followers as they went. They took the naval base of Sandwich and early in September entered the Thames estuary and sailed up to London to confront Edward.

London was the largest and richest city of the kingdom, with an estimated population of 15,000 to 20,000. Godwine had a hard core of mercenaries in his force, eager for pillage and rape: the Londoners appear to have agreed secretly to take his side, or at least give no assistance to the king.

Edward had a fleet of forty ships and their crews, his housecarls and local levies, and had sent north for reinforcements. His Norman advisers urged him to make another stand against the Godwine family, but 'then bishop Stigand intervened with God's help, and the wise men both inside and outside the city, and advised that hostages should be given as surety on either side, and so it was done.'* Many Normans at

*Anglo-Saxon Chronicle (E)   21

once fled from London, some seeking the safety of the Norman castles in the Welsh marches, others, including the Archbishop of Canterbury and Bishop Ulf of Dorchester, taking ship for Normandy.

A meeting of the *Witena gemot* was held and Godwine's earldom restored to him, as were the lands of his sons, with the exception of Swein, Godwine's eldest son, who had died whilst on a pilgrimage. The queen was also reinstated, yet Godwine does not appear to have had it all his own way, and was forced to concede something in return. (Oleson says Godwine appeared before the king as a supplicant, and was granted the kiss of peace.) Although the Godwine family received back its lands, it made no gains, as one would expect of the victor of such a clash, and it is possible therefore that Godwine was now compelled to reaffirm, or give for the first time, his assent to William's succession, in return for the reinstatement of lands: short of civil war he would have had no other option.

The *Witena gemot* also made a promise of good laws for the whole nation 'and they outlawed all the Frenchmen who had promoted injustice and pronounced unjust judgements and counselled evil within the realm, with the exception of as many of those whom they decided that the king was pleased to have about him, who were loyal to him and to all his people.'* Amongst the Normans allowed to stay was the Earl Ralph, William, Bishop of London, and Richard fitz Scrob in Herefordshire.

Shortly after this Bishop Stigand, a close associate of Godwine's, was appointed Archbishop of Canterbury, a post he was to hold, in spite of the anathema of successive popes, until after the Norman conquest of England. It was a controversial appointment reflecting Godwine's still considerable power, for in the eyes of Rome Stigand represented all that was bad in the old-fashioned Scandinavian type of church government: he retained the bishopric of Winchester after his appointment; his family had strong landed interests and Stigand was something of a capitalist; his brother, a bishop, was married; and he did not make the traditional journey to Rome to receive the pallium from the hands of the Pope, but at first used the one abandoned

*Anglo-Saxon Chronicle (C)

by his predecessor in his rapid departure for Normandy.

Edward seems never to have recovered fully from the confrontation with Godwine and although he continued to discharge all the formal duties of a king, and never lost touch with public affairs, he apparently abandoned all attempt to control them and concentrated more and more on his religious interests.

Godwine died in 1053, to be succeeded as Earl of Wessex by his heir, Harold Godwineson. With a king whose grip on his realm was already weakening, Harold slowly rose to a position of absolute power. Some historians believe Harold began plotting to secure the throne itself, or at least the means of remaining the power behind the throne, from the day of his father's death, for if the dynamic William of Normandy was allowed to succeed Edward, Harold's power would be sharply curbed. Certainly Harold's manipulation of the earldoms over the next few years points towards such an aim, advancing the fortunes of his own family and removing any dangerous rivals.

In 1055 Tostig Godwineson received the earldom of Northumbria as a result of the death of Siward, whose heir had been killed in an expedition against Macbeth the previous year. (His other son, Waltheof, was only about nine years old.) Tostig was the queen's favourite brother, and appears to have become a great favourite of the king also, so perhaps did not need Harold's help to obtain his promotion, but at about the same time Earl Aelfgar of East Anglia (Leofric of Mercia's son) was outlawed and Harold attempted to gain that earldom for his brother Gyrth. There is no apparent reason for Aelfgar's outlawing, but it is generally believed Edward took the action because of pressure from Harold: it is possible Aelfgar opposed Tostig's appointment.

Aelfgar raised an army in Ireland, allied himself with Gruffydd ap Llywelyn, king of Gwynedd and Powys, and did so much damage to Herefordshire that Edward had him reinstated. Leofric died in 1057 and Aelfgar became Earl of Mercia: Harold took the opportunity to slip Gyrth into the vacant earldom of East Anglia. Ralph of Hereford also died in 1057 and Harold himself took over these lands: not long afterwards

Leofwine Godwineson was given a new earldom embracing Kent, Essex, Bedford, Hertford and Surrey.

In 1058 Aelfgar was again outlawed: 'Aelfgar was driven out of the country, but he soon returned with violence through the help of Gruffydd. In this year came a pirate host from Norway; it is tedious to tell how it all happened.'*

The fighting which followed was far more serious than the chronicle implies. According to Irish and Welsh sources, it was in fact a devastation of a large area of England carried out by Magnus, son of Harald Hardrada of Norway, with the help of Gruffydd ap Llywelyn, and the Norwegian fleet was a full-scale invasion attempt by men gathered from the Orkneys, Hebrides and Dublin.

Aelfgar was reinstated but died in 1062 and the earldom of Mercia passed to his eldest son Edwin, who was, however, too young to make use of the military resources of his earldom. Harold seized the opportunity to end the troublesome Mercian and Welsh alliance by breaking the power of Gruffydd. In the two lightning campaigns of 1062 and 1063, Harold and Tostig succeeded in stabilizing the perilous Hereford border, extending effective English overlordship to the lands between the Wye and Usk, and ruining all attempts by Gruffydd to unite the Welsh. In 1063 the Welsh princes brought Harold the head of Gruffydd, surrendered hostages to him and Edward, and swore oaths of fealty and homage to the king. Harold was now at the peak of his power and was henceforth referred to as the Duke Harold: 'No subject of the English crown had ever been at once so powerful in relation to other noblemen and so great a figure in the country at large.'†

However, it is possible that Harold had no personal aspirations to the throne itself, but rather sought to supplant William's claim by other means. In 1054 the Anglo-Saxon Chronicle states: 'Bishop Ealdred [of Worcester] went oversea to Cologne on a mission for the king, and was there received with great ceremony by the emperor. He stayed there almost a year. . . .' The chronicle makes no mention of the purpose of the bishop's visit, but it has been interpreted as an attempt by King Edward to bring the last surviving member of the house of

*Anglo-Saxon Chronicle (D)   †Stenton, F. M. *Anglo-Saxon England*

Cerdic, Edward the Aethling, Edmund Ironside's son, back from Hungary to become the king's heir. This does not make sense, for we know with a fair degree of certainty that King Edward had already promised the throne to William. He could gain nothing but trouble from the return of the last prince of the royal blood. Possibly the bishop's mission was only to find out if either of Edmund's sons had survived.

It is far more likely that it was Harold, not Edward, who instigated the return of the aethling. The king had no heir, and there was no claimant to the throne except William of Normandy. If Harold could get the aethling to return to England, might he not be able to arouse popular sentiment so as to eventually ensure the throne remained with the house of Cerdic? In addition, as instigator of such a move, would he not only maintain his position of power behind the throne under King Edward II but also incur the gratitude of all the English?

Whoever Bishop Ealdred was really representing, and whatever his real mission, he returned empty handed in 1055. If he had been seeking the return of the aethling one must consider the prince's point of view. Edward had lived in Hungary for some thirty-seven years, since the age of about one year. He was married to a Hungarian princess, held a high position at the court, and he and all his family spoke Magyar as their native tongue: there was no reason on earth why he should forsake such a position for the uncertainty of a trip to England, where he *might* one day become king, or (just as likely) be murdered. Yet we know he did come to England in 1057, which suggests either further pressure was applied, or applied for the first time at a later date if Ealdred had been merely seeking news of the aethling's survival.

We know also that Harold went on a pilgrimage to Rome some time before 1060, and P. Grierson has indicated convincingly that Harold was at St Omer on 13 November, 1056, when he placed his signature on a document for Count Baldwin V of Flanders. We know also that Harold travelled through France, and St Omer was one of the pilgrim and trade routes taken by the English. It was possible for Harold to have visited Rome after the defeat of Gruffydd (he received his enemy's head on 5 August) and to have arrived back in St Omer by mid-November: Robert of Jumièges also did the return trip in under three months. Alternatively, Harold may have only just arrived on the Continent in November.

Direct communication between the English and Hungarian courts was not possible in the 11th century, but on 6 December Baldwin was in Cologne to see the Pope, and it is possible Harold might have accompanied him, for the Pope was the one man in Europe who could be of effective assistance in securing the return of the aethling to England.

Prior to his elevation (in 1054), Pope Victor had been governor of Bavaria for Henry III and was certainly in a position to help anyone wishing to open negotiations with Hungary. In addition, the Pope moved to Bavaria for Christmas, remaining there until February. If Harold went to Bavaria, he would have been within reasonable distance of Hungary, and have stood a better chance of persuading the aethling where his real responsibilities lay. It is even possible that Harold might have visited the aethling in person. Whatever happened, Harold would probably have accompanied the papal party on Pope Victor's pilgrimage to Rome before returning to England – perhaps even accompanied by the aethling.

We know only that Edward the Aethling arrived in London in the first half of 1057, although his arrival is the first entry in the chronicle for that year. King Edward did not see the prince, either because the Norman faction at his court objected or because the king himself found the situation extremely embarrassing in view of his promise to William: to allow the aethling into his court might have been interpreted as recognition of his claim to the throne. The prince was kept waiting in the background, and died suddenly without ever seeing his uncle the king. No cause of death is recorded and no accusations made. The king is unlikely to have instigated the prince's death, but there must have been Normans at the court who wished him dead and had the means to ensure his quiet removal from the scene. Edward the Aethling had after all given his life for a country called England which he cannot have loved, and almost certainly did not want.

The prince's death ruined Harold's hopes of supplanting William, but Harold seems to have been content now to play a waiting game. The prince's son and two daughters had been taken into the king's household. The son, Edgar, could have been no more than five years old in 1057: the king was about fifty-four. Edward might be expected to live another ten years, and that was all the time Edgar needed. If the king died in 1067 or even later, as he might well do, Edgar would be of an age to take the throne – with the Godwinesons behind him.

Not until 1064 was there another dramatic development in the story – Harold's visit to Normandy. The simplest and probably the most reliable source for the events of 1064 is the Bayeux Tapestry. According to this source, Harold was sent on a mission to the Continent by King Edward. He sailed before a strong wind to Ponthieu (there is no indication of a shipwreck), where he was arrested by the local count. Ponthieu had recently been brought under Norman overlordship and William soon obtained Harold's release. After entertainment at the Norman court, Harold accompanied the duke on an expedition against the Count of Brittany and was present at the surrender of the latter's castle at Dinan. Here William 'gave arms to Harold', probably implying that Harold became William's man. The next scene is inscribed 'William came to Bayeux where Harold took an oath to Duke William.' Harold then returned to England and reported to the king.

The Bayeux Tapestry was made for public display soon after the events it portrays and during the lifetime of most of the participants; for these reasons, it is hardly likely to portray incidents which are entirely fictitious. However, it cannot give information on the reason for Harold's journey, or tell us the nature of his commitment to the duke. For these we must turn to the chroniclers. The Anglo Saxon Chronicle is silent on the matter, and our earliest references are William of Poitiers and William of Jumièges, both Normans. The chronicles of both writers confirm the events portrayed in the tapestry, although William of Poitiers' detailed account places the Breton expedition *after* Harold's oath, while William of Jumièges' brief chronicle does not mention the expedition at all.

27

However, it is clear from these sources that it was at the king's instigation that Harold went to Normandy, almost certainly with the aim of compelling Harold to confirm his father's oath to recognize William as the successor to the English throne – thus cancelling out Edgar. Harold was the most powerful earl in England, but no one earl could defy the king without risking civil war – and perhaps, as a direct result, a Scandinavian invasion, thus losing all. Harold would have learnt this lesson in 1051, when the entire Godwine family, despite its immense power, had been exiled. There was also the possibility that if Harold refused to carry out the king's instructions, his own brother Tostig, the king and queen's favourite, might be sent instead, and in doing so usurp Harold's position as Earl of Wessex.

Regarding Harold's pledge once in Normandy, William of Jumièges says only that Harold returned to England with many gifts, 'having sworn fealty about the kingdom with many oaths'. William of Poitiers goes into considerable detail, setting down the oaths in the full legal jargon, as witnessed by reliable men:

(i) 'that he would be the *vicarius* [deputy or, in a legal sense, executor] of duke William at the court of his lord, king Edward, as long as he [Edward] should live.'

(ii) 'that he would employ all his influence and resources to assure him [William] the possession of the English kingdom after the death of Edward.'

(iii) 'that he would meanwhile hand over to the custody of his [William's] knights the castle of Dover, fortified at his own effort and cost.'

(iv) 'also he would similarly hand over, amply provided with supplies, other castles in various parts of the land where the duke should order them to be fortified.'

In addition, Harold paid homage to William, and in return was confirmed by the duke in all his lands and dignities. He then returned to England, loaded with gifts and accompanied by his nephew Hakon, specially released in his honour – although Harold's younger brother Wulfnoth was held by William until the Conqueror's death in 1087.

William of Poitiers' account is carefully worded and obviously describes the full ceremony of feudal commendation, comprising fealty, homage and investiture, whereby Harold became the vassal of William, but with the articles cited appended at the end of the normal oath of fealty. There is no reliable evidence to discredit this account, while the accusation that Harold was tricked into making oaths on sacred relics does not appear until the 12th century (made by Wace, an unreliable source). Also, we know that Harold, whilst Earl of Wessex, did at some time refortify Dover at his own expense.

Therefore, there is no reason to doubt that Harold's visit to the Norman court in 1064 was a decisive victory in the power game for King Edward, bringing Harold to heel by making him honour the king's nomination of William as heir to the throne, and recognize the other points of the 1051 agreement which had provoked Godwine to open rebellion.

In the autumn of 1065 there occurred another incident which was to have a dramatic effect on the events of the following year – a revolt in Northumbria. Tostig's appointment to the earldom may not have been popular, especially as heirs survived from two great local families (the houses of Siward and his predecessor Eadwulf), but there had been no voice raised against his appointment at the time, except perhaps that of Aelfgar. He had proved his value as a soldier and courtier, and had a certain reputation for piety, but as the governor of an earldom he was harsh and uncompromising, imposing heavy taxes, and too frequently at the king's court in the south when he should have been with his subjects. The Anglo-Saxon Chronicle says: 'All the men of his earldom were unanimous in repudiating him, and outlawed him and all those with him who had promoted injustice, because he robbed God first, and then despoiled of life and land all those over whom he could tyrannize.' He was also accused of treacherously murdering, in his own chamber in York, the thegns Gamel, son of Orm, and Ulf, son of Dolfin, who visited him under sworn safe conduct. (Orm and Dolfin were landowners who presumably attempted to stand up to Tostig, and were perhaps too strong for him to tackle openly.) In addition, Cospatric, heir of the native earls of

Bernicia, had recently been killed at the king's court, and it was believed the queen had procured his death in her brother's interest.

As a result of Tostig's misgovernment, 200 thegns of Lincolnshire, Yorkshire and Northumbria united to declare him an outlaw, then advanced on York and 'slew all his retainers whom they could catch, whether English or Dane, and seized his stock of weapons in York, his gold and silver and all his treasures which they came to hear of anywhere there.'* Support for the thegns was widespread and an invitation was sent to Morcar, brother of Edwin of Mercia, inviting him to become their lord and leader. Morcar accepted and when he joined the rebels they advanced into the midlands, drawing recruits to their cause from the Mercian shires of Nottingham and Derby, and concentrating around Northampton. Edwin himself joined them there with an army of Mercians and his father's old allies – the Welsh. It was a full-scale uprising, not against the king himself, but against one of his leading officers.

The king, with Tostig and such of the *Witena gemot* as he had been able to summon, moved from near Salisbury to Oxford and sent Harold, as his chief counsellor and military commander, to Northampton to open negotiations with the rebels. Harold returned with envoys bearing a 'request' that the rebels be allowed to have Morcar as their earl. While these envoys were with the king, the rebels 'did much damage around Northampton: not only did they slay men and burn houses and corn, but carried off all the livestock they could find, amounting to many thousands. They took many hundreds of captives, and carried them off north with them, so that that shire and the other neighbouring shires were for many years the poorer.'† They also sacked Peterborough.

We do not know precisely what happened during the negotiations, but apparently Harold tried to persuade the rebel leaders to come to an agreement with Tostig. The rebels refused to back down, even for the king, and demanded that Tostig be banished and Morcar recognized as their earl. Tostig is reputed to have accused his brother of complicity in the revolt and may well have done so in the heat of the moment – everyone must

*Anglo-Saxon Chronicle (D and E)   †Anglo-Saxon Chronicle (D)

have recognized long ago that Tostig was Harold's chief rival – but there is not a scrap of evidence that Harold was anything but a conscientious mediator. In fact the brothers had worked together with notable success in the recent Welsh wars, and Tostig's accusation, if made, would perhaps have been provoked by anger at the fact that his brother, whom he had so loyally supported in the past, should now fail to automatically support him, instead of first considering with a level head his loyalty to the kingdom and its unity.

The king was advised by his counsellors, including Harold, that it was far better that one man should suffer than the kingdom should be split by civil war, for the prospect of such a conflict was daunting in the extreme. With Mercia and Northumbria united against the south, there was a question whether the south could win such a war. Furthermore, vast areas of the kingdom would be devastated, and in the background hovered the spectre of a Danish invasion to exploit the schism. Edward had no choice but to keep his kingdom united, even at the expense of his favourite, and must have been greatly relieved that the Godwine family had not united to form an opposition party.

Harold was sent back to Northampton on 27 October to announce the king's decision to grant the rebels' demand for Morcar as Earl of Northumbria. He also renewed the laws of Knut, which insinuates that Tostig may have been tampering with the local Scandinavian laws and customs. The rebels departed peacefully to their homes. Tostig, his family and all his supporters left England and, as in 1051, sought refuge with his father-in-law, Count Baldwin of Flanders.

Harold's position was considerably weakened by this revolt, for the young sons of Aelfgar were now at least the equal of the Godwinesons, while the intervention of a Mercian army and the popular rising of the northern people showed that these peoples identified with Edwin and Morcar in opposition to the West Saxon house. Yet the rebels had no desire to depose the king and split the kingdom, only to remove a hated earl, and that they had sought the king's permission to assume a new earl illustrated their loyalty to the crown. Furthermore, the union with Mercia through the sons of Aelfgar in a way linked Northumbria not only to Mercia but through that earldom to the south, so that indirectly the rebellion had instigated a move towards nationhood. But, across the Channel, Tostig fumed and plotted how to regain his lost earldom, while the king, hitherto apparently in the best of health, abruptly began a physical and mental decline.

Edward was sixty-three at the time of the rebellion. There was no suggestion at this or any previous time that he suffered ill health. He was grievously upset by the banishment of his favourite, and must have seethed with rage at his impotency to control events in his own kingdom. Perhaps the climb down at Northampton brought back all his memories of other clashes, when he had been forced to submit first to this earl, then that one, in order to balance the power of one against the other, and how for years Harold Godwineson had dominated him, and Godwine before that.

In the weeks following the rebellion, the king's depression worsened into a state of morbidity. Perhaps he felt he had done enough for England, that the Godwinesons were balanced now by Edwin and Morcar, and that the succession was guaranteed to pass into the hands of a strong ruler who would be able to control all the earls. By December he was grievously ill and the date for the consecration of his beloved Westminster Abbey was brought forward to the 28th so that he might attend. But he was too ill by then, and remained bedridden in Westminster Palace, from the 28th growing weaker and weaker, developing a raging fever and finally lapsing into a coma. On 5 January he died, only ten weeks after his surrender to the rebels.

There were many lay and ecclesiastical magnates of the realm in London for the consecration of Westminster Abbey and the Christmas feast – and no doubt also because it was known the king was seriously ill. Some gathering of the *Witena gemot* was therefore inevitable as Edward's death drew near, and his successor was named on the very day that the king died.

It is clear Edward had always intended that William of Normandy should be his heir. He had been constant in this aim, and twice stood up to the Godwines to achieve it. But a king of

England had no right as such to promise the throne to anyone, for at a king's death the final decision rested with the *Witena gemot*.

It was customary for the *Witena gemot* to recognize the successor nominated by the dying king, normally the king's eldest son, so as to avoid the dangers of a disputed succession. Where there was no such heir, the most eligible member of the royal family was chosen on a selection basis, whereby the candidate sought to secure the support of the leading magnates. When Edward died he left no heir and the only surviving member of the royal house was Edgar, who was still too young (about fourteen) to control the country. But there were several foreign candidates.

William of Normandy was Edward's choice and therefore prime candidate, but there were also the two Scandinavian kings to be considered. Their claim stemmed from Knut's reign, for on his death the Scandinavian 'empire' had split into Norway under Magnus, and Denmark and England under Hordaknut. Magnus attacked Denmark and in 1038–39 a treaty was made between him and Hordaknut that in the event of the death of either of them without heirs their dominions should pass to the other. Hordaknut died without an heir in 1042 and thereafter Magnus endeavoured to claim both Denmark and England. He was on the verge of success in Denmark when he died in 1047, and his claims were inherited by his father's half-brother, Harald Hardrada. For nineteen years Harald Hardrada fought his contemporary, Sven Estrithson, who claimed to have been named as successor by Magnus, for control of Denmark, and had it not been for these endemic wars it is likely that England would have reverted to being a part of Scandinavia. Sven and Harald signed a peace treaty in 1064, leaving both free to pursue their claims to England in 1066; Harald through the contract made between Magnus and Hordaknut, Sven as the son of Knut's sister and grandson of Sven Forkbeard, King of England 1013–14. However, Sven, as cousin and friend of Harold Godwineson, was to stand aside in 1066 and did not press his claim until after the conquest.

In fact the *Witena gemot* passed over all three candidates and chose Harold Godwineson, although we do not know why. Harold cannot have expected to be king, or indeed plotted such an elevation, prior to 1064. It is possible he may have determined to seize the throne then, due to the king forcing him to recognize William as the successor, but not probable, for at this date he still had Edgar to secure the throne for the English royal house. Edward's illness was unexpected and sudden, and in November 1065 (at the earliest) Harold must for the first time have known for certain that the king was going to die before Edgar was old enough to succeed to the throne. Only then is Harold likely to have begun to campaign to secure the throne for himself.

If he did conduct such a campaign, he faced enormous difficulties. He had not a drop of royal blood in his veins (his mother was a sister of Knut's brother-in-law, but this was hardly a qualification) and was the son of a self-made man. The choice of a commoner was unprecedented, politically dangerous in the 11th century, and, by introducing elective rather than selective means, would create a precedent which in future generations might enable the throne to pass to the man with the greatest army – rule by might alone. Such a step was revolutionary, but if Harold was not chosen, who else was there? The *Witena gemot* had a limited choice: a Scandinavian king once more, either the mercenary Harald Hardrada, who had no hereditary claim, or Sven Estrithson; or William of Normandy, the illegitimate offspring of the duke of a duchy considerably smaller and poorer than England, whose only hereditary claim to the throne was that his great aunt Emma had married two kings of England and was King Edward's mother; or Harold Godwineson.

The *Witena gemot* would have recognized Harold's personal attributes: he was an astute and experienced statesman, a strong administrator yet admired for his tolerance and understanding, and had guided king and kingdom for the past thirteen years. He was popular with the people of Wessex and East Anglia (his old earldom) and also in Hereford and elsewhere along the Welsh border, where his role as scourge of the Welsh had secured him a special place in the hearts of the people of the

34

marches. But the choice of Harold would mean a break with tradition and the old dynasty: it was not easy to abandon the ancient house of Cerdic, even if it was easy to ignore the foreign claimants. Edgar was the natural choice, not Harold or William, but Edgar could not hold the country together or defend it against the wrath of a frustrated Duke of Normandy: Harold Godwineson could.

Apart from Harold's obvious qualifications, and his power to persuade other leading magnates to support him, there is one other possible influence on his election. As he lay dying, the king is reported to have said, stretching his hand towards Harold: 'I commend this woman [the queen] and all the kingdom to your protection.' The source of this comment, the *Vita Edwardi Regis*, was written immediately after the conquest by a careful historian who had close contact with the important people present at the king's death – notably the queen, who commissioned the work, Bishop Stigand, and Robert fitz Wimarc, one of the king's few remaining Norman friends and a relative of William. Wimarc did not deny the remark was made, but, of course, it is open to different interpretations: did Edward mean that Harold should be his successor, or only that he should be regent (*vicarius* as in the oath of 1064) until William could arrive to be crowned, as Godwine had been regent between the death of Hordaknut and the coronation of Edward himself? The biography was written at a time when all supporters of Harold were being persecuted: perhaps the chronicler did not dare put Edward's words in their precise form, and deliberately made them equivocal?

Like everything else to do with Harold's election to the throne, we shall never know the truth, but we do know his election was announced the same day that the king died and there appears to have been no opposition to the choice, for not even the few remaining Normans fell from power by opposing it, and none fled the country as they had on Godwine's return to power in 1052.

Harold was crowned with what has always been termed indecent haste – on 6 January, the same day that Edward was buried. On the face of it, Harold was grabbing the crown, for he

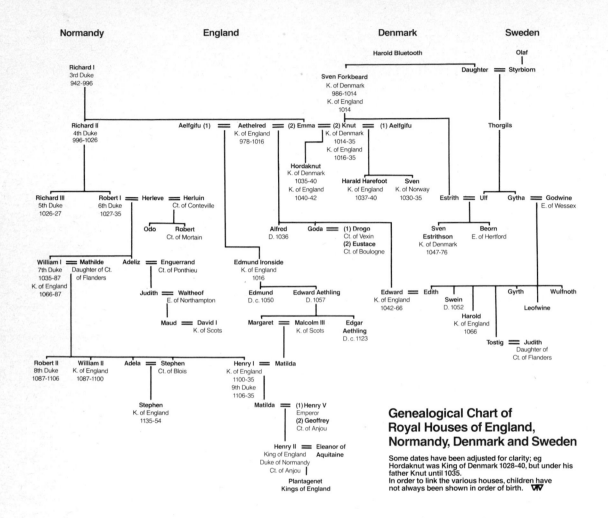

Normandy **England** **Denmark** **Sweden**

**Genealogical Chart of
Royal Houses of England,
Normandy, Denmark and Sweden**

Some dates have been adjusted for clarity; eg
Hordaknut was King of Denmark 1028-40, but under his
father Knut until 1035.
In order to link the various houses, children have
not always been shown in order of birth.

became king before anyone outside London knew that Edward
was dead, and this *fait accompli* must have done much to
influence contemporary opinion. But great state occasions were
normally held on the feast days of the Church. Edward's funeral
took place on Epiphany: the next great feast day was Easter. To
wait three months for the coronation, knowing that William
was bound to make some attempt to claim the throne, was to

court disaster, and Harold had never been one to hang back when one swift move might decide the issue: it was a bold trait he inherited from his Viking ancestors. For better or worse, he was now king of England, although his position was precarious.

Across the Channel was William, who had been named as heir to the throne by King Edward, and whom the great earls of England – and particularly Harold himself only some eighteen months previously – had recognized as the next king of England. Harold's accession to the throne would be a slap in the face to William when the news reached Normandy, and the duke could not afford such a tremendous loss of prestige: he would have to make some move against the usurper. Across the northern seas were Harald Hardrada and Sven Estrithson, either of whom might invade England to seize the throne or to regain control of the Danelaw: after all, it was only thirty years since England had been part of Knut's Scandinavian 'empire'. In the west was the possibility of a renewed Welsh attack if the English were engaged elsewhere, and similarly the Scots could be expected to raid south of the Tweed. And in Flanders remained Tostig, who could not be expected to support Harold, but who might support another in order to regain his earldom.

Harold began his reign with the sure knowledge that he would have to fight to keep the crown: the only questions were, from which direction would the first attack come, and would the whole of England support him?

2
The English

In 1066 England was a rich country with extensive trade, an advanced political structure and a system of national taxation which worked. Such well-developed techniques of government should have meant a strong monarchy, but in the fifty years from 1016 to 1066 England was ruled by kings with Scandinavian and Norman sympathies as well as Anglo-Saxon ones, and as a result she was subjected to much civil strife in this period. By 1066, therefore, England was still not a nation, and the English were far from being one people, though they were all subjects of one king and there were signs of an increasing unity, such as the refusal to be drawn into civil war in 1051, and the tightening of the links with the north in 1065.

In Edward's reign the blending of the various races which made up the English had only just begun. Knut had divided the kingdom into four great earldoms, and in 1066 four great earls still controlled most of the country – the earls of Wessex in the south, East Anglia in the east, Mercia in the midlands and Northumbria in the north. Northumbria was the largest earldom and had originally been settled by the Angles. Wessex was the most heavily populated and prosperous, and had been settled by the Saxons and Jutes – the latter in Kent, part of Hampshire and the Isle of Wight. East Anglia and Mercia had also been settled by the Angles, but the Scandinavian invasions had established the Danelaw over large parts of these two earldoms and Northumbria, imposing a Scandinavian aristocracy on the earlier settlers. The precise extent of the Danelaw in the 11th century cannot be determined, but the heaviest Scandinavian settlement was in Leicestershire, Lincolnshire, Nottinghamshire and Yorkshire, and it is probable that Scandinavian lords also ruled in Derbyshire and Northamptonshire.

The earldoms were divided into shires, corresponding roughly to the counties before the reorganization of the early 1970s, and the shires were further divided into hundreds. The earls administered their earldoms in the king's name, keeping the peace, dispensing justice, imposing and collecting taxes to maintain both their own and the king's states (the earl took a third of certain revenues), levying and commanding the military forces of the earldom, and representing its interests in the *Witena gemot*. An earl was thus a political officer, general and admiral, responsible for the defence of his earldom by sea as well as by land. He was also a courtier and statesman, and his position at the king's court frequently necessitated long absences from his earldom. Therefore, the routine business of each shire was carried out by a shire-reeve, or sheriff, who was appointed by the king.

The sheriff was responsible for administering the royal estates and collecting royal taxes, enforcing the laws and customs, maintaining a 'police' force, commanding the military levies of the shire, dispensing justice in the courts of the hundreds and, in the absence of the earl, presiding with the bishop in the shire court. In the larger towns a port-reeve, also appointed by the king, administered the affairs and courts of the town. All minor appointments in earldoms, shires and towns were made directly by the earls and reeves.

The earls had originally been appointed by the king, but by the 11th century the rank was hereditary. They were powerful men, but they were still answerable to the king and each earl had only one voice in the *Witena gemot*, while their sheriffs and

39

bishops were royal appointees. Therefore, a strong king could so balance the power of his great officers that anyone who resisted him could be sent into exile by the others.

Beneath this hierarchy of king's officers was a landed class known as thegns. In the early days of the Anglo-Saxon settlement of England a thegn had been a companion of a warlord and therefore a member of a warrior class, but by the mid-11th century there were Danish and Norman thegns as well as Anglo-Saxon ones and the term seems to have been applied to almost every rank of men from serf to noble: the Domesday Book lists thegns who were obliged to do the ploughing and harvesting. This situation arose because, although the true thegn had once been distinguished by the holding of five hides of land, by the 11th century the rank had become hereditary and brothers might share the five hides on the death of their father. In addition, if a peasant became the sole possessor of a five-hide unit of land (as he might well do in time of war), he was promoted to thegn and became entitled to the rights of a thegn. If his son and grandson held the land in their own right, the rank became hereditary. Under these laws, thegns could eventually end up with diminutive estates, for the division of the five hides between brothers, and again between their sons, did not carry with it the loss of rank. Thus the Manor of Salden in Buckinghamshire is assessed in the Domesday Book at a little over three hides, held by four thegns, each of whom owed allegiance to a different lord. On the other hand, a thegn might acquire large estates, scattered over many shires: such men are usually called king's thegns and they served in close attendance on the king, the older men as his counsellors, the younger men as bodyguards and lesser officials. The earls had their own great thegns, and both the king's and earl's thegns had lesser thegns under them.

Below the thegns were the ceorls or peasant class, freemen who at their most successful were independent farmers with one or more hides of their own land (hide, meaning household, may originally have defined the area of land needed to support a family), and who formed the backbone of the kingdom, based as it was on a rural economy. There were probably three main classes of ceorls, although the boundaries between the classes are blurred. First, the *geneats*, who paid rent for their land to their overlord and gave service when needed as a mounted bodyguard, messenger, or attendant at the hunt. The *geneat* may even have served as a bailiff on a large estate, for he was a man of some standing, and his agricultural duties were limited to boon-works at harvest time. *Geneat* originally meant a companion, and this implies that the class originated from the lord's household. Second came the *kotsetla*, who paid no land rent, but in exchange for five acres or more was liable to his overlord for all types of heavy duties at the rate of a day a week throughout the year, or three days each week in harvest time. Third was the *gebur*, who in return for a small holding and his initial stock might pay an annual rent of money, corn and livestock, and was also bound to contribute regular labour to his overlord; two days in every week of the year, three days in harvest time, and three days from Candlemas to Easter. On his death his land reverted to the lord's estate.

A prosperous ceorl could rise to become a thegn, but an impoverished one might just as easily sink into slavery. The economy depended considerably on slave labour, and slaves were obtained from prisoners of war, impoverished men who sold themselves as bondsmen, and the offspring of freemen who were sold because of poverty and in times of famine. The *gebur* was a lowly peasant, but he belonged to a privileged class compared to the slaves and was a freeman with the right and duty to bear arms for his king and country.

The right of every freeman to bear arms was a Germanic tradition perpetuated by the Anglo-Saxons, as was the tradition that it was dishonourable to leave the battlefield on which your lord had been slain. This meant the potential military strength of England was enormous, while the military organization which had been developed over the centuries of Anglo-Saxon evolution was at least as sophisticated as any in western Europe. The island's defences were regarded as formidable by most foreign observers, and operated on three distinct levels – shire, earldom and kingdom. The shire force consisted of local levies led by the sheriff, a prelate or sometimes the earl, and acted in defence of its own territory: it could deal effectively with any localized raids and was frequently called on to cope with coastal piracy. More serious threats could be dealt with by the earl's force, consisting of his thegns and household troops, and incorporating levies from more than one shire. A critical threat to any part of the realm was countered by an army drawn from a number of earldoms and led by the king, or by an earl in his name.

The troops who made up these forces were also divided into three main classes – professional soldiers known as housecarls, who formed a small but permanent force, mercenaries hired on a temporary basis, and the shire levies or fyrd. The most important and effective of these three classes was the housecarls. The term housecarl is generally applied to the English as well as Danish warriors who were employed on a regular basis as household troops by the great earls, but it has a special connotation for the unique and closely knit body of professional soldiers who served the kings of England.

This corps of royal housecarls was probably introduced into England by Knut in 1018 and became both the nucleus and the spearhead of any Anglo-Saxon army. All its members were experienced, professional warriors, who continually practised their trade, and were accustomed to living, training and fighting together as a unit. Their laws and code of honour bound them to faithful service to their paymaster and each other, even unto death, with an inflexibility which we cannot fully comprehend today. The exact nature of the organization of this distinctive company of warriors is obscure, but we can gain a general impression from Norske sources which describe similar companies in the service of the Scandinavian kings; in fact the laws and regulations of Danish housecarls seem to have been based on those governing the housecarls of Knut. These laws specify that the housecarls should receive their wages and subsistence from the monarch in peacetime as well as in war, individual warriors could only leave the organization on New Year's day, and all defaulters or internal disputes should be dealt with by the housecarl's own assembly, the huskarlesteffne, which met periodically with the king.

42

Loyalty to the king and to each other was the core of the housecarl's code, and defaulters were treated harshly: treason was punishable by death and confiscation of property, while the murder of a fellow soldier meant death or banishment. These were harsh punishments compared with the parallel civil ones, where exile and compensation respectively were the norm.

The royal housecarls were financed principally by the Danegeld or national land tax, originally raised to buy off Danish raiders, and the heregeld or army tax, which had been instituted by Knut to pay Danish mercenaries. There does not seem to have been anything like these taxes anywhere else in Europe, and they were the main reason why the king was able to maintain a large standing army of professional soldiers: the strength of the royal housecarls in 1066 has been estimated at 3,000. Edward abolished the heregeld, but not the Danegeld, in 1051, perhaps believing his promise of the throne to William would secure him a powerful ally against the Scandinavians, but it seems to have been reinstated in the closing years of his reign, for several passages in the Domesday Book strongly suggest it was in effect at the time of his death.

Three thousand men was a considerable army in the 11th century, and the royal housecarls must have been capable of withstanding on their own almost any serious threat to the realm. However, during normal times they seem to have been scattered about the realm in small garrisons at important ports and towns, where they are said to have also served as tax collectors, or perhaps more appropriately tax enforcers. Their main force was divided between an unknown northern site called Slessvik, almost certainly near York, and barracks at Wallingford in Berkshire, strategically placed to protect London and the capital Winchester.

All the housecarls were mounted to enable them to be concentrated swiftly at any threatened point in the kingdom, but historians are divided over the question of whether the horses were used as mounts in battle or merely as transport. There will always be doubt over the answer to this question, for accounts of Anglo-Saxon battles before 1066 are scarce and often vague, but to this writer it seems fairly certain that the

Housecarl in mail
hauberk and iron helmet,
armed with kite shield,
sword and two-handed
broadaxe.

Select fyrd man in
ordinary clothes but with
a padded jerkin for extra
protection.

Great fyrd man in
everyday dress and armed
only with spear and shield,
and a long dagger in place
of a sword.

housecarls could and did operate as mounted as well as foot soldiers.

Horses were plentiful in England, and the king, his thegns and the shire levies had all been riding to battle (and conducting mounted pursuits of defeated enemies) since at least 755. Admittedly the Anglo-Saxons traditionally dismounted to fight on foot once at the battlefield, but by the mid-11th century the professional fighting men of England were as up to date in their equipment and tactics as any fighting force in western Europe, and it seems unlikely that such a professional force would not have adopted the tactics of its contemporaries.

It must be remembered that some of these housecarls would have seen service elsewhere – the Danes were 'hired guns' who had seen wide service, possibly as Norman household troops, perhaps even as Varangian Guardsmen in Byzantium – and they were familiar with the long-established Frankish mailed horseman. Indeed, Norman soldiers of fortune had been recruited into England by Edward, and some English and Danish housecarls had actually fought Norman cavalry in Scotland in 1054, when Earl Siward of Northumbria heavily defeated the forces of Macbeth, which included a large number of Norman mercenaries, and in the mounted pursuit killed many of these Normans, thus confirming they were horsemen. Harold Godwineson had personally participated in a campaign with the Norman cavalry in 1064, and as commander of the English army is unlikely to have ignored the lessons he learned then. Some of Edward's Normans also tried to train Anglo-Saxon infantry in Norman cavalry tactics: in 1055 the Norman Earl Ralph of Hereford taught the local select fyrd to fight on horseback, but when they confronted Aelfgar and his Welsh allies, 'before a spear was thrown, the English fled, because they had been made to fight on horseback'. The D version of the Anglo-Saxon Chronicle reads: 'And after a brief encounter they were put to flight, and many were slain in that rout,' while the quotation from the C version above continues: 'Many of them were slain, about four hundred or perhaps five. . . .'

This makes it debatable whether the mounted English in fact fled 'before a spear was thrown', and in any case these were not housecarls but local levies, men accustomed to fighting on foot in the steep, broken and timber-clad hills of the Welsh marches. Neither they nor the terrain were suited for cavalry, and these local men had long since learned that the only way to deal with the Welsh was on their own terms – on foot and lightly armed. Harold knew this by the Welsh campaign of 1063, when his housecarls abandoned not only their horses and hauberks but also their axes, donning leather jerkins and relying on spear and javelin to beat the Welsh with their own tactics. Yet the reverse was true of Tostig's force in the same campaign: operating in the flat plain bordering the north coast, Tostig and his men remained mounted, utilizing the advantages the terrain gave to cavalry.

There is only one source which gives an account of Anglo-Saxon cavalry in action, the *Heimskringla* of Snorri Sturluson, which was for a long time discredited because of errors over the family relationships of the Anglo-Saxon leaders. R. Glover as far back as 1952 pointed out that the Anglo-Saxon Chronicle makes similar errors about Norske leaders, but is not discredited because of them, and more than fifty years ago R. W. Chambers pointed out that the Chronicle and *Heimskringla* agree in all other details of the battle concerned – Stamford Bridge. This battle is dealt with fully later, so it is enough to say here that if Snorri's saga is accepted as a faithful account of the battle (that account originating from Norwegians who fought in the battle but not recorded by Snorri until 150 years later – although he used other accounts written only fifty years after the battle) then there can remain no doubt about the ability of the housecarls to fight as mounted warriors.

Other mercenaries were employed besides the housecarls, and these are often referred to as *hired* or *hiredmenn*, although it is not clear if these are temporary troops or troops engaged on a more permanent basis like the housecarls. For example, Tostig's English and Danish household troops are referred to in one version of the Chronicle as housecarls, but another version calls them *hiredmenn*. (*Hired* meaning household, gives *hiredmenn* as retainers or members of the household.) It seems likely that, during the reign of Edward, housecarls were recruited on a

47

permanent basis by the great earls as household troops. During the Northumbrian revolt of 1065, Tostig lost 200 of his household troops: as some survived and escaped, a figure of between 250 and 300 'housecarls' seems a reasonable estimate of the strength of an earl's following.

There are numerous other references to mercenaries, who are clearly not housecarls, in the pay of the king or earls. One such group was the *lithsmen*, an ambiguous term thought to mean sailor in Anglo-Saxon, but which means warrior in Norske literature. The men certainly seem to have been of Scandinavian origin, for they apparently fought in the old Viking tradition, equally at home on land or sea, and it seems likely that *lithsmen* were mercenaries who came in their own ships, under their own leaders, and who were engaged to fight either on land or at sea, as the occasion demanded.

It was *lithsmen* who manned the forty ships sent by Edward to chase off Godwine in 1052, and in 1066 some of the men who marched north with Harold to fight Harald Hardrada are termed *lithsmen* by the Chronicle. They may have been rehired annually, from spring until autumn, for Edward is recorded as dismissing nine of his fourteen ships of *lithsmen* in 1050, and the remaining five in 1051, yet used forty ships of *lithsmen* in 1052. Thus they were professional fighting men, accustomed to fighting together and loyal to each other and their leader. They were probably equal to the housecarls in quality, although lacking the housecarls' total loyalty to their paymaster.

Florence of Worcester describes another group of mercenaries as *butsecarls*, but the Chronicle refers to this same group as *burhwaru*, or garrison. The term *hiredmenn* was applied equally to *lithsmen* and *butsecarls*, and the latter seem to have performed maritime duties as well as fighting on land. To all intents and purposes they may be regarded as the same as *lithsmen*. *Lithsmen* and *butsecarls* would have been supplied with horses when necessary for their land activities, but would not have fought as cavalry.

The housecarls and mercenaries, although an élite force and probably in total equal in strength to any Scandinavian army which might invade England, were only a small part of the military potential of England, and the rank and file of the Anglo-Saxon army was the fyrd, a reservist or territorial force.

There were two distinct types of fyrd, named the select and great fyrds by Hollister in his *Anglo-Saxon Military Institutions*. The great fyrd was only called out in times of local emergency, and consisted of *every* freeman in the threatened area. These men had the incentive of fighting in defence of their own lands and homes, but they were poorly armed, untrained, almost entirely on foot, and therefore awkward to control or manoeuvre. The obligations of this 'citizen's army' were limited, the main restrictions so far as the commanders were concerned being that the men were entitled to return home at night, and if they were required to serve outside their own area then they had to be paid. These restrictions meant the great fyrd was not widely used.

The select fyrd was completely different, truly a select body of men who were well equipped, mostly if not all mounted – though not capable of fighting as cavalry – and organized in shire units of a manageable size under their own sheriffs. (They might be grouped with other shire units under their earl, or even the king, in the field, but retained their separate unit identities and may possibly have been divided further into groups of perhaps sixty warriors.) As well as local service, they were also eligible for national service anywhere in the kingdom for a total period of two months annually, and were therefore accustomed to working together as a unit.

The obligation to serve in the select fyrd was based on a national assessment of landholding. The most complete description of this obligation is found in the Domesday Book passage relating to Berkshire: 'If the king sent an army anywhere, only one soldier went from five hides, and 4 shillings were given him from each hide as subsistence and wages for two months. This money, indeed, was not sent to the king, but was given to the soldiers.'

In other words, one soldier had to be sent for every five hides of land, and whoever owned those five hides was responsible for his pay and maintenance for two months. The soldier might be the sole owner of the five hides, in which case he collected 20

Spearheads with moulded sockets found in the River Thames at Mortlake. English, Vikings and Normans all used spears with heads of these types for hand-to-hand fighting, though the sockets of English spearheads were more often split at both sides.

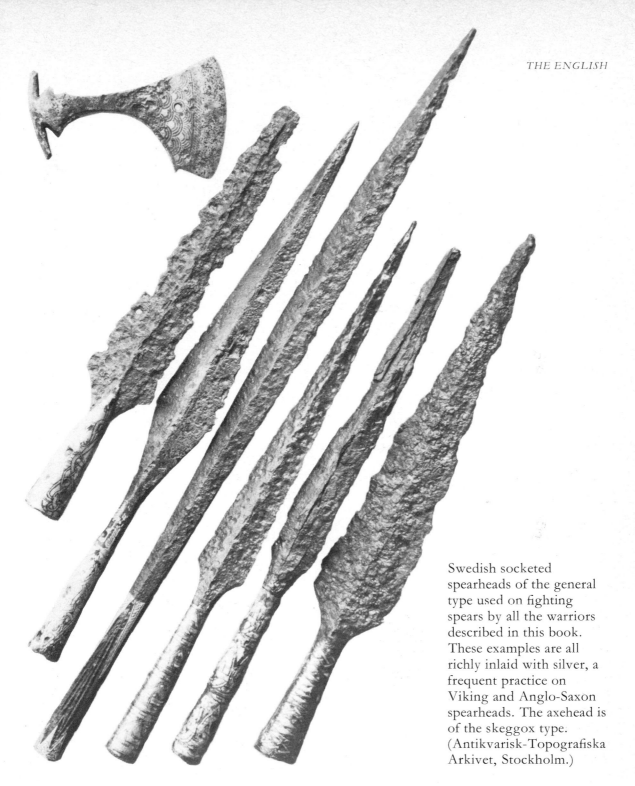

Swedish socketed spearheads of the general type used on fighting spears by all the warriors described in this book. These examples are all richly inlaid with silver, a frequent practice on Viking and Anglo-Saxon spearheads. The axehead is of the skeggox type. (Antikvarisk-Topografiska Arkivet, Stockholm.)

Swedish socketed
spearheads illustrating the
various types for different
roles; a 'lance' form, the
broad-bladed fighting
spear, and two smaller
heads for throwing spears.
Note the first two are
inlaid with silver, whereas
the other two are plain.
(Antikvarisk-Topografiska
Arkivet, Stockholm.)

Winged spearhead found
in the River Ouse,
Cambridgeshire. The blade
is damascened, and the
socket richly ornamented
with silver, copper and
gold. By the 11th century
such spearheads were
probably used only for
hunting.

shillings from his subordinates, or perhaps from his own
income. Alternatively, he might possess no land of his own, and
collect 20 shillings from the men who held the five-hide unit of
land which sent him. Or he might be a small landowner within a
five-hide unit, supplying part of the 20 shillings from his own
income and receiving the remainder from his fellow landholders within the five-hide unit.

Many of the select fyrd would therefore have been thegns,
but when no thegn was available – either because the unit of five
hides was part of a larger estate held by one thegn, or because
the land was held by a ceorl or ceorls – it would also contain
peasants. A great number of these would have been *geneats*, the
aristocracy of the peasantry, who were experienced horsemen
and able to afford the necessary equipment and weapons. It is
significant that this intermediary class between thegns and
peasants is also referred to as *cnihts*, the term the English later
adopted for their horsed warriors in preference to the French
chevalier. Similarly, not all thegns were obliged to serve in the
select fyrd, for five hides might be held by two or more thegns,
only one of whom was liable for service.

It has been argued that military service before Hastings was a
duty of the aristocracy, owed to the king at a personal level and
not because of landholding, yet the *Rectitudines Singularum*

Personarum, made in the half-century preceding the conquest, clearly describes the Thegn's Law as follows:

'The law of the thegn is that he be entitled to his book right (land protected by charter), and that he shall contribute three things in respect of his land: armed service, and the repairing of fortresses and work on bridges. Also in respect of many estates, further service arises on the king's order such as service connected with the deer fence at the king's residence, and equipping a guard ship, and guarding the coast, and guarding the lord, and military watch, almsgiving and church dues and many other various things.'

However, as we have seen, a man did not *have* to be a landowner to serve in the select fyrd, and thegn and peasant, landowner and landless man, all ranked as equals in the select fyrd, fighting side by side in every important battle from Maldon in 991 to Hastings in 1066. Selection for the select fyrd was an honour as well as a duty, and it is probable that the same man was sent from each five-hide unit every time the fyrd was mustered. Service was personal in that the summons to the muster, although conducted at shire level, came direct from the king, and there are indications that the select fyrd may have been a royal force in the sense that it would only serve the king; it was, after all, led by the king's own officers, the sheriffs, with any under-officers appointed by those sheriffs. Such an attitude would have prevented the select fyrd of the shires from being used by their earls to revolt against the throne, and may be one of the reasons why, after the conquest, the fyrd invariably appears on the side of the monarch, never on the side of the rebels.

The five-hide assessment system described was that appertaining to Berkshire: we cannot now tell if precisely the same system was used in all other shires, for the nature of landholding differed in the various regions, and much was held by custom but not by law. The Berkshire hide, for example, was probably forty acres. The hide in Dorset and possibly some other southern and western shires was also about forty acres, but in Wiltshire it was forty-eight and in other regions a hide of 120 acres was common. (At this date an acre may not have been

4,840 square yards but merely the amount of land a plough team of eight oxen could plough in a single day.) However, the hide seems to have been regarded as a standard unit of assessment regardless of its size – a fiscal and military unit rather than a real one – and it is likely therefore that the Berkshire system prevailed in all parts of the kingdom where hidage existed.

Known hidage figures for the 11th century give multiples of ten, thus Cambridge, Oxford, Colchester and Shrewsbury were assessed at 100 hides each, each contributing twenty men to the select fyrd. Huntingdon, Chester, Bedford, Ipswich, Warwick and Maldon were assessed at fifty hides each; Northampton and Sudbury at twenty-five; Bath, Cheshunt and Shaftesbury at twenty; Worcester at fifteen; Dorchester, Hertford, St Albans and Wareham at ten; Malmesbury, Exeter, Bridport and Yarmouth at five. Tewkesbury was assessed at ninety-five hides; Barnstaple, Lidford and Totnes at five hides between them.

From charters and passages in the Domesday Book we know that in the Danelaw the military service and obligations were assessed in carucates or ploughlands. The carucate had the same function in administrative and fiscal matters as the hide, and it is fairly safe to assume the two equate when it comes to military service, but unfortunately there is no known source for the amount of fyrd service owed per carucate unit: it may have been one man for every six carucates, but this cannot be proven. Leicester, which was assessed by carucates, sent twelve men to the select fyrd, but we do not know the number of carucates involved.

Kent was assessed in sulungs and juga, the former usually being taken as the equivalent of two hides. In East Anglia, because of the strong Scandinavian influence, there were numerous independent holdings, creating an extraordinary ratio of freemen, or sokemen, many of whom were free to choose their lord, so that manor and village bear no clear relationship to one another. The leet was the sub-unit of the region for the Danegeld, with twelve leets to a hundred. There were ten carucates to the leet, so the fyrd service must have been fixed at some standard ratio of men to carucates, leets or

55

hundreds, although it is now impossible to determine that ratio.

Some idea of the total territorial force available to an English king can be determined from The Tribal Hidage, a late 10th-century copy of an earlier manuscript, which lists the total hidage for England, excepting Northumbria, at over 230,000 hides – capable of yielding a select fyrd of 46,000 men. The hidage assessment figures were drastically reduced during the 11th century; by the date of the Domesday Book some shires were down to half their original figure; but even so a select fyrd of between 20,000 and 25,000 men must have been available in 1066.

In some cases towns were allowed to make payments in lieu of service, the rate corresponding to the cost of hiring replacements. This was a legal alternative but not a right, and could only be granted as a privilege by the king. Oxford, for example, was allowed to satisfy its obligation by paying £20 to the king instead of sending twenty men. Some other major towns paid special taxes, in addition to the Danegeld, to contribute to the cost of the king's mercenaries. If there was no arrangement to pay in lieu of service, and men were not sent to the muster, then a fine known as the fyrdwite was levied. This was hardly ever less than 40 shillings, twice the cost of sending a man, and was frequently as high as 100 shillings. This system of finance – Danegeld, special town taxes, fyrdwite and payment in lieu – yielded a high revenue, which enabled the king to maintain his large professional army of housecarls and mercenaries. There was no other system like it in western Europe and it was entirely due to such advanced fiscal methods that England was so rich and strong: the payment in lieu of service, for example, predates by at least a hundred years the Anglo-Norman scutage system, which did not become common in western Europe until about 1300.

In theory the select fyrd could be summoned to serve for a period of sixty days, but in practice such a long period of service was rare, partly because most crises could be dealt with in a short time, and partly because a large force could not be provisioned for such a long period without a great deal of prior organization. Military campaigns conducted by the king against the Welsh or Scots were normally several years apart and entailed much less than the annual obligation, and the fyrd was not summoned merely for training. On the other hand, the king expected – and received – unlimited service from the select fyrd in times of national crisis, and the fyrd might be summoned a number of times in one year: it was mustered five times in 1016.

Arms and Armour

The arms and armour of the English army varied in quality rather than in nature, the professionals being heavily armoured and equipped with the best weapons, the great fyrd unarmoured and bearing any object which could be used to stab or bludgeon a man to death, and the select fyrd somewhere between these two extremes.

The most common weapon was the spear, not just for the fyrd but also for the professional soldiers and even the magnates: it was the traditional weapon of Woden and remained the weapon *par excellence* among Germanic people even in the 11th century. In the laws of Knut (1020–23), the heriot or war trappings of the various ranks underline this:

'An earl's as belongs thereto, namely 8 horses, 4 saddled and 4 unsaddled, and 4 helmets and 4 coats of mail and 8 spears and as many shields and 4 swords and 200 mancuses of gold.'

'And next, the king's thegns, who are closest to him: 4 horses, 2 saddled and 2 unsaddled, and 2 swords and 4 spears and as many shields, and a helmet and coat of mail and 50 mancuses of gold.'

'And of the lesser thegns: a horse and its trappings, and his weapons or his healsfang in Wessex; and 2 pounds in Mercia and 2 pounds in East Anglia.'

'And the heriot of the king's thegn among the Danes, who has right of jurisdiction; 4 pounds.'

'And if he has a more intimate relation with the king: 2 horses, 1 saddled and 1 unsaddled, and a sword and 2 spears and 2 shields and 50 mancuses of gold.'

The above suggests that twice as many men were armed with spear and shield as were armed with mail shirt, helmet, shield, spear *and* sword, i.e. the difference between a housecarl or mercenary and a member of the select fyrd, and that all were normally mounted.

There were two types of spear, a light throwing spear and a stouter thrusting one. Manuscripts frequently show warriors holding two spears in the shield hand and a third in the right hand: presumably two of these would be throwing spears and the third retained for hand-to-hand fighting. The shafts varied in length according to type and the owner's size. No Anglo-Saxon shaft has survived, but the position of the heads and ferrules found in graves indicates lengths of 1.50 to 2.75 metres. A German shaft which has survived is 2.10 metres, and 2 metres seems to have been a common length, with the longest shafts for the thrusting type.

The heads of these spears are found in the graves of rich and poor alike, and range from 7 to 60 cm in length. They are usually leaf-shaped with a rib running up the centre of the blade. The socket is usually split at the sides, being hammered tight on the shaft and secured with a rivet and often leather thong lashing also.

The Anglo-Saxon sword had a broad, two-edged blade between 75 and 80 cm long, with straight edges and a rather rounded point. The width of the blade was about 55 mm and the weight around 0.68 kg. A wide, shallow groove (the fuller) down the centre of both sides of the blade served to lighten it without loss of strength. The hilt had a crossguard which almost always curved towards the blade; a grip of wood or bone, bound with cloth, leather, cord or even silver wire; and a heavy pommel to counterbalance the weight of the blade. In the 9th and 10th centuries the pommels were of the types now called tea cosy and brazil nut, after their shapes, but in the 11th century a few disc-shaped pommels appeared and some of the older three- and five-lobed pommels of earlier times remained, for swords were the most prized of weapons and were handed down from father to son. As late as Knut's reign men below the rank of thegn did not have swords, and even in 1066 a large number of the select fyrd would have had only spears and long knives.

The scabbards for these swords were made from two thin

laths of wood, covered in leather, and with the mouth and tip protected by metal. The inside was frequently lined with fleece, the lanolin in the wool preventing rusting, and its spring helping to hold the blade firmly in the scabbard. The 'lay' of the wool was upwards, to enable the sword to be drawn easily. The scabbard was slung on the left hip, either by a baldric over the right shoulder or on a waist-belt. Both belt and baldric were frequently ornamented and the buckles were generally of bronze, sometimes copper, and not infrequently gilded, embossed or enamelled, and some were set with garnets or other stones.

All warriors, from the highest to the lowest, also carried a single-edged knife known as a scramasax. This was used to finish a felled opponent and in the case of the peasant classes took the place of the sword. Therefore its length varied according to its role, and examples range from 7.5 to 75 cm in length. However, the average size for most of the hundreds found is around 15 cm from point to hilt. This was probably the knife usually referred to as the handseax: the extremely long examples were sometimes called langseax. Most blades were broad, heavy and with an angled back edge sloping in a straight line towards the point, and were often inlaid with copper or bronze wire. The guard, if any, was insignificant; the grip of wood, sometimes carved; and the tang usually without a pommel. Some of the longer knives have a grip long enough to be clasped with two hands. The scramasax was carried in a sheath of folded leather, the edge riveted together on the side of the cutting edge and suspended on the thigh from the waist-belt by small bronze loops.

The reigns of Knut and Harald Harefoot saw the introduction into England of the two-handed Danish axe as a major weapon of the professional soldier. However, its use in the English army was not nearly so widespread as most writers would have us believe, and it was used only by some of the housecarls and Danish mercenaries, who were but a fraction of the whole army. That it was not a common weapon amongst the Anglo-Saxon soldiery in general is proven by the rarity of its occurrence at archaeological sites, and it has therefore been described fully in the chapter on the Vikings, with whom it is most commonly associated.

A smaller, single-handed axe was used by some of the professional warriors, and may have been employed as a missile at times. Stone hammers and clubs were also used as missiles, the former being merely a heavy stone lashed to a long wooden handle. Such a weapon cost nothing, was easily made and totally expendable. Thrown in much the same way as the modern hammer in athletics, and from behind the shield wall, it fell from the sky with deadly effect, its weight plus the velocity of its descent making it capable of inflicting injuries which mail armour could do nothing to prevent.

The Bayeux Tapestry and contemporary manuscripts show slings being used to hunt birds, but slings were probably used by members of the fyrd at Hastings to supplement the limited missile power of the army. The sling was a simple leather strap with an open pocket at the middle for the projectile, and it hurled with considerable force either stones or fired clay balls, which were carried in a wallet. Stones, propelled either by hand or by catapult, are still used today by country people to knock off the odd pheasant at dusk.

There has been much argument in the last two decades about the use of the bow as a weapon by the English army of 1066. The Anglo-Saxons were keen huntsmen, and many contemporary illustrations show them using the bow for hunting, but apart from Snorri Sturluson's account of Stamford Bridge there is no clear indication of the bow being used in war, for in the Anglo-Saxon language the same word is used to describe both an arrow and a throwing spear. Nor do the heriots listed in Knut's laws make any mention of the bow.

The aristocracy was skilled in the use of the bow for the hunt, but were unlikely to carry it as their weapon in war; for the spear and the sword were the weapons of warriors. Similarly the housecarls and mercenaries were too valuable as an élite heavy infantry to be allowed to linger in the rear as archers. However, it is highly unlikely that any army of such high quality as the Anglo-Saxon one, and with such recent battle experience against the Scandinavians – who had a strong tradition of the use of a war bow – would have completely ignored the bow as a weapon of war. Nor should the strong Scandinavian influence in England itself be forgotten, and it is more than likely that the men from the Danelaw also had a strong tradition of the use of the bow in war. It can safely be assumed that archers were a recognized part of the normal English army of the 11th century, most likely peasants who fought in their everyday clothing and were armed only with the bow (of all the 'Norman' archers illustrated in the Bayeux Tapestry, only one wears a mail hauberk), but what proportion of the army consisted of archers must remain a mystery.

Bows are rarely found on archaeological sites because of the decay of wood, but several traces have been found in graves in England and these would seem to indicate a length of about 150 cm. Surviving examples found in Germany, which may be taken as typical of Anglo-Saxon bows, range from 120 to 320 cm in length: 180 to 210 cm seems to be an average figure. These staves are of yew, slightly curved, thickest at the middle and tapering towards the ends. Metal has been found on the ends of a few, and it is possible horn was also used to tip the staves. It would appear, therefore, that the bow in use in the mid-11th century was little different to the medieval longbow, except that the string was not pulled back to the ear, only to the chest, suggesting either a weaker or more rigid stave, or merely inferior ability as archers. Nevertheless, these bows were capable of piercing mail at up to 45 metres and, with a trajectory, had an effective range of up to 90 metres.

Arrow heads are not commonly found and can be confused with the small heads used for throwing spears. They appear to have been leaf-shaped and some were barbed, with a tang or socket for the shaft. Shafts which have survived are about 60 cm long, somewhat thicker towards the head, and had four flights. Quivers which have survived also point to a short arrow of about 60 cm: the quivers were cylindrical and were carried over the right shoulder or on the left hip.

Mail armour was only worn by the housecarls, some mercenaries, great lords, and the richer thegns of the select fyrd: the bulk of the army would have worn everyday clothing, sometimes with the addition of a leather jerkin. The mail shirt was made from thousands of metal rings arranged so that each one had four others linked through it. The individual rings were either punched out of sheet metal or made from drawn wire wrapped round a former, the ends then flattened, overlapped and riveted together. The punched rings were often used in alternate rows with the riveted ones, but some mail consisted of all riveted links. Eleventh-century mail shirts were of knee length, had wide sleeves reaching to just below the elbow, and were slit from hem to crotch at front and back so that they hung down either side of the saddle when the wearer was mounted. There was a slit from the round neck opening down the centre of the chest, and this was closed by laces. The great lords sometimes had mail shirts with long sleeves reaching to the wrists. A mail hood, known as the healsbeorg, was also worn by the professional warriors to protect head, cheeks and chin: this term became corrupted to hauberk and was eventually applied to hood and mail shirt together.

Helmets were also worn by the professional warriors, magnates and thegns, and were of the form now referred to as the spangenhelm. This could be hammered out of one piece of iron, either including a nasal guard or with this bar added later, but was more often of the framework type – a brow band and four iron arches, with the spaces between them filled by metal plates. In Knut's time the lesser thegns had neither mail nor helmets, but by 1066 probably all thegns had helmets, and possibly even some of the *geneats*.

The traditional form for the Anglo-Saxon shield was round, made of two or three layers of wood laid cross-grained, and often faced with ox-hide. Traces of such shields indicate diameters of from 30 to 76 cm, but 60 cm would be a reasonable average. According to surviving rivets, the thickness of the shields ranged from 12 to 30 mm. A hole in the centre provided room for the hand to clasp an iron grip across the inner face of the hole, and this hole was protected by a metal boss about 15 cm wide, secured to the shield by four or five rivets. A strap for the forearm would have been used on the larger shields, and the metal fastenings for this on the face of the shield were

62

sometimes embellished and made into decorative plates.

Until the early 11th century the Anglo-Saxon warrior had closely resembled a Viking, wearing a short, lightweight mail shirt, using the round shield, and relying for defence mainly on agility and speed. The adoption of the long and much heavier hauberk had robbed the Anglo-Saxon warrior, particularly the housecarls, of this mobility, and created the need for a larger shield which could give more complete protection. Therefore, by 1066 the housecarls and many of the select fyrd were using the kite-shaped shield, normally associated with the Normans, but the less well-equipped members of the fyrd and the Scandinavian warriors in English pay continued to use the round shield. The Bayeux Tapestry does show some 'house-carls' with the round shield, and these have been interpreted as Norske shields taken at Stamford Bridge to replace the damaged shields of some housecarls. However, the housecarls had six days in London in which to obtain replacement kite-shaped shields prior to marching against the Normans, and it is far more likely that those warriors illustrated in the tapestry with round shields are Danish mercenaries, lithsmen rather than housecarls, whom they would resemble in all other respects.

The Navy

The exact composition of the English navy in the first half of the 11th century is obscure, but we know it contained three main elements: mercenaries – the lithsmen and their ships – who were hired as a small, semi-permanent navy; ships provided as a special obligation by certain coastal towns, including those later known as the Cinque Ports; and a general territorial obligation to perform sea duty and to subscribe to the building of ships when necessary.

In the case of the territorial obligation, in certain regions the five-hide units were combined into larger districts of 300 hides to cope with the construction of a ship, and these were called ship-sokes. Thus a ship-soke not only produced a ship when ordered, but also sixty warrior-seamen, the number of men needed to man a typical ship of the period. Inland regions probably paid to the king a tax, known as ship-scot, in place of the coastal towns' obligation to build and equip a ship.

It would appear, therefore, that the select fyrd and ship-fyrd were one and the same, expected to serve on land or sea depending on need, and led by the same commander, who was thus both general and admiral. However, the men selected by each unit of land to serve in the ship-fyrd may not have been the same men that served in the select fyrd, and not all inland areas were obliged to send men to serve at sea. Leicester, for example, owed twelve men for land service, but, if the fyrd was to serve at sea, sent four horses as far as London to carry arms or supplies instead. Another example is Warwick, which normally sent ten men to the select fyrd but supplied four boatswains or £4 in lieu if the fyrd was to serve at sea. The ships themselves were manned partly by seamen from the coastal areas and partly by the mercenaries, who doubled as soldiers.

In 1045 Edward mustered thirty-five ships off Sandwich, and a much larger fleet at the same place in 1046. In 1049, when Godwine was sent to drive off coastal raiders, he took two of the king's ships and forty-two '*landes manna scipa*' – probably ships manned by the ship-fyrd ('manned by men on national service'*). When Godwine had set sail, Edward 'then gave leave to all the Mercian contingent in the fleet to go home,'† again suggesting this was the ship-fyrd.

Knut had reduced the fleet of mercenaries to a mere sixteen ships, and the permanent navy remained at this strength under his successor. Under Edward it had a strength of fourteen vessels in 1049 and five in 1050, when these last crews were discharged. In 1051 Edward abolished the heregeld, which had paid these mercenaries since Knut's time. Shortly afterwards he instituted a new system under which the Cinque Ports (Sandwich, Dover, Hastings, Romney and Hythe) and Maldon were granted special privileges, including all the monies taken in their courts, exemption from tolls throughout England and from select fyrd service, and in return owed an exceptionally heavy naval obligation. Thus, in 1066, Dover and Sandwich were each obliged to produce twenty ships for the king's service, each with a crew of twenty-one men, a steersman and his assistant. There is no evidence of the service owed by

England in 1066, showing the divisions of the kingdom and position of the roads.

*Anglo-Saxon Chronicle (E)   †Anglo-Saxon Chronicle (C)

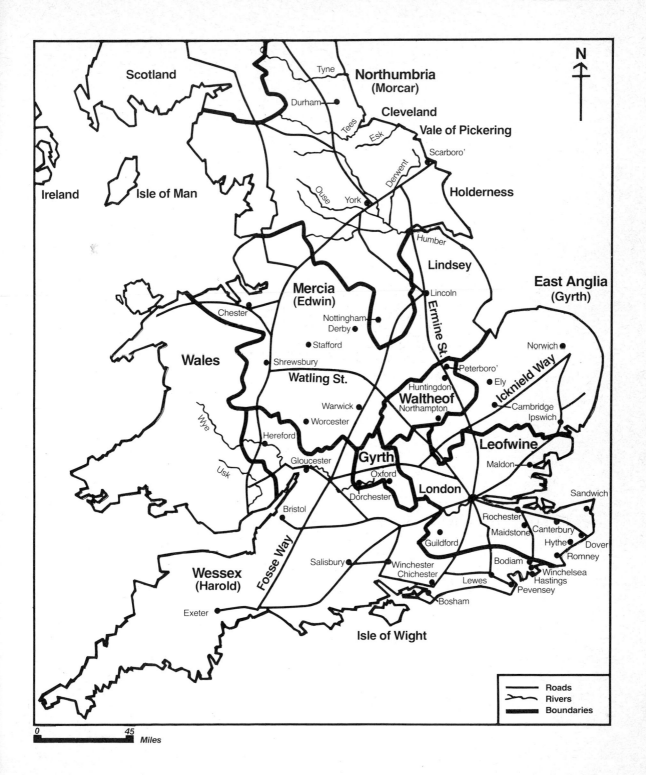

Hastings and Hythe, but Romney seems to have owed one ship with a crew of twenty-one men.

However, the obligation to serve at sea instead of on land remained for the select fyrd, and Scandinavian mercenaries with their ships could always be hired when needed. Therefore, in 1066 the English navy was exceptionally strong, although slow to muster and difficult to hold together, consisting as it did of the ships owned personally by the king and his earls; ships manned and owned by mercenaries; impressed private merchant ships; ships and crews provided by particular coastal towns in return for special privileges and exemptions; and ships built by the old ship tax or ship-sokes and manned by the select fyrd warrior-seamen.

The length of service owed by the ships of Dover was only fifteen days: the same period of service was probably owed by the other Cinque Ports. The length of service for those ships manned by the select fyrd is not known, but the ship-fyrd probably served up to the same two months' limit that it would have served had it been on land.

Sandwich was the main naval base where the fleet mustered, and was to remain so for centuries: Godwine tried to capture it when he returned from exile in 1052, and Tostig made it a major target in his raids of early 1066.

The type of ship used by the English navy does not appear to have differed a great deal from that used by the Vikings: a double-ended, clinker-built longship which was fast and manoeuvrable, single-decked and single-masted with one large square sail, guided by a steering oar which was pivoted on the starboard quarter, and with oar ports cut in the sides. One distinctive feature on many was a break in the row of oar holes amidships and a corresponding gap in the bulwark, possibly as a result of a raised deck to facilitate sea fighting. However, when Alfred decided to tackle the Vikings at sea he 'ordered warships to be built to meet the Danish ships: they were almost twice as long as the others, some had sixty oars, some more; they were both swifter, steadier, and with more freeboard than the others; they were built neither after the Frisian design nor after the Danish, but as it seemed to himself . . . most serviceable.'*

*Anglo-Saxon Chronicle (A)

The Viking ships were built to cross the North Sea and were sturdy, sea-going vessels: the English ships were designed exclusively for work in coastal waters, and could therefore be much longer and higher out of the water, assets which would have made the Viking ships unseaworthy. Therefore, they probably *were* twice the length of the Viking ships, with an average of thirty oars a side, and ranging from 50 to as much as 70 metres in length.

Fortifications

It is often assumed that England had no fortifications prior to 1066, but this is untrue. The Norman motte and bailey castle was designed to give protection to small groups of soldiers in exposed positions in hostile territory: this situation did not arise in England except in the Welsh marches, and here Edward had already made a small start by allowing at least three such castles to be built by Norman soldiers. Robert fitz Wimarc had also been allowed to build a small castle at Clavering in Essex.

Many of the towns were fortified to some extent by the old Roman walls: London and Exeter at least were capable of such a stout defence that William was held up at both places, and it is doubtful if his own Rouen was better fortified than London.

The Anglo-Saxons had also engaged in the construction of their own earthworks (burhs) round their towns in the late 9th and early 10th centuries. These fortifications were a ditch, an earthen rampart and a timber palisade, repeated on a smaller scale for the inner stronghold of the local overlord. The burhs often had wet ditches, probably because the settlements were almost invariably on low land close to rivers.

William of Poitiers considered that Dover had a 'castle' before 1066, and describes both its natural position and artificial defences with some admiration. The Romans had built a lighthouse and a fort on the height to the east of the town, commanding the sea approaches, the valley and the town. In the 1050s Harold had restored these fortifications, constructing an oval enclosure surrounded by a ditch, and a mound topped with a palisade in the Norman style. Within the enclosure were the lighthouse, the church of St Mary, which was probably built in

Knut's reign, some barracks and other buildings. Nothing remains of these fortifications today, but in 1066 William thought them so strong that he would only be able to take them by fire, and he was somewhat scornful of the 'castle's' quick surrender to him.

From the details set out above, it can be seen that when Harold became King of England he inherited a powerful and efficiently organized army and navy, both of which he had commanded for the past thirteen years. The professional fighting men were well equipped with the most up-to-date weapons and defences, and both they and the select fyrd were trained to act together as units under his command, whether on land or sea. They were also experienced in actual combat, veterans of the prolonged Welsh wars and accustomed to dealing with minor Viking raids or major attacks, such as the one in 1058. There must have been at least 3,000 royal housecarls, perhaps a thousand more from the earls' household bands, and possibly another thousand of the Danish mercenaries, who were hired when needed. The select fyrd could provide another 20,000 to 25,000 experienced men, and the shire levies many thousands of untrained and ill-equipped men, who nevertheless had their uses. The Channel ports alone were obliged to supply about fifty ships on demand, at least three times that number could be supplied by the ship-fyrd, and there were the ships of the Danish mercenaries.

Harold himself was an experienced general, who could hold his troops together during the toughest campaign, and seems to have had an exceptional talent for inspiring the respect and loyalty of his men. As victor of the Welsh wars (1057–63) he was the first Englishman to solve the problem of fighting the Welsh on their own ground, adopting the Welsh tactics of striking swiftly with lightly armed troops: only Edward I, with more organized resources, more sophisticated methods and a large castle-building programme, was able to equal his successes.

Harold had been a wise and just ruler of East Anglia before his father's death, and of Wessex thereafter. He was respected throughout the land as a military leader and statesman. With perhaps 25,000 or 30,000 trained warriors and at least 250 warships at his back, he had every reason to feel safe and confident in his new role. But he was not fool enough to underestimate William of Normandy, and on coming to power he immediately devoted himself to ensuring the realm was prepared to defend itself. Thereafter he could do little except wait.

3
The Vikings

When Harald Hardrada became King of Norway in 1047 he took over a realm which was prosperous enough to support his wars with Sven Estrithson of Denmark, but which was still far from being a united kingdom. At this date Norway was divided into a number of provinces ruled by *jarls* or earls, some of whom were strong enough to defy the king. For example, the earls of Orkney acknowledged the overlordship of the king of Norway but were in fact independent rulers, while the settlers in Iceland were ruled by their chieftains as an oligarchy, totally divorced from Norway. In Norway itself the difficult terrain had enabled some earls to establish their own dynasties in the isolated fjords, the most powerful of which was the Earl of Lade (Hlaoajarlar), who held all the land from Trondelag northwards. The King of Norway had no permanent residence, but travelled constantly from one royal estate to another in order to maintain control over his subjects, relying on alliances with these great earls in all parts of Norway for his success and survival as king.

Harald Hardrada, whose name means hard counsel or hard ruler, was not the sort of king to tolerate this situation for long, and he at once set about consolidating his power. One of his first steps was to ruthlessly crush the Earl of Lade, and thus effectively end any possibility of an earls' revolt: thereafter the power of the king grew, while the earls declined in national importance so that by 1066 the title had fallen into disuse in Norway and, unlike their Anglo-Saxon counterparts, the earls had little or no part in the administration of the kingdom.

However, these men remained the natural leaders in their own regions, not least because at this date the opportunities for establishing settlements abroad had diminished considerably, and new settlements were now being founded in the Scandinavian homelands. Some of these new farms were on common land and were regarded as Crown leases, but others were on private land, the lands of the earls and their families. The wealth and strength of these families depended on the support of the freemen or yeoman farmers who worked their lands, and the increased number of settlements on these lands meant more freemen who could be expected to support the earl, because they were his tenants. Others, whose families had held lands under the earl's family for generations, were his men because of the traditional and personal links, and still others were loyal to him because the wealth he accrued from his tenants enabled him to buy their loyalty. This last category was known as his houseband or *huskarlar*, and could include foreign mercenaries, although it was normal for most of the band to be recruited from the earl's own region. These *hirdmenn* or housecarls shared his hall, food, ale, loot and treasury, and in return stood by him come what may, gave their lives for him without hesitation and, in the event of his death in battle, died on the same field avenging him. The size and richness of a *huskarlar* indicated not just an earl's wealth, but also his worth as a leader and as a man.

In the late 9th century Harald Finehair, the first true king of all Norway, had decreed that each earl should maintain a *huskarlar* of sixty warriors, and that beneath him there should be a minimum of four local military commanders, each with a houseband of twenty warriors. Harald Hardrada did much to curb the ambitions of the earls, but is unlikely to have reduced the size of their *huskarlar*, for he depended upon them to form

71

an élite professional corps within the national army.

The freemen mentioned above formed the bulk of the population, supplying the middle class between the aristocracy of the great landed families and the slaves. From this class came the priests, poets, lawmen, builders and master craftsmen, but most importantly of all the farmers. At the top of the class was the *haudr* or landed man, an independent yeoman farmer who lived on and cultivated family lands. He was a man of some substance and importance, head of a household, a man of considerable property, especially in livestock, with influence in the political assemblies of his region and the right to assist at the making of judgements at the local court. Not far below him was the *bondi*, another freeman who farmed, but this time on rented, leased, new or bought land. At the bottom of the scale was the *rekspegn*, a freeman who was not a householder but who might have a smallholding which he rented: he was available for employment by the others, either as a manager or as a hired hand, but although less privileged he still shared the legal rights of the more elevated freemen, in particular the right to bear arms – the distinctive mark of the freeman.

At the bottom of society were the thralls or slaves, who were despised by freemen and regarded as cowardly and stupid. There are some indications that in parts of Scandinavia there was an hereditary slave class before the Viking Age: if there was, it was soon swollen to far greater numbers by the raids of the following centuries, for human beings were probably the most common commodity of Viking trade, either as slaves or for ransom. It was also possible to be reduced to slavery as punishment for certain offences or, in a temporary form, as payment of a debt.

Although the slaves performed all the menial tasks and were essential in agriculture, their numbers were never great in any of the isolated settlements – somewhere between three and eighteen per farm – for slave revolts were common.

Slaves could earn their freedom, usually by working a piece of land for themselves and selling the produce to raise their redemption price. In the 11th century, under the influence of Christianity, they also began to be given freedom for their past services; in Norway the general assemblies of Trondelag and western Norway were obliged to free one slave per year as an act of piety. Also in Norway, a slave was armed if the region was invaded, which might seem a dangerous step, but an armed slave could obtain his freedom as a reward for killing an enemy, and this ensured he attacked the invaders, not his masters.

Under Harald Hardrada, Norway was divided into large 'law provinces' for administrative purposes: for example, the west coast legal federation which was known as the Gulathing Law, the Frostathing Law in the Trondelag districts and Halogaland, the Heidsævislog Law region round Mjosa, and the Ranrike and Vikin Law province, which included Oslo and Tonsberg. Each of these law provinces had a central assembly for law-making and local government. The earls were members of these assemblies, where they were countered by representatives nominated as the king's agents, but the assemblies were so large (up to 400 men) that the freemen remained a notable force, capable of influencing all law-making and political debate.

These central assemblies were also responsible for the military levy known as the Leidang, a levy of ships, men, armaments and provisions called out by the king and supplied by the population on a proportional basis. Each province was divided into small units, each responsible for supplying one man together with his equipment and sustenance: the similarity to the Anglo-Saxon fyrd is obvious and as the Leidang was fully established and highly organized by the early 10th century, it is probable that it was modelled on the English system, which the Vikings found highly effective when used against themselves, particularly under Alfred (871–899). In the west coast regions of Norway three farms together originally sent one man, but later one man was supposed to join the levy for every seven inhabitants.

These individual units were collected into larger units responsible for supplying and fitting out a ship for active service: in western Norway such a unit was called a *skipreida* (ship-providing) district. In Denmark the local officer responsible for the levy was called styræsman, literally helmsman or skipper.

Every freeman was under obligation to turn out if an attack was made on his district, and even the thralls could be armed for such an emergency, but the Leidang was a levy, a selection of the able-bodied men, which could be called out at either national or local level. Therefore, if the king summoned the Leidang, even if for defensive purposes, only a select number of men mustered. In Norway it was customary to summon the whole Leidang for the defence of the realm, half the Leidang for an offensive expedition, although Harald Hardrada did summon the whole levy during the Danish wars for offensive purposes. It is generally accepted that the king had the right to summon the levy annually, but for what length of time is unknown.

The summoning of the levy took time, and for defence purposes was frequently done on the strength of intelligence received of an enemy move: once the fleet was assembled it could only wait, and its main function became that of transport for the quick concentration of forces wherever they might be needed. The command to muster was passed from household to household: in Norway each householder was obliged to pass a token, a symbolic arrow of wood or iron, to his neighbour. Attacks by smaller, raiding forces were countered by an elaborate warning system of bonfires sited on high points.

We can only guess at the strength of a full Leidang. A contemporary poet says that in about 1050 Sven of Denmark had 720 ships. Not all of these would have been large warships, and an estimate of 20,000 men would perhaps not be too optimistic. Another contemporary source gives 200 ships as the strength of Harald Hardrada's fleet, which sailed from Norway in 1066. With an average crew of perhaps forty men per ship, this gives a figure of 8,000 men for the half Leidang, possibly 16,000 men for a full Leidang. (Denmark, with its larger population, could always muster larger forces than either Norway or Sweden.) However, the total number of ships available for a full Leidang may not have exceeded 310, Harald Hardrada's total of 200 probably including private ships belonging to himself and his earls.

In addition to the Leidang, each earl had his personal fleet

manned by his own housecarls. The Norwegian kings in the
11th century also had an élite bodyguard of housecarls or
hirdmenn, and a lower echelon of retainers called *gestir* (guests),
whose pay was half that of the *hirdmenn*. The *gestir* had their own
leader, assembly and quarters, and acted as a kind of police force
for the king, enforcing his justice and collecting his taxes. The
gestir were not likely to be popular, whereas the *hirdmenn* were
heroes all; men hand-picked not only by the king but by the
other housecarls. To be accepted as a *hirdman* was a great
honour, and all newcomers to the group swore loyalty not just
to the king but to the group as a whole, and utter loyalty was
demanded and given in return for admittance. The *esprit de corps*
fostered within such a group was immense, and inevitably
attracted the best Scandinavian fighting men as well as aliens,
for exiles who had lost their land and families could find a new
'family' in the *huskarlar*.

The total force of élite *hirdmenn* available to the king of
Norway in the mid-11th century was quite considerable. In
1062, at the battle of Nissa, Harald Hardrada had 180 ships
belonging to himself and his earls, all manned exclusively by
hirdmenn. This gives a possible total of 7,200 professional
warriors available to the king that year, and therefore
presumably a similar number was available in 1066. By this date
seventeen years of endemic war and 200 years of Viking activity
had bred a hardy race of warrior-seamen and created a highly
organized military structure. Admittedly by 1066 the great era
of the Vikings was over, but the men who followed Harald
Hardrada (often called the last of the great Viking leaders) to
England to press his claim to the throne were experienced
warriors, accustomed to serving together as ships' crews for
many years, and their skill, discipline and strong code of honour
and loyalty to their employer had made them famous as
mercenaries from England itself to Constantinople.

Arms and Armour
For the Viking warrior the sword was the principal weapon, the
badge of rank of the true fighting man, and as such would have
been carried by the magnates, housecarls and the freemen of the

select levy. From the early 10th century the blades were of flexible, high-quality steel, either produced in Scandinavia or imported – particularly from the Rhineland – but the best of the older swords retained their value because of the reputations of the previous owners, and such swords were handed down from father to son to grandson. Olaf Haraldsson's sword, for example, was already old when it came into his possession and on his death it passed to a Swede, whose family used it for another three generations before it was placed over an altar in the 12th century.

The blades of these earlier weapons, made at a time when it was difficult to obtain large pieces of iron and it was necessary to mix inferior metal with that of superior quality to minimize the effect of the former, were made by a process known as pattern welding. The core of the blade was made from three parallel bars of iron, each of which was itself made up of several case-hardened strips placed like a sandwich between two rods of similar iron. (Case-hardening, a core of malleable iron within a skin of iron with a higher carbon content and therefore harder, was achieved by repeated heating in a charcoal fire.) These strips were twisted tightly to weld all parts together, with the rods on the outside of the sandwich filling the spiral grooves created by the twisting. The three bars thus formed were next welded together and another bar of case-hardened iron welded all the way up each side and round the point to form the cutting edge. Finally the blade was tempered and quenched to give it hardness and flexibility, and treated with acid, which caused markings like those on a snake's back to show up in the fuller: this was the twisted rods of the core, with the carburized parts showing a lighter colour than the softer iron. Such a blade might take a month to manufacture and in the mid-10th century was valued as equal to the cost of fifteen male slaves or 120 oxen.

Including the 10 cm tang, the Viking sword was usually no more than 90 cm in length: a sword as long as 95 cm was a rarity and all swords were intended for use in one hand. The blades were similar in shape to the Anglo-Saxon ones; straight, broad, two-edged blades with a fuller down the middle of each side, and a rather rounded point. The Vikings loved richness and

Viking warrior with short
mail shirt, iron helmet,
and wooden shield for
defence.

Viking spearman in
everyday dress and armed
only with helmet, shield,
spear and probably a long
dagger in place of a
sword.

Viking archer in ordinary
clothes, wearing a helmet
which probably had
leather panels between the
metal arches.

colour in their weapons and dress, and their sword hilts were often richly chased and gilded, or inlaid with copper, silver, gold or niello. Many such hilts were made in Sweden. The crossguard curved towards the blade, also in the Anglo-Saxon fashion, while the pommels were of triangular or semicircular shape, usually divided into three, five or even seven lobes. The tang was covered with wood, bone or horn, and this was sometimes sheathed in leather. The grip thus formed was little wider than the width of a man's hand, indicating that it was not normal or necessary to employ two hands, though some Vikings frequently did so, and Harald Hardrada is alleged to have used his sword in this manner, presumably scorning the use of a shield in order to add more weight to his blows.

The scabbards for these swords were of the same basic construction as the Anglo-Saxon ones, and were normally suspended from a waist-belt, though occasionally a baldric might be used.

A popular alternative to the sword was the long-handled broad-bladed battle-axe, which could cleave through any armour and the man inside it, or literally slice the head off a horse. There were many varieties of axe head, but the two main types were the bearded axe and broad axe. The older bearded axe, or *skeggox*, dates from the 8th century and was probably developed from a woodworker's tool. Over the years the blade was slowly increased in size until the upper and lower points of the cutting edge were some 23 cm apart, with a convex cutting edge between them. This was the broad axe, first popular *c.* 1000, and the most common Viking axe of the 11th century. The cutting edge was often made of specially hardened steel, welded onto the head. Both types of axe had angular necks and were sometimes beautifully decorated with silver inlay on the blade and neck.

From the illustrations on the Bayeux Tapestry it would appear the broad axe had a haft about 1.25 metres in length, often with a slight curve to it, like a modern axe helve. The axe was held in the shield hand, i.e. behind the shield, if a spear was also carried, but frequently a warrior would be armed with only an axe, and if he carried a shield this was slung over his back on a strap to leave both hands free. The axe was held with the left hand uppermost so that it was swung from the left shoulder to catch an opponent on his unshielded side. There was little defence against the broad axe's immense power and both attacker (who was unprotected when striking) and attacked relied mainly on agility to survive. Many axemen worked in partnership with a man armed with shield and sword or spear, who covered them when engaged.

The spear did not have the social implications of the sword and battle-axe, but was nevertheless a major weapon for all ranks, useful as a missile and as a long-handled weapon in the opening phase of a battle, thereafter discarded by at least the professional warriors in favour of the sword or axe. The throwing spears were much like the Anglo-Saxon ones, with small, plain heads: the thrusting spears had broad heads for cutting and thrusting, and were frequently richly inlaid with geometrical patterns in silver across the base of the blade. All Scandinavian spearheads were socketed and usually leaf shaped, with a rib up the centre of each side, giving a lozenge-shaped cross-section. The rivets which attached the heads to the hafts often formed additional ornaments to the socket.

Most men also carried a small, single-edged knife at their belt, with a simple handle of wood or bone. These were employed for a variety of everyday tasks, but the Norwegians had a liking for the Anglo-Saxon langseax, a large single-edged knife which was virtually a short sword and could have had little use except as a weapon. It was probably carried by the spear-armed freemen to serve as a sword in hand-to-hand fighting.

Archery was popular throughout Scandinavia: earls made and strung their own bows, the sagas frequently mention flaxen bowstrings and barbed arrows in the battle scenes, and the Norwegians in particular are referred to by Saxo Grammaticus as famous bowmen. Snorri Sturluson also gives a description of Harald Hardrada wielding his bow throughout the night at the battle of Nissa in 1062. However, it is doubtful if the bow attained its rightful place in Scandinavian land warfare before the 12th century, and in the 11th-century land battles it seems to have been used only by men who carried spears as their main weapons, i.e. the lesser warriors. Such bowmen were relatively few in number, mainly because the Scandinavian ideal of warfare was individual prowess – which could not be attained by standing off and firing arrows – and it is even possible that archers had to be detailed in order to provide a sufficient number.

Bows are rarely found and those which have been identified as Viking ones cannot be regarded as typical. A yew bow found in Ireland, alongside a Viking type of sword, was 185 cm long and

Axe-head of the 10th century from Mammen in Jutland. It is richly inlaid with silver wire but would have been used in battle as well as for ceremonial purposes. (Nationalmuseet, Copenhagen.)

Axe-head of early skeggox form found in the River Thames near Whitehall. The skeggox first appeared in the 8th century and was probably developed from a carpenter's axe.

Viking axe-heads illustrating the development of the broad-bladed two-handed or broadaxe (bottom) from the earlier single-handed skeggox (top). The broadaxe, first popular *circa* 1000, was the most common form of axe used by the Vikings and housecarls in the 11th century.

Head of a Viking broadaxe with ornamented brass socket, found by Old London Bridge.

81

Broadaxe with a large part
of the original wooden
handle, found in County
Mayo, and probably
Norwegian. The surviving
handle is 66.5 cm in
length, the cutting edge of
the blade 17.8 cm.

of D cross-section. Other examples range from 150 to 180 cm.
Bundles of arrow heads have been found in many graves and
usually have leaf-shaped blades between 10 and 15 cm long: a
few have a trefoil cross-section with three cutting edges. There
are also the barbed arrows mentioned in the sagas, though these
have not been found in graves. Many of the arrow heads are
tanged, but some are socketed. The four flights were glued in
position and secured with tarred twine. Cylindrical quivers
were used.

Very little is known about the armour worn by Vikings, as
there are few illustrations and grave finds have not included
sufficient fragments to reconstruct a Scandinavian mail shirt.
The armour is well documented in poetry, in words like
hringserkr (ring-shirt) and byrnie, and was assembled in the same
manner as Anglo-Saxon mail, but was of a lighter and more
flexible construction and reached only to the hips, with short
sleeves and a simple round neck opening. The full-length
hauberk, with sleeves to the elbows and reaching to the knees,
and made with heavier links, was probably only ever worn by
the great leaders and by some of their housecarls. Mail armour
was never as common amongst the Vikings as we are given to
believe and the majority of Scandinavian warriors would have
made do with either their everyday dress or have used tough
leather jackets or jerkins of padded linen, some of which were
partially covered by metal rings attached individually.

The chief means of defence for the Viking was the shield.

HIC : V VILLELM : DVX INTERRO

Almost all Viking shields were round, but there is some evidence that in the 11th century the kite-shaped shield was introduced, and it would have been surprising if it had not been, for the Vikings, as professional fighting men, had always adopted the latest and best of weapons and defences, never hesitating to abandon traditional styles in favour of more efficient ones.

The round shields were made of thin layers of wood laid cross-grained liked modern plywood, or from several boards fitted side by side. There was a hole in the centre to enable the bearer to hold an iron handgrip fastened across the hole, and the hand was protected by an iron boss, usually hammered out of a single piece of iron, though the Norwegians from Ireland often used a boss made from a flat sheet of metal which was merely 'rolled' to form a cone. The boss was secured to the shield orb by rivets, and there was frequently leather, metal strip or small metal plates reinforcing the edge of the shield.

These shields seem to have been larger than the Anglo-Saxon shields on average, being up to a metre in diameter. Many were

Duke William and probably his half-brother Odo, Bishop of Bayeux, receive news of the position of the English army before Hastings. (From the Bayeux Tapestry.) Both are armed with a mace, William having a wooden one and Odo a wooden handle with the trilobate metal head common to both English and Norman maces. The tapestry portrays the English using their maces as missiles.

83

Fragment of leather
scabbard belonging to an
Anglo-Saxon scramasax,
found at Hexham,
Northumberland. It bears
an interlaced ribbon
pattern. The fragment is
11.2 cm long by 6 cm
wide. (British Museum.)

Opposite
A series of gold and
enamel equipment mounts
from the Sutton Hoo find
(late 6th, early 7th
century). The hinged
mount at top centre, and
buckle panels to its left
and right, were found
beside the sword scabbard,
as were the flat belt panels
below. The hinged panel
must have had its lower
end attached to a second,
narrower belt, which held
the scabbard tilted
backwards. The buckle to
the right, having a narrow
opening, must have been
for this second belt. The
larger buckle was for the
waist belt. The plates
were attached to the belt
by the gold rivets which
are still in place. The
buckle on the right is
7.7 cm long. (British
Museum.)

brightly painted, the most popular colour being red, with blue,
yellow and black as other common colours, and decorated with
dragons, ravens, etc. Despite the reinforcements, it was not
unusual for a shield to be hacked to pieces early in a fight; the
sagas frequently mention shields shattering, but the boss
and grip were riveted together and could still be used as a

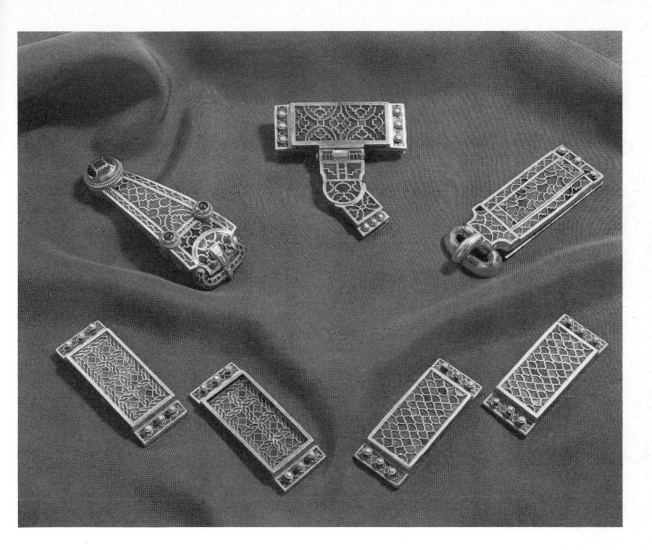

mailed fist, or the shield of a fallen man might be seized.

In battle the round shield was initially carried at arm's length in order to break the force of any weapon striking the shield and to keep away from the body any weapon which pierced it. For the in-fighting it was held close to the body so that it could not easily be knocked aside, and was used both to parry blows and as an offensive weapon; the edge was often used to strike at a spear shaft to break off the head or to knock the spear away, and

85

the boss was forcibly thrust into an opponent's face or chest to throw him off balance.

Many helmets are known from the 6th century Vendel period, but only a few fragments survive from the Viking Age and it is difficult to be precise about the form of helmet worn in the 11th century. The most remarkable find, in the 10th-century Gjermundbu grave, shows a simple rounded cap built up from four ribs and a brow band, with a spike on the crest and a nose and eye guard, the latter of spectacle shape. Similar helmets have been found in the pre-Viking Age graves at Vendel and Valsgärde in Uppland, Sweden, and there is also the helm of St Wenceslas in Prague Cathedral, which is of this general pattern and dates from pre-935. A helmet from Lokrune in Gotland takes the same form and has a nose guard decorated with interlace ornament which is normally associated with the 10th or 11th centuries. It would seem that mail face guards were suspended from the eye guards of some of these helmets: these guards were of fine mesh and did not reach to the mail shirt to cover the neck. Some had cheek pieces added instead of the mail.

Only the magnates and their housecarls would have been able to afford helmets, and the men of the levy would have been either bare-headed or have worn a leather cap, possibly of the Phrygian type. Most housecarls would have had the simple conical helmet now referred to as the spangenhelm.

It is possible that a few of the magnates may have also worn some form of greave; a sensible defence as the legs were unguarded by the round shield, and contemporary accounts often mention men having their leg or legs chopped off. No greaves have been found, and illustrations of them are rare. The first illustration is dated *c.* 890 and shows a Dane and two companions with thin metal plates attached to the front of their stockings and reaching from knee to instep. An example at the beginning of the 11th century also covers the foot. Greaves do not seem to have been used much after the end of the 11th century, by which date the kite-shaped shield, which did afford some protection to the legs, was becoming more popular.

In the late 12th century laws were laid down to regulate the weapons which male adults should own. This is more than a century after 1066, but gives a fair indication of what must have been an even greater lack of armour in the preceding century:

Sweden: shield, sword, spear and iron hat for each man. One mail coat or protective jerkin and a bow and three dozens arrows per rowing bench. An axe might be used instead of a sword.

Norway: shield, sword or axe, and spear for each man. A bow and two dozen arrows per bench.

Denmark: shield, sword, spear and iron hat for each man. The styræsman also had to provide, with the help of his neighbour, a horse, a coat of mail, and a crossbow and bolts, along with a man to use the latter.

The Ships
The high-prowed 'dragon ship' has become the accepted symbol of the Vikings, an awe-inspiring weapon which was so constructed that it was able to strike swiftly across the dangerous North Sea at the coasts of Europe, yet could also penetrate to the rich valleys inland via the rivers, or be drawn up on sandy beaches or on islets, where the heavier vessels of their enemies could not follow. It was the most revolutionary of all the Vikings' weapons: long and narrow with a large sail which gave fast sailing speeds, yet light enough to be rowed so that it was not dependent on sails alone. Small wonder the mere sight of these ships was sufficient to cause the local populace to flee in terror.

Our knowledge of these ships and their construction comes from a variety of sources: from memorial stones and scrimshaw on wood, from contemporary Scandinavian poetry and western European literature and the later laws and sagas, and from surviving examples, particularly the Tune, Oseberg and Gokstad ships found in burial mounds on the shores of Oslofjord in Norway, and the ships found in Roskildefjord in Denmark.

There were a number of different types of ship and these were classified roughly by size and also named. The smaller warships were listed according to the number of paired rowing places (called a *sess*) they contained, e.g. a *fimtansessa*, or fifteenbencher. According to the Gulathing Law, the smallest vessel which could be counted by benches was a thirteen-bencher (*prettansessa*). The standard levy ship all over Scandinavia seems to have been the twenty-bencher, though some were smaller, while others had as many as twenty-five or even thirty benches. The space between the benches was called *rum* (room or space), and it was also customary to describe a ship by the number of *rum* it had.

The chief ocean-going vessel was named the *knorr*, though a general term for trading vessels was *kaupskip*. The *knorr* was a bulky maid of all work, essentially a sailing craft with just a few oars fore and aft for manoeuvring in harbour. An 11th-century example found in Roskildefjord is 15.5 metres long and 4.5 metres in the beam.

General-purpose vessels used around the fjords were the *skuta*, with up to thirty oars and built for speed, and the *karfi*, with twelve to thirty-two oars: the Gokstad and Oseberg ships probably belonged to the latter class. The origin of the term *karfi* is unclear, but a late Norwegian text suggests the name might apply to a ship fitted out for the levy but smaller than the longship, which was the real warship.

Of the longships, the commonest type was the *snekkja*, which had twenty benches. A later and larger type was the *skeid*, with possibly as many as thirty benches. The largest of all was the *drekar* (dragon), probably so named because of its ornate prow.

To understand the construction of the Viking ships it is best to take a look at the three finest surviving examples. The Oseberg ship was built of oak about AD 800. She is 22 metres long, 5.25 metres midships, 1.5 metres from gunwale to keel and has fifteen oarholes along each side. Her prow and stern posts are 4.5 metres high. The mast step was cracked and had been repaired and strengthened: she was probably an old ship, refitted for her last 'voyage' as a burial ship (her oars and mast were new).

The Tune ship is also of oak, built at the end of the 9th century, 20 metres long, 4.25 metres in the beam and about 1.40 metres deep. There are eleven oarholes each side. This ship is of shallow draught, extremely light and with a low freeboard, but the upper two strakes have been raked strongly outwards, giving an extra buoyancy when the ship heeled over and helping to keep out the spray. This made her a more seaworthy craft than the earlier Oseberg ship.

The Gokstad ship is again of oak, built in the late 9th century, 23.3 metres long, 5.25 metres in the beam and 1.95 metres deep, with a draught of only about 90–95 cm and therefore a freeboard of about 110 cm. She represents a considerable advance in ship-building techniques over the Oseberg ship, having an improved type of mast step, two extra strakes above the one with oarholes, giving about 75 cm more freeboard, and a keel cut from a single oak tree, which draws nearly 30 cm more water at the centre and so allows her to sail closer to the wind.

The hull is also more efficiently shaped, built of sixteen strakes, nine of which are below the waterline. The strakes were riveted together, each overlapping the one below, caulked with wool-yarn and tar, and lashed to the frames by means of pliable spruce roots which passed through holes in cleats which had been left free-standing when the plank was cut. This method of construction gave considerable elasticity in rough weather, together with a lightness because fewer ribs were needed. A replica built in the late 19th century was sailed across the Atlantic in 1893 in twenty-eight days. During the stormy crossing the captain recorded in his log that the ship undulated with the waves, the bottom and keel rising and falling by as much as 2 cm, and the gunwale twisting as much as 15 cm out of true, yet the vessel remained watertight. The captain reported that she could sail at ten knots and sometimes more, and the rudder 'had the advantage of never kicking, as a stern post rudder would certainly have done. One man could steer in any weather with merely a small line to help.'

This rudder looks rather like a large oar and was attached to the starboard side at the aftermost frame by a tree root which passed through the rudder itself, through a large wooden block which acted as a pivot and through the side of the ship and the frame. The gunwale at this point was reinforced with a heavy plank, to which the head of the steering-oar was strapped. A straight tiller bar was inserted into the head of the steering-oar at right angles. The steering-oar, which extended below the keel, could be raised when the ship was beached by releasing the strap and swivelling the oar on the pivot block.

The mast was stepped in an elaborate housing some 3.75 metres long, fastened to the ribs, and at deck level passed through a mast-fish some 5 metres in length. The mast could be lowered or raised at will and was locked in its upright position by an oak wedge: when lowered it rested above the deck on two crutches, which were used to house the oars when the ship was under sail. A forestay, shrouds and almost certainly a back stay supported the mast.

Only short fragments of masts survive and it is impossible to judge with certainty the length of the mast or the depth of the sail. On the Gokstad ship the mast was 30 cm thick and heavy, but because it was intended to be frequently and quickly lowered it is unlikely to have been as long as this indicates, and when lowered its truck may well have remained within the ship, giving a possible length for the Gokstad ship of perhaps only 10 metres.

The width of the sail may be judged from surviving spars, that of the Gokstad ship being about 12 metres, that of the Oseberg ship 12.7 metres: the sail would probably have been about 11 metres across. The short mast and wide but low sail would have lessened the need for ballast and special shrouds, for the lateral force of the wind would have created less leverage than on a ship with a higher mast and taller sail, and the short mast would have been another important factor in the ability of the Viking ships to be fast and light. The sagas describe the sails as all red, or white striped with red or blue, but the Gotland stones usually depict them with a checkered pattern.

A considerable manoeuvrability could be achieved using sail and rudder, but although the vessel could sail close to the wind, she could not tack into the wind. Therefore, when headwinds were encountered, the sail was lowered and the crew either began rowing or awaited a favourable wind, depending on the circumstances.

There were sixteen circular oarholes in the third strake from the top on each side of the ship, each hole having a slot across it to enable the blade of the oar to pass through. The rowers faced aft and were seated, though no traces of rowing benches have been found. In the Oseberg ship were found iron-bound chests which are the right height for use as rowing benches: it is probable these served the dual purpose of a store for weapons and equipment, to prevent them getting rusty, and as rowing benches, for it is notable that they are exceptionally long and are raised on bench-type uprights.

When under sail the oarholes were closed by circular wooden covers, which swivelled on nails. A batten was fastened inside the gunwale and the shields of the crew could be tied to this when the vessel was at anchor. The shields could not be hung thus when the ship was being rowed, and the sagas make it clear that the shields were hung on the gunwales only when a ship was in harbour: nevertheless, several Gotland stone carvings portray ships under sail with shields arranged along the gunwales.

The Gokstad ship was not a longship but probably a general-purpose vessel which could serve in the levy as one of the smaller vessels. On the other hand, the ships portrayed on the Gotland picture stones are warships, and these illustrations show that, although the longships were probably larger than any of the surviving examples, they must have been very similar in appearance to the Gokstad ship, some having richly carved prow and stern posts like the Oseberg ship.

The longships described in literary sources are often considerably larger than the Gokstad ship, with tall sides which enabled them to tower over their adversaries in battle. The most famous longship of this size is the Long Serpent, built by Olaf Tryggvason, probably in 998: she is reputed to have been thirty-four *rum*, i.e. with thirty-four pairs of oars and therefore having a length of about 37 metres. Harald Hardrada had a similar ship with thirty-five pairs of oars built for his wars with Denmark, but the only surviving vessel of anything like this size is an 11th-century warship found in Roskildefjord, which is estimated to have been 28 metres long and not more than 4.8 metres in the beam, with perhaps twenty-five oars a side. Her worn keel shows she was often hauled up onto land, and she could probably hold about sixty warriors: Olaf's Long Serpent is said to have carried 250 men.

We know that warships with thirty or more pairs of oars were used in the 12th century, but this does not necessarily mean that such large ships were common in the 11th century: of some 500 recorded boat burials in Norway only five are longer than 20 metres. Admittedly smaller boats are more likely to have been used for burials, but this evidence does suggest that most of the ships in a fleet would have been of the smaller type, the twenty-bencher mentioned earlier being perhaps the most common warship of the 11th century. The Long Serpent is an isolated example for the earlier period, and an exceptional ship for her day to judge from the vivid description accorded her building in the literary sources. She was also built to help Olaf in his struggle for power in Scandinavia – she was designed to operate in coastal waters, not to make stormy North Sea crossings. Great strain was put on the keel by the flexible construction of the Viking ship, and this meant the keel had to be cut from one length of timber. Therefore, the length of the oak trees available determined the length of the ships which were intended to make voyages across the North Sea. The longest known one-piece keel to survive is 20 metres, and it is unlikely that many oaks in Scandinavia could have yielded straight timber much longer than this. Twenty-five metres – for the twenty-bencher *snekkja* type of longship – would seem to be a reasonable allowance for maximum length likely to be available, though such a restriction need not be placed on ships designed for purely coastal work.

A classic example of a ship that had a keel made of more than one piece of timber was the *Mariasuden*, built by King Sverrir of Norway in 1182–83. She was lengthened after the keel and nine strakes had been laid, gave at the seams when launched, and earned a name as a notoriously bad ship.

The Vikings did a great deal of their voyaging within sight of land and it was customary to seek a landing place at dusk and drag the ship out of the water for safety during the hours of darkness. But many voyages were also made across miles of open sea, and some navigational aids were needed. They did not have a magnetic compass, but from observations of the sun's position at dawn and dusk they were able to compile an azimuth table; one such table compiled by an Icelander in the early 11th century has survived. Used in conjunction with a simple bearing-dial they could find the four points of the compass, a vertical pin on this dial casting a shadow to show North at sunrise and sunset, and a horizontal arrow as an indicator. The Vikings may also have had a fair idea of latitude and followed a basic principle still used in the medieval period, whereby a ship sailed to the latitude of its destination, then turned at right angles to follow this parallel until land was sighted. Their knowledge of the winds and observations of bird and whale movements in the different seasons may also have assisted them. They could judge their speed only by the strength of the wind and the size of the bow wave, but ocean speeds of around nine to ten knots seem to have been normal, though the largest ships had a traditional day's sailing of 100 miles at four knots.

Tents were carried both for camping ashore and to give some shelter at sea when under sail, the canvas being draped over the mast, spar or oars rigged amidships between the crutches mentioned earlier. The sagas mention that large skin bags called *hudfat* were used to store weapons and gear during the day, but served as two-man sleeping bags at night. Fresh water was probably carried in skin bags also. The staple diet at sea was dried and salted fish or meat, with water, beer or sour milk to drink. Each ship had a large cauldron for communal cooking purposes, and that of the Gokstad ship could hold thirty-two gallons.

At the beginning of 1066 Harald Hardrada had no plans to attack England – in fact one of his first actions when he became king in 1047 had been to despatch envoys of peace to England. But in 1047 Harald had planned to seize Denmark. By 1066 this ambition had been thwarted, and his army and fleet had lain idle all through the campaigning season of 1065. Accustomed to being mustered annually for the wars with Denmark, his fleet of over 400 ships, with perhaps 7,000 housecarls and at least 12,000 levies available to man them, was ready and eager to carry war and destruction anywhere he commanded. In 1066 all Harald needed was a target.

In his teens Harald had fled from Norway and, after a stay in Novgorod, had travelled farther east to take service in the Varangian Guard of Byzantium. For ten years he campaigned from the Greek islands to Asia Minor, from the Caucasus Mountains to Jerusalem, taking part in at least eighteen battles and rising to become commander of the Varangian Guard. He emerged as a brilliant commander, audacious, courageous and ruthless, but by no means incautious; quick to perceive an enemy's weakness and exploit any advantage. Snorri Sturluson describes him thus: 'All who ever followed him in his battles and campaigns agree that in sudden peril he always took the course which everyone – afterwards – realized was the best.'

Snorri also says of Harald: 'He was brutal to his enemies and dealt ruthlessly with any opposition to him. King Harald was exceptionally greedy for power and valuable possessions. But he was very generous to those of his friends he liked.' Such a man, known as the Thunderbolt of the North and regarded as the last great leader in the Viking tradition, was unlikely to pass up any opportunity of seizing land, wealth and fame, and in the summer of 1066 a man came to his court who offered all of these in exchange for one bold strike – the crown of England, all the great wealth of the land which had poured forth the fabulous Danegeld, and the opportunity to follow in the footsteps of Knut, the most powerful and greatest Viking of them all.

4
The Normans

In 1066 William of Normandy, duke of a relatively small duchy and a vassal of the King of France, invaded and conquered the great and strong kingdom of England. It is difficult to explain how he was able to bring such a perilous enterprise to a successful conclusion, and still more difficult to explain how he was able to undertake that enterprise in the first place, for when William, bastard son of Robert the Magnificent (derisively named William the Bastard by his vassals because of his parentage), became the seventh Duke of Normandy in 1035, at the age of only seven or eight, the duchy was still very much a minor state whose ill-defined borders were everywhere threatened by her neighbours. Internally the duchy was ravaged by private wars between the great landed families, and split into Upper Normandy, where lay the capital of Rouen and the strongest Frankish influence, and Lower Normandy, where the Scandinavian influence and customs of William's Viking ancestors remained the strongest. For twelve years after William became duke, from 1035 until 1047, the duchy was in a constant state of anarchy, the young duke's court a shambles, and, with almost all his guardians murdered, William had frequently to seek refuge to survive. The situation came to a head in 1047 when the whole of Lower Normandy rose in open rebellion, headed by the duke's own officers, and William was saved only by the intervention of Henri of France, who led an army into Normandy and defeated the rebels at the battle of Val-ès-Dunes, near Caen. Within twenty years of this battle William was head of a united and strong state which was virtually independent of France and capable of conquering England. To understand this contrast between the weakness of Normandy at the beginning of William's reign and its strength in 1066, it is necessary to show how William's dynamic personality forged a new state, harnessing the vigour of the Normans to expedite his own policies and ambition.

Any feudal society was normally a decentralized one, with the powers of government chiefly in the hands of the local magnates, and William's childhood and early youth had been a nightmare struggle for survival against the power of these magnates. The decisive victory of Val-ès-Dunes, which crushed all open rebellion to William's authority in Normandy until 1053, gave him, at the age of twenty, the power to change all that, to forge a state over which he had absolute control, so that he would never again have to hide from his own vassals.

One of his first steps was to oust from power all those who had opposed him and to give their landed property to his loyal companions in arms. It was a pattern he was to follow until his death. Using a mixture of the old Scandinavian system of exile, the Carolingian right of confiscation, his rights as a feudal suzerain and sheer autocracy, over a period of years William seized the lands and property not only of those who opposed him but also those who were too old or inefficient to actively support him militarily and in council. He also displaced the powerful illegitimate and semi-legitimate descendants of the previous dukes, who controlled the counties of Evreux, Mortain, Eu and Arques, replacing them with his own men and the other sons of his own peasant mother, his half-brothers Robert and Odo becoming Count of Mortain and Bishop of Bayeux respectively.

William had inherited vast domains of his own, and he also

gave much of this land to his chosen followers, not only securing by the gift the loyalty and predominance of those he trusted most, but also creating new vassals, who, because they were obliged to supply him with knight service in return for the land, further increased his military power.

By this method William created a new aristocracy, one which was still of the ancient Viking blood, but which consisted almost entirely of trusted companions in arms, friends and relatives; a hand-picked group of men who gave him utter loyalty and as a consequence rose to the highest positions in the duchy. The houses of Montgomery, Montfort, Beaumont, Ferrers, Mowbray, Warenne and Clare all date from this period of violent upheaval in the distribution of landed property: all men who were to make their mark in England.

Another of William's early changes was the founding of a new capital at Caen to serve as the chief base of his power in Lower Normandy. He also made the laws and customs of both Upper and Lower Normandy uniform, thus healing the breach between the two halves of his duchy. This new unity, and the powerful backing of his new aristocracy, now enabled William to tighten up the fuedal system adapted in Normandy by the first Viking settlers from that of the Carolingian kings, instituting a much more centralized form of government. The jealously guarded rights of private war and blood feud between his vassals, although not entirely abolished, were considerably reduced: castle-building was permitted only under licence and on condition that the castles be handed over to William on demand: the minting of coinage, generally a valued privilege of the magnates, was controlled exclusively by William: and the administering of justice, although still shared by William with the magnates and the Church, was now regarded more as a delegation of his authority than as a right. Even the Church could not escape his control as William personally appointed its bishops and most of its abbots, so that almost all the leading ecclesiastics were soon members or close relatives of his family, or members of his new aristocracy. He and his leading magnates founded at least twenty religious houses between 1035 and 1066, all of which owed military service for their lands and thus

97

further increased William's military power, but although generous to the Church, William left no doubt as to who was master in Normandy. When Pope Alexander II tried to restore an abbot whom William had deposed, William sent word that he would gladly receive papal legates in matters of faith and doctrine, but would hang from the tallest oak of the nearest forest any monk who dared to resist his authority in his own land.

By 1051 William could look to his borders – Flanders in the north, Brittany in the west, and Maine and Anjou in the south. Flanders was one of the strongest French fiefs, but the count was a cousin of William's father. William cemented the friendly relationship by marrying the count's daughter Mathilde, sometime between 1051 and 1053. The Bretons to the west were little more than individual tribes and presented no organized threat, but Anjou was different. Under Geoffrey Martel this comparatively small county had risen to become the dominant power on the Loire, claiming Maine – once annexed by the first Duke of Normandy but never held – and in 1051 seizing the two border fortresses of Domfront and Alençon between Maine and Normandy. Alençon was actually on Norman soil, though held by the virtually independent marcher family of Bellême, and William responded by besieging and taking both fortresses.

In 1058 his uncle, William of Arques, who had refused to allow William's forces to enter his territory during the siege of Domfront and had withdrawn his knights from William's army, proclaimed himself the rightful duke. He was backed by another of William's uncles, Mauger, Archbishop of Rouen: between them the two men controlled most of eastern Normandy. When William laid siege to the castle of Arques, his uncle appealed to Henri I for help. Henri, who now saw William's increasing strength as a threat to French suzerainty, marched into Normandy at the head of a large army, but was defeated by William at St Aubin-le-Caulf. Arques fell to William in January 1054 and in the February Henri, allied with Geoffrey of Anjou, again invaded Normandy. William crushed this invasion at the battle of Mortemer. Geoffrey and Henri made a minor raid in 1057, but were defeated by William at Varaville.

William did not follow up any of his victories by attacking the king, whom he continued to treat as his feudal overlord, and even after he became a king in his own right, William seems to have rendered the military service he owed the King of France as a vassal.

Both Henri and Geoffrey died in 1060, leaving William without a king or rival capable of withstanding him. (Philip I of France was only a boy and under the guardianship of the Count of Flanders – William's father-in-law.) By 1063 he had united Maine with Normandy, and the following year crushed the Bretons, thus establishing himself as undisputed master of north-west France. By this date he was no longer known as William the Bastard, but as William the Great.

An authority such as William now wielded required considerable income for its maintenance, and while no Norman fiscal records earlier than 1180 survive, it is possible to trace back to William's time most of the sources of revenue which appear in detail in the rolls of the exchequer a century later. William had his own estates and forests scattered throughout the duchy, and these, together with large possessions in certain towns – he sold half of Coutances to its bishop, for example – and the receipts from his feudal dues, yielded a great variety of payments in kind. He also owned mills, saltpans, fishing rights at certain points on rivers and the coast, and received customs and tolls and the fines and forfeitures of justice. He had a monopoly of wrecks and treasure trove, all whales and other 'great fish' landed, rights over markets and fairs, and the profits from coinage. But most important of all was the considerable and regular cash revenue which was collected by his local government officers, the vicomtes.

At this date the King of France had as local representatives only the semi-feudal agents on his farms. He received their dues in labour, produce and military service, and had to travel round his kingdom living off his vassals, as it was more economical to move the king and his court than the food. This situation was typical of the age and could only be changed by the development of a revenue in money – such as the various taxes in England – and the collection of taxes demanded a strong and

Norman infantryman, probably a *vavasseur*, in quilted coat and leather hood, but otherwise equipped as the knight.

well-organized system of government.

The distinctive feature of Normandy under William was the administration of local government by public officials instead of feudal lords. The duchy was divided into large administrative districts known as vicomtés. Each vicomté was administered by an official called a vicomte who was responsible for maintaining order and administering justice in the duke's name, commanding the duke's troops in the vicomté and guarding his castles, and collecting all the ducal revenues, including those from the duke's own estates. From the revenues thus collected the vicomtes rendered to William a fixed sum of money each year. With this regular income behind him, William could establish a permanent court and pay cash for whatever he needed beyond that received in feudal dues, whereas his king and other neighbours had still to bestow revenue by the primitive method of granting so many measures of grain at the mills or so many measures of wine from the vineyards. This freedom to negotiate for services outside the confines of the feudal system of payment in kind was to greatly influence the military forces available to William in 1066.

Norman (or mercenary in Norman pay) archer in everyday clothes. The helmet may have had leather panels.

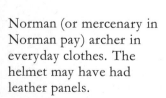

100

The vicomtes were initially appointed by the duke, although the position may have become hereditary. They were frequently required to attend the duke's court or *curia*, and therefore took some part in the duchy's government: they might also be specially commissioned to hold an inquest or execute a decision of the court.

The chief officers of William's *curia* were the Chamberlain, responsible for the internal organization of the duke's household; the Seneschal, the duke's deputy (William fitz Osbern, as Seneschal, governed England after the conquest in William's absence); and the Chancellor, responsible for drafting the title deeds of his grants of land and abbeys. The office of Chancellor was always filled by a priest, and was closely connected with the duke's chapel, which provided all his clerks to run the fiscal and secretarial sides of the central administration. There was also a Butler (responsible for the supply of wines and custody of the duke's plate) and a Constable (master of the horse and an important command in the army), but apart from these five officers there seems to have been no fixed

Norman knight in hauberk and iron helmet, armed with kite shield, spear and sword.

Viking sword, probably 11th century, with three-lobe pommel. The blade is typical of Anglo-Saxon, Viking and Norman swords of this century, as is the crossguard.

entourage. Therefore, when William summoned a council to discuss and assent to important matters of state, that council consisted of his personally chosen household officers and members of his family, together with any of his counts, bishops and vicomtes who were at the court at the time. This meant the composition of the council was very fluid, but it usually contained only those men who were closest to the duke and depended upon him for their rank: thus the duchy was governed by a small group of interrelated great families who were in turn controlled by the duke.

By 1066, therefore, William was a king in all but name, ruling without question over a united duchy and effectively controlling not only the potential rivals of Church and aristocracy within his dukedom, but also the neighbouring states of Maine and Brittany. Normandy under William was stronger than it had ever been, its army expanded and tested in the long series of successful feudal wars of the 1047–64 period. However, William's people were his vassals, not his subjects, and his army, despite its quality and strength, remained a purely feudal one.

William held his lands from the King of France in return for homage and military service. He granted large estates to lay and ecclesiastical magnates, or tenants-in-chief, and all these tenants owed him homage and military service in return. The magnates then granted part of their lands to lesser tenants, who owed fealty and military service to them. This was the system for raising military forces in all feudal societies, but in Normandy there was one important difference – the military service was systematically assessed and attached to specific pieces of land

known as a knight's fee, or *fief de haubert*. These pieces of land might vary in value or extent, but whoever held them was liable to provide the service of one knight, mounted and fully armed, in return for each fief. The fiefs were normally granted in units of five or ten and the period of service due is regularly quoted as forty days in the documents of William's reign.

It is plain that by the mid-11th century knighthood was a status and an honour as well as an obligation. It was conferred upon a young man by a ceremony, usually described as the bestowal of arms, after an apprenticeship as an *armiger*. The sheer expense of a knight's war horse and hauberk, and the necessity to be free of other commitments so as to serve the long apprenticeship, inevitably meant that knights had to be members of the aristocracy. However, not all young Norman knights could be enfeoffed, or landed, for some must have been heirs or younger sons without lands of their own, while some knights may have lost their inheritance, either through their own or their father's opposition to William. These landless knights therefore took service with a lord in the hope of acquiring lands as a reward for their services: in the meantime they were supported by that lord. The enfeoffed knight was socially more elevated, but both the enfeoffed and landless knights were members of the upper class, served their apprenticeships at the court or in the military household of a magnate, then undertook a variety of military employments, such as envoy and escort. Most importantly of all, they devoted almost all their time to practising and exercising their military skills, so that a Norman knight was in effect a professional soldier.

The word knight did not exist as such at this date, the Latin term *milites* being used. This had originally meant simply

Anglo-Saxon swords and scramasaxes of varying sizes. The sword pommels are of the type now known as 'cocked hat'. The great length of some of the scramasaxes should be observed, also the slight curve of two of these single-edged weapons.

103

'soldier', but by the beginning of the 11th century in Normandy it was being used to identify the magnates only, while their vassals were termed *barones*. By about the same date a third term had been introduced in Normandy – *vavasseur*, a second class of *milites*, or the lesser tenants of the *barones*. These *vavasseurs* were half-way between the Norman aristocracy (descended from the Viking settlers) and the peasantry (descended from the original Frankish peasants), and their ancestors were probably native landholders who had been allowed to retain their estates at the founding of the Norman state. They were not members of the Viking aristocracy and did not receive the status of knighthood, but had equipment and weapons similar to those of the knights, although perhaps of inferior quality because of the expense.

Therefore, each magnate, or tenant-in-chief, and the barons under him, was served by a contingent of feudal knights and *vavasseurs* who gave military service in return for lands. The landless knights, and a third type of knight – the stipendiary knight, who served for pay alone – formed part of a separate group, the lord's *familia* or warrior band. Every great lord was compelled in self-defence to keep a *familia* whose size bore no relation to the amount of military service he owed his overlord,

Typical crossguards and pommels of the 10th and 11th centuries; from left to right five-lobe, 'tea cosy' and 'brazil nut' pommels.

Silver Anglo-Saxon
pommel of the 9th
century, found in London.
The design of whirling
snakes is inlaid with niello.
Length 9.5 cm. (British
Museum.)

but rather reflected the individual lord's wealth and standing. In
a sense the *familia* was therefore akin to the Viking and Anglo-
Saxon houseband or *huskarlar*, in that it served a lord in return
for maintenance and reward – either in land or money. The
landless and stipendiary knights formed only a percentage of
the *familia* and we can only guess where the other members of
the bands came from, but all were heavily armoured and fought
as cavalry: like the war bands of the Viking and Anglo-Saxon
earls, the *familia* must have attracted foot-loose or exiled
professional fighting men from all parts of Europe.

William's army was therefore divided into a number of
natural units, each containing feudal and paid contingents and
commanded by its own lord, and this gave some organization
and cohesion. This was probably one of the reasons why
William was able to maintain such a high state of discipline in
his armies – for example, the 'wait and see' tactics employed in

Hilt of a Viking sword found in the River Escaut at Termonde, Belgium. The guard and pommel are covered with plaques of bronze decorated with incised double scroll figures. The pommel is of the three-lobe type with strands of bronze between the lobes.

the campaigns leading up to Mortemer and Varaville, and the campaign in Brittany, all of which required an unusual degree of discipline and control. But such division also had its disadvantages, inherent in the feudal system. Although William exerted considerable control over his magnates, and the feudal system was far more advanced in Normandy than elsewhere in Europe at this date, Normandy was still not nearly so well organized or so centralized as England was to be under his rule. The crucial point is that at this date the military potential of any feudal system was by no means exclusively at the disposal of the ruler, for the under-tenants each had direct obligations to their overlords. William himself was not obliged to serve the King of France with *all* his feudal host, but only a part of it. In the same way, his own magnates were not obliged to bring all their feudal troops to assist the duke (and none of their *familia*), and the greater part of the knight service owed to a Norman magnate was in fact for the use of that magnate alone. For example, the duke could claim the service of only ten knights out of the thirty-three who owed service to Robert de Cureio, and only twenty out of the 120 who owed service to his half-brother Odo, while Odo had an obligation to supply only ten knights to the King of France. Therefore, even for the defence of the duchy, William could not call upon the *familia* of any lord, or upon *all* the feudal knights of Normandy, as Harold of England and Harald of Norway could call upon their entire select levy and all housecarls for the defence of their realms. Thus the total number of knights owing military service to the duke was small: the feudal survey of 1172 reveals that out of a total of about 1,500 knights in Normandy at that date, only 581 were available for the service of the duke. Furthermore, it was no part of any tenant's feudal obligation to follow his lord overseas: military service was only owed for the defence of the lord's domain.

The Norman knight was, of course, a copy of the mailed cavalryman the Vikings encountered in France when they first settled in that country, and there is nothing to show that the Normans contributed anything original to the training or equipment of the individual mounted warrior, rather they

106

assimilated the long experience of the Franks, who had been using armoured cavalry since the end of the 8th century, and used it to further their own ends. The first known record of the Viking aristocracy of Normandy abandoning their traditional practice of fighting on foot occurs in 993, when the Duke of Normandy sent a mounted contingent to fight in the army of his overlord, the King of France: by the mid-11th century therefore the Normans were practised cavalrymen and were regarded as the finest armoured cavalry of the time. On the other hand, the pastures of Normandy were rich in horses, and it is more than likely that an unrecorded skill in the stable had made the Normans the best trainers of horses in France, for the Norman war horse of the 11th century, heavy enough to carry an armoured man yet nimble enough to be capable of the manoeuvring and flexibility demanded in the mounted warfare of the time, must have been the final product of generations of skilled breeding and experience in stable management. Great technical skill as a rider must also have been needed to handle in battle a shield, spear or sword, *and* the reins, all the time manoeuvring to seek an advantage, and this – according to the Bayeux Tapestry – mounted almost exclusively on stallions that were accustomed to joining in the fighting with hooves, teeth and forehead.

The mounted knights were the main force of the Norman armies in the 11th century, but William was well aware of the valuable role played by infantry and especially archers, although he had no force of his own to match the select infantry levies of England and Norway. The only infantry force available to William under the feudal system was the *arrière ban*, a general levy of the peasantry to defend the duchy in times of emergency: Wace mentions the calling out of the peasantry in 1057 when the king of France invaded Normandy. The right to summon the *arrière ban* dated from Carolingian times, but William was careful to perpetuate this ancient right in his charters, and from the care with which his magnates reserved this obligation as regards their dependants and even townsmen, it would seem he held the magnates responsible for producing this levy when needed. Archers were present at Varaville in 1057,

107

Hilt of a Viking sword found in Dublin. The point of the sword is missing but the surviving part is 92 cm long.

and infantry were used at the sieges of Domfront and Alençon in 1051, of Mayenne in 1063 and the campaign in Brittany in 1064. The local *arrière ban* was most likely called out to provide manual labour at sieges, and may also have provided archers and slingers. However, the infantry in Brittany can only have been specially hired foreign mercenaries, for the *arrière ban* was not liable for service outside Normandy, and William is known to have also employed mercenaries at the sieges of Domfront and Alençon.

Arms and Armour

The distinctive arms and armour of the Norman horse soldier were his lance, shield and hauberk. All three are well portrayed on the Bayeux Tapestry, and a verbal description of the Normans on crusade in 1107 is given in Anna Comnena's 'Alexiad': 'Their chief weapon of defence is a coat of mail, ring plaited into ring, and the iron fabric is so excellent that it repels arrows and keeps the wearer's flesh unhurt. An additional weapon of defence is a shield which is not round, but a long shield very broad at the top and running out to a point, hollowed out slightly in the inner side but externally smooth and gleaming with a brilliant boss of brass.' Anna had never seen the Bayeux Tapestry, yet her description could be of any of the Norman knights portrayed on that masterpiece.

The coat of mail or hauberk weighed about 14 kg and was of the same general construction and style as the mail armour described for both the Anglo-Saxon housecarls and the Viking leaders: heavy iron rings interlaced to form a flexible garment which reached to the knees, with wide sleeves ending just below the elbow, and slit from hem to crotch at front and back so that the flaps thus created hung down either side of the saddle when the wearer was mounted. Many of the hauberks illustrated on the Bayeux Tapestry have some form of fastening, possibly a flap, across the throat, but as many are shown without any form of opening apart from the round neck, and these may possibly have had a slit at the back, running down from the neck opening, which was then closed by straps. Quite a few others are shown with a square panel of some kind on the chest,

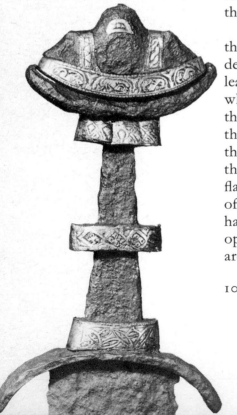

Hilt of a sword found in the bank of the River Witham near Lincoln. The silver plates are inlaid with niello. Dated 9th century. (Sheffield City Museum.)

108

marked by a broad band of material. The panel may simply have been another form of fastening for a flap, or an additional protection, either of mail or plate, attached to the hauberk to defend the chest.

William, his brother Odo, and Count Eustace of Boulogne, are also shown on the tapestry as wearing mail leggings, and Count Conan of Brittany is similarly portrayed for the Brittany campaign. Probably only the greater magnates had leg armour and, as they normally fought on horseback, such leggings must have been of mail only on the outer face, with leather or textile on the inner side, to prevent chafing of the thighs.

The distinctive kite-shaped shield covered the entire left side of a mounted man from shoulder to ankle at a time when armour alone was not sufficient protection against a lance thrust or sword or axe slash, and although apparently clumsy, it must have been much easier to use in its static all-covering position than the earlier round shield, which had to be moved rapidly to fend off blows, and this with the hand which also controlled the reins. When using the lance or spear, the shield was hung from the neck by an adjustable strap called the *guige*. For hand-to-hand fighting with sword, mace or axe, the shield was held more securely by passing the forearm through two vertical straps (*enarmes*) on the upper back of the shield, with an oblong pad for the forearm to rest against, and with the left hand grasping the reins. There was sometimes an additional strap to be grasped in the left hand if fighting dismounted.

The shield was normally of linden wood, faced with leather and often reinforced with metal plates or strip around the edges. The boss was not necessary but continued to appear on some shields as part of the ornamentation-cum-reinforcement. The average width of these shields was around 55 cm, the length about 1.25 metres and the thickness around 16 mm. As Anna Comnena says, the shield was slightly cylindrical, curving towards the body to afford better protection and to present a deflecting surface towards the enemy.

The third Norman defence was the iron helmet, a simple conical helmet with a nose guard and of exactly the same form as

Hilt of the Abingdon sword, 9th century, with pommel and crossguard inlaid with silver plates. The guard is 12 cm long. (Ashmolean Museum.)

that described under the Anglo-Saxons and now referred to as
the spangenhelm. Helmets were worn by all knights and the
vavasseurs.

Norman spearheads took a number of forms: leaf-shaped
with a rib running up the centre of each side of the blade; a
sharply pointed vee shape with barbed ends; the winged spear
of the Carolingians, another leaf-shaped blade but with one or
two crosspieces on the socket as part of the head; and the
barbed type with crosspieces at the socket. All four types are
shown on the Bayeux Tapestry, but the winged spear seems to
have been only used for the hunt. The barbed heads were
probably for throwing spears or javelins, the leaf-shaped heads
for use as an early form of lance and in the hand-to-hand
combat, using the point for thrusting and the long cutting edges
for slashing.

The fact that the Norman knight had been using these spears
from horseback since at least 993 does not mean that the
Norman cavalry charged home with the spear used as a lance,
couched under the arm and delivered with great impact. In 1066
the Norman knight was still an individual warrior, not part of a
regimented unit, and nothing like the later cavalry charge
existed: if it had, nothing would have persuaded the knights to
charge the famous shield wall formation of the Viking and
Anglo-Saxon infantry, where they would immediately have
been pierced by a spear or two, or chopped down by a two-
handed axe. It is noticeable also that no source mentions or
illustrates the Anglo-Saxon infantry opposing the Norman
cavalry by using their spears to provide a thicket of points, as
they would surely have done to make charging horses refuse.
No, the Norman knight of this period was little more than a
mounted javelineer, who attacked the enemy by hurling his
throwing spear or spears at close range in an attempt to create a
gap in the enemy's line, and used his thrusting spear, either
over- or under-arm, to probe for weak spots in a man's defences
during individual hand-to-hand combats.

Knights also carried a sword, or sometimes an axe or mace.
The swords and their scabbards followed very much the pattern
described for the Anglo-Saxons and Vikings, with hilts

following the Scandinavian style. The axes were single-handed weapons with short hafts, used in place of the sword, and the maces were also short-hafted, single-hand weapons with metal heads, which were sometimes of bulbous trilobate shape. Axes and maces were not widely used, probably through personal preference, and the sword was the distinctively knightly weapon.

The saddle used by a knight had a tall, upright pommel and cantle and was secured by breast-band and girth. Long stirrup leathers were used to give a straight-legged seat, and simple prick spurs were universal.

The lower class of mounted soldier, the *vavasseur*, was also armed with spear and sword, but although some may have had mail hauberks and iron helmets, the majority probably wore simple caps and jerkins of stout leather, and it is this writer's belief that in 1066 William's infantry in England consisted to a large extent of lesser knights and *vavasseurs* whose horses could not be shipped across the Channel.

The archer element was probably supplied by both feudal levies and mercenaries; certainly it had to be exclusively the latter in England. Wace describes these men in England as 'well equipped, each bearing bow and sword; on their heads were caps, and to their feet were bound buskins. Some had bound strong hides round their bodies; and many were clad in frocks, and had quivers and bows hung to their girdles.'

The bows used were known as the 'Danish bow', i.e. similar to that employed by the Vikings, some 150 to 180 cm long and drawn only to the chest. Although comparatively ineffective against troops with shields, an arrow from such a bow could penetrate a hauberk and kill the wearer at ranges of up to 45 metres, and, with a higher trajectory, arrows could be sent some 90 metres. Quivers were mostly worn at the waist.

The importance of archers had been much promoted by Charlemagne, only for their use in warfare by the Franks to decline after his death, but William appears to have fostered the arm and developed a considerable body of mercenary archers, whose tactical value was fully appreciated by him. The Normans were to continue to exploit archery in warfare in England after the conquest, of course.

111

Shipping

By 1066 the typical Norman magnate was so much a product of generations of assimilating the Frankish way of life that he was no longer the owner of longships and their warrior crews, in the fashion of his Viking ancestors, but the possessor of a castle and a force of mounted knights. It is possible that William's father, duke from 1027 to 1035, had a small navy of some sort, but by 1066 the only ships available to William were a handful of longships maintained by himself and one or two of the greater magnates, and the fleets of merchantmen and fishing vessels.

The reason why the Normans so totally abandoned the sea may be found in the coastline of the duchy. Along this particular stretch of the coast of Europe there is hardly any sheltered water and very few decent harbours, these few being mostly in river estuaries, where the difference between high and low tide could be as much as 12 metres. Dangerous five-knot tidal streams also scoured the promontories. Any vessel which put to sea from one of these harbours had to stay at sea until such time as there was a tide to enable it to return, and during this waiting period the vessel – which was incapable of manoeuvring against the wind – was completely at the mercy of the wind and weather. Such conditions did not encourage either fishing or coastal trading, and there were therefore few ships, few experienced seamen and no naval tradition in Normandy such as existed in England and Norway.

The few longships maintained by William and his magnates followed very closely the method of construction employed by the Vikings.

Thus, it is clear that in 1066 William's army was quite small and consisted almost entirely of mailed horsemen who were not obliged to serve overseas; his naval resources were almost nil, with no naval tradition to enable him to fill the gap by commandeering existing vessels and impressing seamen; and the physical limitations of his duchy meant that his funds were insufficient to hire the vast force which would be needed to invade and conquer such a strong kingdom as England.

But William had anticipated succeeding Edward to the throne of England for the past fifteen years, and he was not the type to allow a usurper to rob him of a kingdom. Within weeks of Harold's accession, William would be taking the initial steps towards creating the greatest invasion force to be launched since the days of the great Roman empire, not to be surpassed until the invasion of Malta in 1565 by the mighty Ottoman empire – yet all he could rely on to back him were a few friends and the treasury of a small duchy about the size of Wales.

Normandy and her neighbours in 1066.

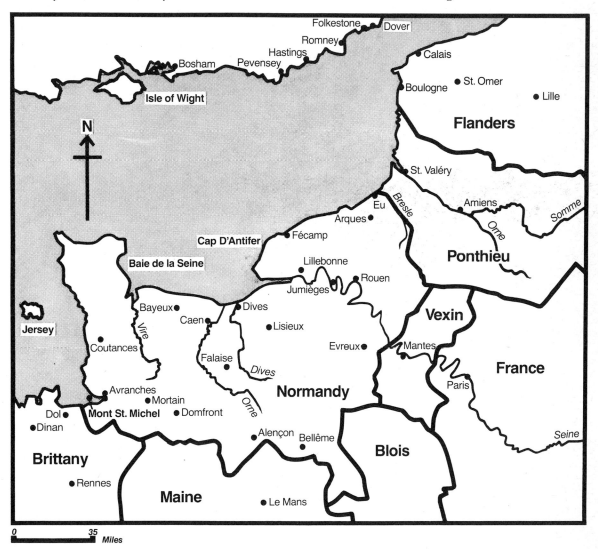

5
The
Storm Clouds
Gather

According to Wace, William was about to begin a hunt in his deer park near Rouen when, on or around 10 January, news arrived from England that Harold Godwineson had been crowned. The hunt was abandoned at once and the duke returned to his palace at Rouen, his face so dark with anger that none of his courtiers dared approach him. For fifteen years he had expected to become King of England on the death of Edward, and only eighteen months previously had had that expectation confirmed by the oaths of Harold himself. All Normandy knew William expected to become King of England: if he accepted the situation, his loss of face would be enormous and, in a society ruled by the strong, his humiliation in this matter could possibly promote the end of his absolute power in his own duchy. He had to take action to reverse this *coup d'état*, but how?

William of Jumièges, a usually reliable source, records that William's father had once planned to invade England on Edward's behalf, had collected an invasion fleet, and actually set sail for England. However, the fleet had been forced by unfavourable winds to seek shelter in the bays of Jersey, and the invasion of England had deteriorated into a landing at St Michel to impress the duke's authority upon the Bretons. This story is unconfirmed and must be treated with caution, but if it is true it would have been in William's mind in January 1066, and it is not impossible that, with such a precedent, William might have envisaged an invasion of England from the very moment he received news of Harold's coronation. But William had risen to his present position by pursuing a chosen path with cautious, clear-thinking thoroughness, not by impulsive reactions to events. Whatever his long-term plans might have been at this stage, he began his counter moves slowly and with great care.

His first step was to open a diplomatic offensive in order to gain for his cause the moral approval and political acquiesence of western Europe. An official protest was at once sent to Harold, demanding that he renounce the throne in William's favour. The exact terms of this protest are unknown, but are not really important. Harold refused, as William must have anticipated: the true purpose of his protest had been to formalize the issue and create an air of legality for his future moves. A second embassy was then despatched to London, offering a compromise: that Harold should marry William's daughter, failing which William would claim his rights by force. William is unlikely to have been satisfied with the distant prospect of a grandson becoming King of England one day; again his aim was to create for feudal Europe an image of a prince determined to pursue his rights at the point of the sword, but only after fair warning to his adversary, and at the same time warn the English people that supporting Harold could lead them into war. Harold replied that, as King of England, he could not enter into a political marriage (or rather betrothal, as William had only been married about fourteen years, and his eldest daughter could not have been more than twelve) without the *Witena gemot*'s permission, and that body was opposed to a foreign queen. With this refusal of a generous compromise, William was free to begin his second maneouvre.

Some time in the spring an embassy was despatched to Rome to appeal for the judgement of the Pope against Harold as self-perjured, sacrilegious and a false executor, guilty of profaning the relics of the saints of the Holy Church, of usurping the throne of England promised by Edward to his kinsman William, and of complicity with his father Earl Godwine in the murder of Edward's brother Alfred, and the expulsion from his see and from England of the true archbishop of Canterbury, Robert of Jumièges. No record of the resulting proceedings at Rome has survived, but there is no evidence that Harold was ever summoned to appear at Rome to answer the charges; they were clearly a matter of expediency for Rome and William rather than a true hearing.

Normandy under William had been exceedingly generous to the Church, and William could be expected to be even more generous as King of England, but the real importance of this embassy was that it presented to the Pope an opportunity to bring the erring Church in England firmly back into the fold. The English Church was guilty of tolerating amongst its clergy the denounced custom of marriage, delay in paying the annual tribute initiated by Knut and known as Peter's Pence, and in having in the Archbishop Stigand a religious leader who was unrecognized by Rome, unable to either consecrate bishops, bury Edward or crown Harold, and who had obtained his pallium only by bribing Pope Benedict X, whose own election had been so irregular that he had been driven from office by reformers in less than a year. It was also a chance for Rome to promote its recent decision in favour of the hereditary principle in monarchy as opposed to the elective monarchies of England and Germany, to create a precedent whereby a Christian king held his realm as a fief of the Church of Rome, as William now swore to hold England.

When some cardinals objected that the Church was lending her authority to an armed intervention in the affairs of an unoffending Christian state, they were overruled, and the Pope authorized William to invade England, restore obedience to the See of Rome, and re-establish the tax of Peter's Pence. William was honoured by the receipt of a consecrated banner, and a hair of St Peter set in a diamond ring. Finally, a papal Bull, excommunicating Harold and his supporters, and giving William official sanction for a crusading expedition against England, was entrusted to the duke. Thus by the spring of 1066

William had established his claim to the throne of England as just, and achieved for any invasion of England the status of a Holy Crusade.

An invasion could not be undertaken without a great army and fleet, and William had neither: his raising, equipping, provisioning and maintenance of a large army and fleet during the summer of 1066 is the most remarkable part of the whole history of the conquest of England. In this instance his first step was to call a meeting at Lillebonne of the greatest men in his duchy and ask them for the support which he so desperately needed, but which they were not obliged to provide under their feudal obligations. All the men present at this meeting owed their position and wealth to William personally: without hesitation or exception they pledged their lives and their treasure to his service in an armed invasion of England to defend his rightful claim to the throne. But they also warned him that they spoke as individuals, not as tenants-in-chief on behalf of their barons, and advised him to summon all the barons of Normandy to a great assembly so that each man might give his own consent to accompany an expedition which was outside the normal obligations owed to the duke.

This second assembly was also held at Lillebonne. William explained to his barons the case against Harold, his plans for an invasion, and revealed to them the Pope's judgement and Bull of Excommunication. He invited them to help him with men, ships and money, then withdrew so they might debate in private.

Uproar broke out when William left the assembly. It had never been part of the feudal obligation to one's lord to follow him overseas, and the barons were afraid of creating such a precedent. Wars also cost money, and their coffers were low after the recent campaigns against Maine and Brittany. Nor were they seamen, and much shipping would be needed to cross the Channel, which was known to be guarded by a great English fleet manned by experienced sailors. A Norman fleet might never reach England, and even if it did the English army was both large and expert: defeat would not only mean financial ruin but death on a foreign shore, for there could be little hope of retreat once the invasion force had landed.

Although many barons were influenced by the Pope's part in the affair, others were reluctant to risk wealth and life in such a dangerous enterprise, and the assembly broke up without reaching any definite conclusions. Abandoning all attempt to gain the collective support of his barons, William next summoned them to him individually and offered them wealth and glory in return for their support. His great magnates had already pledged their support in writing, and with their overlords already committed – and alone in the duke's overbearing presence – the barons succumbed one by one, the duke's clerks scrupulously recording their promises of men, ships and money, and the favours William promised to bestow upon them in return. Thus an ambitious monk, Remi of Fécamp, promised twenty knights and a ship in return for a bishopric in England, and others lent their support in return for other offices, lands, money, and even well-to-do English brides. William had each transaction recorded in a ledger and issued each man with a sealed guarantee.

Once the leading men of the duchy had promised their support for William, and the news of his lavish rewards had spread, others came forward eagerly to offer their services in anticipation of a rich return, or at worse absolution for their sins: farmers gave produce from their farms to feed the growing army, merchants and craftsmen gave goods and credit to assist in equipping the invasion force, and clerics gave money to build the ships and pay the mercenaries. For William 'advertised' his Holy War far and wide, offering good pay and the rewards of the victor to all who would serve under him. He had a good reputation from his past campaigns as a military leader and generous paymaster, and he had the backing of the Pope: volunteers now rode to his court not only from all parts of Normandy and its satellites of Maine and Ponthieu, but also from Ile de France, Flanders, Anjou, Picardie, Aquitaine, from Germany, and even from the Norman colonies beyond the Alps in southern Italy and Sicily. Some were great lords with their followers, such as Count Eustace of Boulogne, but many were landless knights attracted by the lure of adventure and the prospect of a fief in England, while others were mercenaries, some of whom had no doubt fought for William in his other wars and been well rewarded for their services. Florence of Worcester speaks of the numberless horsemen, slingers and infantrymen who were taken into William's pay at this time: William's army, although at least fifty per cent Norman in origin, was also to contain mercenaries and adventurers from all over northern Europe, and all his army and navy served him not as a result of any feudal duty, but as crusaders fighting for the Church, and for loot and the promise of rich reward in land.

As soon as William had the support of his barons he issued orders for the gathering of the invasion fleet. As we saw in the previous chapter, his own fleet was small, even allowing for the commandeering of merchant and fishing vessels. Some ships were hired or purchased from Flanders and France, but there was still nothing like the number needed to transport an army, its horses and equipment across the Channel, and several hundred more ships would have to be specially built. Normandy was rich in oak forests at this date, and the timber buildings of the age meant there was no shortage of skilled carpenters. The relatively few shipwrights available were probably each allocated several teams of experienced carpenters and commissioned to build a number of ships. It is possible that some form of 'liberty ship' was devised, with templates for the various parts issued to each team, so that mass production methods could be employed by the inexperienced builders, or at least so that they could work without constant supervision. It is equally likely that there was a mad scramble to obtain the services of the shipwrights and each magnate then strove to fulfil his promise to William as best he could. However the problem was tackled, the beaches of the Cotentin peninsula (on which 900 years later other invasion craft were to land, travelling in the opposite direction), the small harbours between Le Havre and St Mère-Église, and the estuaries of the Seine, Dives, Bresle, Orne and Vire, were soon the scene of furious activity.

While the army assembled, and the fleet to carry it was being built, William was busy arranging for the safety of his flanks and

119

rear during his absence in England. Envoys had already been sent to the Holy Roman Emperor and the King of Denmark to seek their military support. Sven Estrithson, who had only recently managed to hold on to his own kingdom, refused to give military aid but entered into some form of alliance with William, either promising not to pursue his own claim to the English throne or not to support his cousin Harold. The Emperor Henry IV of Germany was a minor, and those who governed in his name also refused William direct aid, though they agreed to defend Normandy against aggression from any quarter during William's absence in England.

William now rode to meet Philip of France to secure aid, offering to pay homage to the French king for the kingdom of England – an irony of history. Philip's advisors feared that William, once King of England, would become too powerful, and they argued that if the French supported him and he was successful it would be costly in money and knights for but little return, while if he were defeated France would incur the

Bow of the late 9th century Gokstad ship. This Norwegian ship was probably a general purpose vessel, but would also have served in the levy as one of the smaller ships when required. (Universitetets Oldsaksamling, Oslo.)

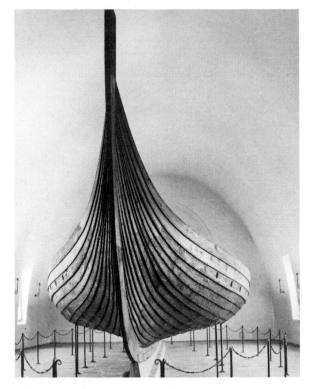

animosity of England. All William could extract was a promise of friendly neutrality.

He then rode to the court of Baldwin of Flanders at Lille. William planned to leave Mathilde and his fourteen-year-old son Robert in charge of Normandy and he knew he could rely on Baldwin to keep a protective eye on his own daughter. But Baldwin proved too prudent to commit himself to actually assisting William's invasion, even though he was harbouring Harold's brother Tostig.

These refusals of military support were a bitter blow to William's hopes; not one state had promised any military assistance. But ironically these refusals of direct aid were to create for William a unified command, unfettered by the rivalries and divisions of all joint feudal enterprises: there would be no quarrelling between dukes and kings, for now William would be the sole leader, all would obey his commands, and all victories and gains would be his alone. Nor was William really to lose any great military support, for although the

Detail of the construction of the Gokstad ship. (Universitetets Oldsaksamling, Oslo.)

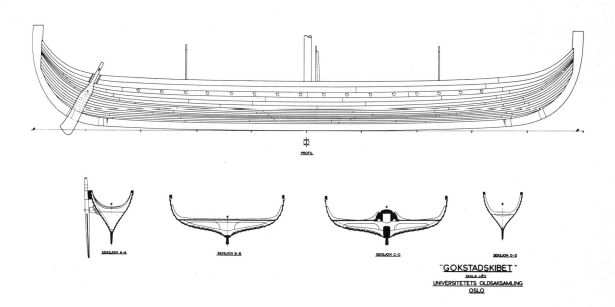

SEKSJON A-A   SEKSJON B-B   SEKSJON C-C   SEKSJON D-D

"GOKSTADSKIBET"
SKALA 1:40
UNIVERSITETETS OLDSAKSAMLING
OSLO

various dukes and kings refused him aid, men of all ranks came from France, Germany and Flanders in great numbers to swell the ranks of his army. Also, William could still rely on the continuing friendship of Baldwin, and to a lesser degree of Philip of France, and this meant that all the harbours of northern Europe, from the Scheldt to Finisterre, were either under his personal control or in the hands of allies or men

Iron-bound chest found in the Oseberg ship burial. The bench-type ends suggest such chests doubled as rowing benches, as no fixed benches have been found in Viking ships. (Universitetets Oldsaksamling, Oslo.)

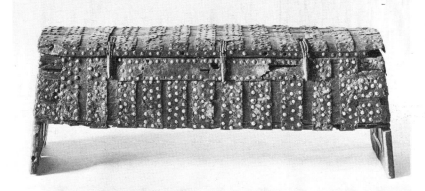

Leather shoes found in the Oseberg ship burial. (Universitetets Oldsaksamling, Oslo.)

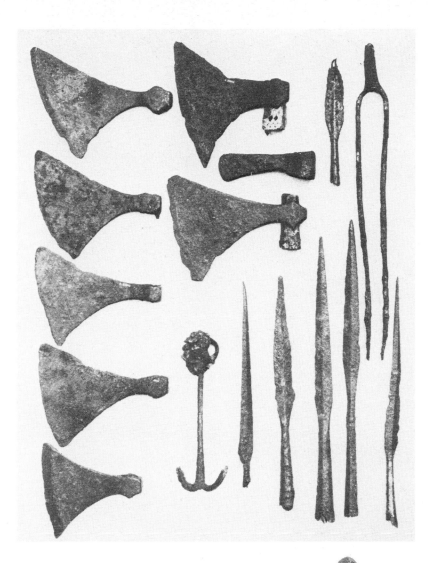

Weapons and tools, dated *circa* 1000, found close to Old London Bridge and clearly part of the equipment of a Viking ship. Illustrated are seven broadaxe heads (two having unusual decorated brass sockets), one skeggox or perhaps a tool, six spearheads (two inlaid with silver), a pair of fire tongs, and a four-pronged grappling iron, possibly for naval warfare.

Below
Helmet from the Sutton Hoo ship burial, probably made in Sweden in the 6th century. The iron is covered with impressed bronze sheets and silver and bronze gilt additions. Height 31.8 cm approximately, the helmet having been much reconstructed: compare with next illustration. This is the type of helmet worn by Viking chieftains prior to the Viking Age, but which is believed to have survived into the 10th and possibly 11th centuries. (British Museum.)

7th century Vendel warrior's helmet found at Uppland, Sweden. The crown is covered by impressed bronze sheets. No Viking helmets of the 11th century have been found yet, but it is believed the richer warriors wore helmets of much the same type as that illustrated here and in the preceding photograph. Most would not have been so richly decorated, but may have had a spike at the crest. The cheek guards were sometimes replaced by mail, which was suspended from the helmet edge and nasal bar to cover the face, leaving only two eye openings. (Antikvarisk-Topografiska Arkivet, Stockholm.)

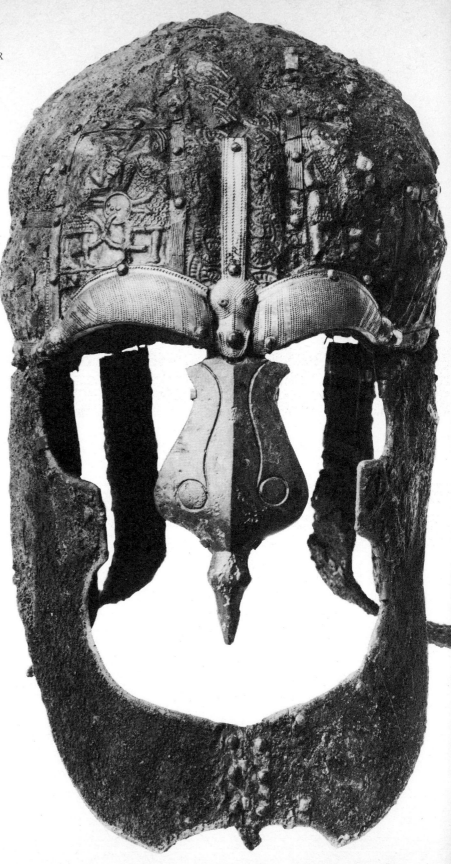

Framework of a 7th century Anglo-Saxon helmet found at Benty Grange, Derbyshire. Horn plates were originally attached to the iron bands. The boar crest is a Celtic emblem, but it is mentioned in a number of passages in Anglo-Saxon literature. By the 11th century metal plates were often used to form a completely iron helmet: by this date the boar crest was no longer used. (Sheffield City Museum.)

bound to him by feudal ties, and all were therefore open to his ships.

William's old enemy, Anjou, was at this time too busy with civil war and a feudal dispute with Brittany to threaten the safety of Normandy in William's absence, but nevertheless some time during the summer there was one sudden threat to all William's plans, for Conan, Duke of Brittany, chose this opportune moment to issue a challenge to William – yield Normandy to him or he would invade that duchy as soon as William sailed for England! For a brief time it looked as though William's ambitions would be thwarted by this one duke, but, fortunately for William, Conan's chamberlain proved sympathetic to Normandy. Conan was poisoned, and with his death the last barrier to the fulfilment of William's ambitions was removed. Shortly after this event a strong contingent of Bretons joined the invasion army.

The first of the new ships was launched in May and moved to

the estuary of the Dives, which at this date was a large tidal lake, providing an excellent anchorage for a large fleet. More and more ships gathered here during June and July, but it was not until early August that William's fleet was at last ready.

The number and size of William's ships has been debated endlessly, but no accurate estimate can be given. It does not help to consider the number of men, horses and amount of equipment to be transported, for the size of William's army is usually assessed according to the size of his fleet. The earliest chroniclers give totals which are hopelessly exaggerated, but Wace quotes a more realistic figure of 696 ships, while Ordericus, who can be counted as one of the more reliable sources, gives 782. A third estimate may be gleaned from the record set down by William's clerks of the ships promised by his magnates. William's half-brother, Robert of Mortain, promised 120 ships; his other half-brother, Odo, 100; and William, Bishop of Evreux, another eighty. William fitz Osbern, Roger of Montgomery, Roger of Beaumont, Hugh of Avranches and Robert of Eu each promised sixty ships: Hugh of Montfort, fifty: Fulk le Boiteux and Gerald Dapifer, forty each: Walter Giffard and Vougrin, Bishop of Le Mans, thirty each: and Abbot Nicholas of St Ouens at Rouen, twenty ships. This gives a total of 810 ships, without those supplied by William himself. The similarity of these three totals – 696, 782, 810 – is tempting, particularly in an age when the strengths of armies and navies were customarily given in round figures by the thousand. But even if reasonably accurate, these figures are at best incomplete, for there is nothing to indicate the size of the vessels, nor, in the third total, can we be sure that all the promises were fulfilled.

It is arguable whether the Bayeux Tapestry can throw any light on the problem. The largest ship illustrated with oar holes has sixteen pairs of oars, the same as the Gokstad ship, which is 23.3 metres long. All the others with oar holes range from seven pairs (one example) to twelve pairs (two examples), with a quarter of the ships illustrated having ten pairs. An average number of, say, eleven pairs suggests a length of between 15 and 20 metres. The smallest vessels are shown as full when holding only four or five men.

Anglo-Saxon warrior from an 11th century manuscript, showing the most common form of Anglo-Saxon helmet illustrated in 11th century manuscripts. Note also the concave shield, the method of slinging the sword – without a scabbard – and the barbed spearhead, also common in contemporary manuscripts.

126

Viking helmet as shown
on the wood carvings on
the portal of the 12th
century stave church at
Hylestad in Norway. Note
the similarity to the
Anglo-Saxon helmet in the
previous illustration.
(Universitetets
Oldsaksamling, Oslo.)

Viking helmet as shown
on the wood carvings at
Hylestad church.
Although of much the
same form as that shown
in the previous
photograph, the crest
suggests it is a 'Phrygian
cap' of leather. However,
the neck and nose guards
deny this, and it may be
that the Phrygian cap, or
at least some examples of
it, was of metal but with a
'crest' as illustrated here.
(Universitetets
Oldsaksamling, Oslo.)

Anglo-Saxon soldiers as illustrated in an 11th century manuscript. Although one carries a shield, it is likely that they are hunting, for all carry winged spears. The hat is that commonly referred to as the Phrygian cap, a type of headgear worn by Anglo-Saxon and Viking warriors in the 11th century and earlier. It is supposed to have been of leather because of its shape, but see comments with previous photograph.

It could be said that these craft are only representative and not accurate portrayals, yet in the sections showing Harold's journeys to and from Normandy in 1064, his ships are illustrated as of English design, with sixteen and nineteen pairs of oars respectively – much larger than the largest Norman ship in 1066. It seems the designer was deliberately portraying the different types of vessels, differentiating between English and Norman ships, and, for 1066, showing the full range of shipping used, from giant flagship down to little boats, some with sails and oars, some with sails alone. If this is so, something may be gleaned from the contents of those vessels. The number of horses shown in the ships of the invasion fleet varies between three and nine, with from two to five attendants (crews excepted): an average of six horses per vessel, together with attendants, would seem a reasonable conclusion. The largest ships could hold about forty men, the more common twenty- to twenty-four-oared vessel between twenty-five and thirty men.

Another snippet of information which may be gleaned from the tapestry is that only about half the vessels illustrated have oar holes. This could indicate that up to half the fleet were entirely dependent on sail: these were probably the transports. The remainder of the fleet could use either sail or oars, and most likely contained a large percentage of warships, which William would need to protect the transports from the great English fleet. Normandy could not have yielded sufficient experienced oarsmen to row half the fleet, but no doubt all except the

11th century helmet of the type now known as the spangenhelm. This was the most common form of helmet amongst the professional fighting men of the 11th century, such as the English housecarls and Norman knights. (Kunsthistorischen Museum, Vienna.)

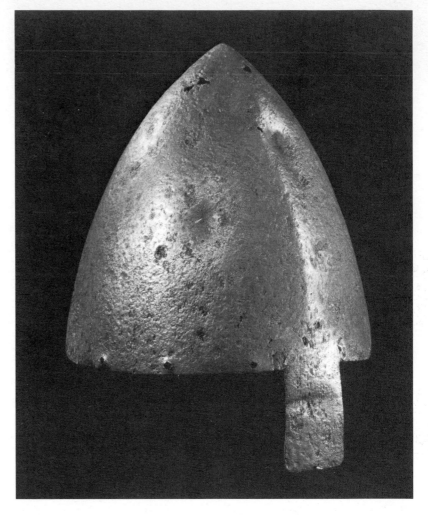

knights were expected to take a place at the oars if the occasion demanded it. The warships could not be counted as carrying anything except their crews, of course.

When one considers that William's fleet had to transport horses, food and wine, tents and tools, and three timber towers, as well as the entire army, its weapons and equipment, and at the same time include a fair proportion of vessels unable to carry anything except their crews, those figures of Ordericus and Wace begin to look more than reasonable. Nor should it be

130

forgotten that in 1142 it took fifty-two ships to carry about 350 English knights and their horses across the Channel, and in 1346 the English expedition to Calais needed 783 ships for perhaps 12,000 men and about 2,000 horses. Fleets of up to 700 ships were also employed in the 11th century by the Scandinavians – who did not normally bother overmuch with horses and supplies – for some of their large raids or invasions, so it is quite possible that Ordericus and Wace's figures may be correct, and that as many as 700 or even 800 vessels were needed for William's invasion of England.

It must be remembered that William would have had a good knowledge of Harold's strength, and been aware that he would have around 4,000 housecarls to deal with, plus the lithsmen and select fyrd: he therefore would not have ventured to invade England with markedly inferior forces. Modern historians usually place the strength of William's army at around 7,000 men. I would estimate 8,000, of which perhaps 2,400 (thirty per cent) would be cavalry. Some 400 ships would have been needed to transport the horses and attendants of 2,400 cavalrymen, perhaps another 260 to carry the knights and infantry. To this total of over 660 ships (including the warships, and remarkably close to Wace's figure of 696) must be added a multitude of transports of varying sizes to convey the supplies and equipment across the Channel. My own estimate is that between 750 and 800 vessels of all sizes must have been involved, and that the invasion force may in fact have been considerably larger – perhaps as many as 10,000 men, including great numbers of seamen and noncombatants who could be used to guard the fleet once it was dragged ashore and who could form part of the garrisons which would be needed at the bases established in England.

No one in western Europe had ever tried to take a mounted army across the sea before, although such expeditions were not unknown to the Byzantines and Normans in the Mediterranean, while the Danes had transported horses to England as early as 892. In 1066 William had no alternative but to take horses across the Channel, for he would need all the cavalry he could muster to defeat the strong English army, and his knights needed their trained war horses. Unlike the Danes, they could not rely on capturing the undersized, untrained ponies of England once ashore.

Amongst the volunteers in William's army were a number of Normans from southern Italy and Sicily. The Norman colonists in the Mediterranean had been familiar with the transportation of horses across the sea since 1038, when Normans fighting for Byzantium had landed on Sicily, and the Byzantines had for a century been using specially designed ships for this purpose. There is no indication anywhere that William employed special ships, or even ramps – the Bayeux Tapestry is almost certain to have included such an innovation had it been used – but he must undoubtedly have benefited from the advice of these men, who since 1060 had launched several amphibious operations of their own against Sicily.

The knights' mounts were almost exclusively stallions, all unaccustomed to sea travel, and liable to cause pandemonium in an open ship at sea. It seems likely that some partitioning or other crude stabling arrangements must have been made to confine these animals once aboard, in addition to hobbling them and securing them by their halters, but we have no details of this, or of how they were loaded into the ships. Sheer legs and slings may have been used to lower them aboard, but it has to be remembered that loading took place in a tidal anchorage. It is difficult to envisage some 2,400 horses being loaded by this method in one or even two tides.

In 1061 the Normans in Italy had dug out a ramp in the cliff near Oranto in order to load their horses on ships at any state of the tide, and it may have been this simple method that William employed at Dives-sur-mer – he had a great many idle hands at his disposal and a large number of such ramps could have been dug prior to embarkation, so that all the horses could be embarked in one day. These ramps would have run parallel to the bank so that the horses could step into the ships at any state of the tide. Unloading in England would not have presented the same problem, as ships were customarily beached and the horses would have needed no encouragement to leap ashore. (The Bayeux Tapestry shows precisely such a scene – two horses, led by one man, jumping into shallow water from a beached ship.) It is possible that a platform may have been built in the bows of those ships carrying horses, with a ramp leading down to the deck. A simple modification of this nature would have greatly facilitated both loading and unloading. Of course, such ramps would also have speeded up the loading of stores and equipment.

William's invasion army and fleet were ready and assembled at Dives-sur-mer by mid-August, but since the ships of this period could not sail against the wind, and only half the fleet had oars, there was nothing for it but to do what all seamen of that time did – wait and pray for a favourable wind; in William's case a southerly wind which could carry his fleet to the south coast of England in the short space of some twelve hours. But day after day the wind frustrated all William's careful planning, and as the days slipped into weeks the initial high spirits of his army must have declined accordingly. Some of those gathered at Dives-sur-mer were his former enemies, some were the traditional enemies of others, and all were accustomed to seizing from the local peasantry whatever they felt they needed. Despite all William's organizing, the resources of the area cannot have been unlimited, and as August gave way to September the prolonged delay in embarkation created, both economically and from a control point of view, a potentially explosive situation. Some probably recalled that William's father had been baulked in a similar venture by unfavourable winds, and no doubt the rumour passed round the camp that God must be against them to withhold a favourable wind for so long.

William's leadership proved up to the difficult task of controlling this polyglot army and overcoming these fears, and a famous passage from William of Poitiers reveals just how unusual a degree of control William had: 'He made generous provision both for his own knights and those from other parts, and did not permit any of them to take their sustenance by force. The neighbouring peasantry could pasture their cattle and sheep in peace either in the meadows or in the open countryside; the crops awaited untouched the sickle of the harvester without being ridden down by the arrogant passage of knights or cut by foragers. Weak or unarmed, any man might move about the district at his will, singing on his horse, without trembling at the sight of soldiers.'

William's army waited at Dives-sur-mer for a southerly wind for a whole month: it was extraordinary weather for the time of year, as much today as in 1066. Then on 12 September the wind changed to blow from due south, and there was a frantic scramble to embark.

To clear the eastern extremity of the Baie de la Seine, Cap d'Antifer, the fleet had to sail some thirty miles due north before bearing north-east towards the south-east coast of England. It must have been late in the day when the fleet sailed, already dark when it rounded the cape. At some time during the night, as the fleet sailed up the Channel, the wind veered to westerly. Disorganized by this change of wind, perhaps already scattered in the darkness, the fleet broke up, each ship making its own way towards the nearest natural harbour, St Valéry-sur-Somme, in Ponthieu. A number of ships foundered, others were wrecked on the shoreline, and many seized the opportunity to desert an enterprise which God had obviously abandoned.

This storm marked the end of summer: the season of the dangerous equinoctial gales had arrived. The wind veered to northerly again, and William's invasion of England was on the verge of disaster. His fleet reassembled at St Valéry, in the mouth of the Somme, to refit and await again a southerly wind. William set about restoring morale and replacing the losses in men and *materiel*: 'Warding off adversity by prudence, he kept secret as far as possible the deaths of those whom the waves had engulfed and had them buried in secret.'*

Perhaps because of the change of venue, perhaps to lift his army's morale, William ordered the doubling of meat and wine rations. But rain set in, followed by squalls, and in their tents on the muddy banks of the Somme the army began to murmur against William. William of Poitiers tells us William was driven to constant exhortation to maintain the spirits of his followers, and there were endless prayers and religious ceremonies in an increasingly anxious quest for a fair wind. By the final week of September William must have almost given up all hope: day

*William of Poitiers

after day the sky was dark with rain, and the tent and horse lines were thick in mud. Winter was drawing near, and still the wind blew from the north and east. In desperation he had the body of St Valéry paraded round the camp. Silver and gold offerings were made by both the high and low in the army, and their prayers implored the saint to intercede on their behalf. When the army retired to its tents that night, 26 September, after forty-five days of continuously contrary winds (apart from the brief period on the 12th), it could have had little hope of any change, and even if they should get a southerly wind, it was now too late in the year to conquer a country the size of England, and a perilous winter would have to be spent on a foreign shore.

Harold Godwineson had made a significant start to his reign by insisting that he be crowned by the Archbishop of York instead of by the unrecognized Stigand, who had received his post through the personal influence of Godwine, and who must now have been an intense embarrassment to Harold. By this gesture Harold turned his back on all the past political and private manoeuvring of the Godwine family, but gestures were not enough. With rival claimants to the throne to north and south, and with all his people not yet reconciled to his rapid elevation from commoner to successor to the ancient house of Cerdic, he had to show that he was an effective ruler, and he had to do it quickly. Florence of Worcester reveals that he did just that: 'On taking the helm of the kingdom Harold immediately began to abolish unjust laws and to make good ones; to patronize churches and monasteries; to pay particular reverence to bishops, abbots, monks and clerks; and to show himself pious, humble, and affable to all good men. But he treated malefactors with great severity, and gave general orders to his earls, ealdormen, sheriffs and thegns to imprison all thieves, robbers, and disturbers of the kingdom. He laboured in his own person by sea and by land for the protection of his realm.'

Harold's overriding concern from the moment of his coronation was to prepare his country for the war that was inevitable. He made sure that throughout the land his officers knew the dangers that beset the realm, and what would be expected of them in the months ahead. Armouries were checked and replenished, and non-perishable provisions stockpiled at strategic points. His ships were refitted for the spring, and no doubt arrangements were made for extra lithsmen and their ships to arrive as soon as possible. Only by one act did Harold risk censure at this stage: he retained the earldom of Wessex, a most unusual and perhaps risky step, but probably justified in view of the known threat from Normandy.

It was almost certain that William, if he risked an armed invasion, would attack the prosperous and heavily populated south, while any Norwegian attack could be expected in the north-east. If Harald Hardrada were to seize Northumbria, or even Northumbria *and* Mercia, the richer and more populous south could still resist, and the north and midlands could eventually be regained. But if William established himself on the south coast and gained control of the south by defeating the king's army there, then Mercia and Northumbria could not be expected to stand alone and must inevitably fall to him. In the military preparations which Harold instigated early in 1066, it was a vital necessity therefore that the administration of Wessex should not be disturbed by a change of earl.

Harold also realized that whilst he could rely on his brothers' support to hold the south and East Anglia, he needed guarantees that Edwin and Morcar would remain loyal to him if their earldoms, with their strong Scandinavian links, were invaded by Harald Hardrada. Neither of these two young earls, and few of their lay or ecclesiastical magnates, had been present in the *Witena gemot* that had chosen Harold as king, and he could not be sure that they were willing to support him. It was many years since a king of England had set foot in the north. Seizing the bull by the horns with characteristic boldness, in February Harold rode to York to meet his earls and their followers, taking with him only a bodyguard of housecarls and Wulfstan, Bishop of Worcester, the most venerated Churchman in England.

The usual mist of time shrouds the course of events at York, but according to the *Vita Wulfstani* the northern leaders 'for the reverence they bore the bishop, easily yielded their allegiance to king Harold'. Both Edwin and Morcar must have realized that they needed Harold as much as he needed them at this time: they would help him against William if he would help them against any attack by Harald Hardrada or Tostig, who could be expected to try to regain Northumbria.

There is a suggestion that during this visit Harold undertook to marry Ealdgyth, sister of the two northern earls. Such a step would have been a logical conclusion to his visit, and, as Harold was as yet unmarried in the eyes of the Church, it would have been a glorious opportunity not only to seal his alliance with Edwin and Morcar, but also to unite by a political marriage the two great houses *and* the realm. The private feelings of Ealdgyth, whose former husband was Gruffydd ap Llywelyn (whose head had been presented to Harold only three years previously), and of Harold, whose common law marriage to Edith Swanneshals was both happy and fruitful, would not have been considered in such a match. However, there are only meagre mentions of the affair in the chronicles and it seems likely that only a marriage contract was drawn up at this time: had there been a marriage, the chroniclers are unlikely to have passed over it so lightly.

Harold returned to Westminster in time for the Easter feast, abandoning the traditional custom of holding it at Winchester, for London, at the angle between the south and east coasts and the junction of the great Roman roads, was the obvious centre from which to control the defence of the realm.

According to the Anglo-Saxon Chronicle, in 1066 Easter fell on 16 April: 'At that time, throughout all England, a portent such as men had never seen before was seen in the heavens. Some declared that the star was a comet, which some call "the long-haired star": it first appeared on the eve of the festival of *Letania maior*, that is on 24 April, and shone every night for a week.'

Today we know this comet as Halley's Comet, but to the uninformed and superstitious people of that time it appeared as an unnatural omen of evil, and perhaps the old men recalled the tales of their fathers, and how a century before a similar sign had heralded a renewal of the dreadful Danish invasions.

The Anglo-Saxon Chronicle continues: 'Soon thereafter came earl Tostig from across the sea. . . .' Tostig had been fretting in exile in Flanders since the previous year. All the time Edward had been alive there had been the hope that he might be reinstated, but now his situation was hopeless, for Harold would not risk another Northumbrian rebellion by reinstating his brother at the expense of Morcar, and in any case Tostig himself now appears to have nurtured such a hatred of Harold that he would not *ask* him for anything. Brother of the King of England, related by blood to the King of Denmark and by marriage to William of Normandy and the Count of Flanders, only a few months earlier Tostig had been the favourite of the King and Queen of England, the ruler of a great earldom, and richly endowed with his own private estates. His wife's brother had kindly given him the district of St Omer, but in his own eyes he was now a man without position, wealth or hope, and humility did not sit easily on his shoulders.

In 1066 there were only four courses Tostig could steer: to settle in Flanders as a minor lord, seek his fortune in new lands, raid southern England in an attempt to gain the earldom of Wessex, as his father, brothers and he himself had done once before, or ally himself with a foreign power and gain a share of the realm by assisting in a full-scale invasion. Exiled Englishmen had frequently returned by force, spilling English blood before being reinstated. A raid on Wessex would have been the logical choice, for Harold had made the mistake of not yielding it to another. Therefore, if Tostig could gain sufficient local support, Harold might well yield it to him in order to ensure peace at this dangerous time. Yet in the event Tostig chose to support a foreign invasion, forsaking honour for gain.

But first he tried to enlist the aid of his cousin, Sven Estrithson of Denmark, in regaining his earldom, riding overland to Denmark, accompanied by his own English followers and by a band of Flemish knights who were now in his service. Sven refused help, but offered Tostig an earldom in Denmark. Tostig rejected this generous offer and the two men parted on not very friendly terms.

On his return to Flanders Tostig learned of William's embassy to Rome and the declaration of a Holy War against England. He began recruiting Flemings to increase his following, and offered his service to William, no doubt in return for Northumbria. William, who could not afford to offend Baldwin, accepted the offer of troops, and in March Tostig and his men moved to Normandy, but it soon became clear to Tostig that William had no intention of entering into any firm contract with him regarding reward in England. When spring arrived, therefore, Tostig decided to attempt to seize Wessex, and requested aid from William, probably in return for help when William landed in England. William had nothing to lose by such a development, and much to gain: he probably gave Tostig permission to recruit ships and men for his venture, but gave no direct aid.

Tostig sailed from Normandy early in May with between thirty and thirty-five ships of various sizes and some 1,200 men, English, Flemish and Norman. He landed first on the Isle of Wight, where the returning Godwines had united in 1052. Then he and his family had been welcomed with open arms: now he was met by bewilderment – the locals had been told to watch for Norman invaders, not the king's brother – then by embarrassment. The islanders gave him provisions and money to speed him on his way.

Tostig now made a series of exploratory landings along the Sussex coast, where in 1052 men and ships had flocked to Godwine's standard. But now no one came to join him, and his mercenaries began to seek plunder in place of recruits. By the time the fleet reached the Kentish coast the landings had deteriorated into raids, burning and looting the villages and killing the people.

The vital port of Sandwich was seized by a surprise attack which encountered little resistance. Tostig now held the main base of the English navy and the gateway to south-east England. Here he succeeded in gaining a number of volunteers and pressed other seamen into service to man the captured shipping. And here he was joined by one of his Northumbrian supporters named Copsi, who had been exiled with him in 1065 and who brought with him seventeen ships and some 700 mercenaries from the Orkneys.

When Harold received news of Tostig's raids he was faced with a crucial decision. Tostig might be doing nothing more than raiding, but he might be conducting a reconnaissance in force to test England's defences for William, or he might be a lure to draw Harold's forces to the wrong area and distract attention from William's main offensive. It would have seemed unlikely that William could have already mustered a sufficiently large fleet to cross the Channel in great strength, but when Sandwich fell Harold suddenly had no choice of action left. Whatever Tostig's true role, Harold could not afford to have Sandwich in the hands of an enemy at this time: he was forced to mobilize his fleet and the fyrd.

By the time Harold reached Sandwich, Tostig had gone, continuing round the south-east coast, with a fleet that now numbered sixty ships, to sail up the east coast. The raiders put into the mouth of the River Burnham in Norfolk and harried the surrounding countryside, then sailed on to the Humber, where they disembarked on the south bank. Tostig's men ravaged this area as cruelly as any Vikings in the past, but were caught scattered and unprepared by the swift reaction of Edwin and the Lindsey fyrd. Returning hastily to their ships, the depleted raiders continued northwards, but found the Yorkshire coast stoutly defended by Morcar's men, alerted by the raids on the Mercian coast. The men from Sandwich and most of the mercenaries now deserted, taking with them all the largest ships and as much of the loot as they could. His fleet reduced to twelve small vessels, Tostig made his way to Scotland, landing in the Firth of Forth, probably at the beginning of June.

Malcolm of Scotland offered Tostig protection but not aid: '. . . the king of the Scots took him under his protection and helped him obtain provisions, and there he stayed the whole summer.'* Some historians believe that Tostig now sailed to Norway to enlist the aid of Harald Hardrada. Snorri says he made such a voyage, and told Harald: '. . . if you want to conquer England, I can ensure that the majority of the

*Anglo-Saxon Chronicle (C)

chieftains there will be your friends and give you support. Compared with my brother Harold, the only thing I lack is the title of king.' Tostig, or his deputy Copsi, had already opened some negotiations with Harald Hardrada, for the Orkneys had recently come under the authority of the King of Norway and Harald's approval must have been needed for the seventeen ships to sail with Copsi.

Tostig certainly spent most of the summer in Scotland, gathering to him fresh forces for another attack on Northumbria, this time in conjunction with his new ally, Harald Hardrada. Harald himself is believed to have issued the summons to arms about mid-June. Both Norman and English contemporary sources are silent about Harald's preparations, yet we know Harold anticipated an attack on northern England from Norway. It could well be that the annual mustering of the large Norwegian war fleet passed unrecorded simply because it had been a regular feature of life for the past seventeen years; but it could also be that Harald Hardrada's muster was accomplished secretly and with a speed that prevented the news of his fleet's departure from Norway reaching either Harold or William in time. Within six weeks of the summons being issued, Harald's forces were mustered and his fleet ready to sail; all he needed to descend on England was a favourable wind.

There was little or no communication between England and Norway at this date, but Normandy and Norway were in close contact, mainly because of trading. Harald must have known of William's preparations for an invasion of England and he would have had no desire to land in a kingdom already conquered by the Normans. But Harald must also have known in June and July that William was not ready to sail and, at the beginning of August, that the wind which now carried his own fleet southwards would be holding William's fleet in port, and at the same time preventing the English fleet from sailing northwards. All the time the wind blew from the north Harald could call the tune, and that summer it blew almost continuously from the north and east for nearly two months.

No Norman fleet had followed in the wake of Tostig's raids, while messages from Edwin and Morcar informed Harold that the raiders had been driven off and had retreated northwards. Harold could draw reassurance from Tostig's defeat at the hands of the northern earls, it showed the north was alert and capable of protecting itself, but he had now committed all his forces by summoning the fleet and the fyrd, with no sign of the Norman invaders. His spies must have informed him during May and June that William's fleet could not be ready before July at the earliest, yet Harold decided to hold the fyrd in the field until that fleet arrived, rather than dismiss the select men and summon them again later. With hindsight this was a fateful decision, but the advantages of having the fyrd assembled were that the time until the Normans arrived could be utilized in organizing the defence of the realm to the utmost efficiency, and when the invaders did arrive they could be met at the coast rather than allowing them to establish a firm base before the fyrd could arrive.

There were some 150 miles of coastline to be defended. Harold took the only course possible and concentrated the select fyrd at strategic points on the coast, one of which was the Hastings–Pevensey area, and held the élite housecarls and part of the select fyrd of the south coast as a mobile reserve, using the fleet for their transport. At this date there was virtually no possibility of intercepting the Normans at sea. Given that the Normans must come on a southerly wind, and that ships of this age could not sail against the wind, there was no way Harold could arrange a mid-Channel interception. Therefore, the only use for the fleet was as transport for his reserve – movement by sea was faster than movement by land, given a favourable wind, and if the wind was unfavourable then the troops could still be landed to march overland.

Leaving the defence of the coast to his local commanders, Harold took the fleet of some 700 vessels from its mustering point at Sandwich and sailed to the Isle of Wight, together with his reserve of housecarls and select fyrd. The craft were more than likely drawn up on the eastern beaches until needed. Just across from the Isle of Wight was Chichester harbour and

Bosham, Harold's home. It is probable that he established his headquarters here, where messengers from London, Kent or Sussex could reach him, for a short boat trip would take him to his fleet. When the Norman fleet was sighted and had passed the Isle of Wight, he could set sail and follow them to their landing point, where his fleet and its soldiers could hold them until the select fyrd could concentrate.

Harold was to remain at the Isle of Wight until September: he would only have done this if he considered that William was a more serious threat than Harald Hardrada, Edwin and Morcar could deal with Harald unaided, or Harald's fleet would not be ready before William's.

By the end of July neither the Norwegians nor the Normans had come, and Harold's forces had been held in a position of readiness for two months, the normal limit of service for the select fyrd. By his superb organization of supplies, Harold was able to hold the fyrd in position for a further six weeks, in total a period longer than any previous king had been able to hold an army in the field, and almost twice as long as William had to hold his invasion force together. But by early September there was still no sign or news of an invasion from Normandy, the last of the supplies were exhausted, and men were beginning to slip away to their homes: the harvest had not yet been reaped and winter was not far off. In medieval times, August and September were crucial months, during which the peasants had to not only reap by hand the harvest of crops but store them so they would not rot, slaughter and preserve most of their livestock, and cut sufficient timber to ensure they would not die of cold during the long winter months. If these tasks were not completed before the winter set in, then famine and death must inevitably follow.

In 1066 the equinox commenced on 16 September. No invasion would be feasible after that date and the watch along the coast could be relaxed – just as it was relaxed at this date in the times of Philip of Spain, Napoleon and Hitler. But medieval people lived by the Church calendar, and Ember Week, which marks the transition from summer to winter in the Church's year, began on 14 September. The seamen would need several

143

days to sail home, beach their ships and secure for the season of gales and the winter: so 8 September, the Nativity of St Mary, was probably the traditional date for an English fleet to disperse.

The Anglo-Saxon Chronicle states: 'When the festival of the Nativity of St Mary came, the men's provisions had run out, and no one could keep them there any longer: they were therefore given permission to return home.' But Harold does not seem to have allowed his forces to disperse even then, and it is possible that he had by now received news that Harald Hardrada's fleet had left Norway and that Tostig was again on the move, and was merely returning his reserve to London so as to be in a position to deal with an attack from either north or south in these last few days of the campaigning season. For Harold's fleet did not disperse to its individual ports, but sailed for London. Unfortunately it was caught in the first of the equinoctial gales and severely battered, many ships being either lost at sea or using the excuse of the storm to put into their home ports on the south-east coast to refit.

Harold himself did not go with the fleet, but landed with his reserves. There is some evidence that he then took a circuitous route to London, dropping off large groups of housecarls at strategic points along the south coast, keeping some of the fyrd men from the coastal areas on duty, releasing others, and arranging a system of reliefs to maintain the watch for a while.

The exact date that he arrived in London is unknown, but it was probably about the 15th, for he had been in London only a day or two at the most when he received the news that invaders had landed in the north. The period of waiting was at an end, the time for action had arrived. Harold now had only two choices – keep his reserve in the south against the possibility of a Norman invasion, or march it 200 miles north (the contrary winds and state of his fleet prevented movement by sea) to deal with Harald Hardrada, trusting that he would be able to return in time to deal with William. He chose the latter course, well aware that it was a calculated risk, but he must by now have known that the Norwegian invasion force was much larger than might be expected from Normandy. On 20 September Harold and his reserve troops began their famous march north.

144

6
The
Northern Invasion

Harald Hardrada summoned half the Leidang for his invasion of England and by the beginning of August had about 200 warships, a considerable number of transports and smaller craft, and some 7,000 men assembled off the Solund Islands at the mouth of Sognefjord, north of Bergen. But his summons had gone farther afield than the Norwegian homeland, and many more men and ships were yet to join this great invasion fleet – from the Shetlands, Orkneys and Norwegian-controlled parts of northern and western Scotland, from Iceland and the Faroes, and from the Hebrides, Ireland and the Isle of Man.

With the aid of the same northerly winds which were keeping William landlocked in the Somme, the Norwegian fleet sailed south-west in early August, Harald and part of the fleet to the Shetlands, the remainder to the Orkneys. Here were mustering the ships from Iceland, Ireland and the other Norwegian colonies, to make up a total of almost one hundred ships and perhaps 3,000 men.

Harald moved to the Orkneys about mid-August and waited there, probably in Scapa Flow, for the last of his levies until the

The Vikings' love of
horses is well known, and
grave finds have revealed
that they were greatly
influenced by the Magyars,
themselves famous
horsemen. These
archaeological finds
suggest – as do this and the
following illustrations –
that the Vikings made far
greater use of the horse in
battle than is at present
considered likely. And if
both the Normans and
Vikings were proficient
cavalrymen in war, then
why not the professional
soldiers of the English
army, who were at least
their equal in fighting
skills? This illustration is
from a 12th century
tapestry, found in the
village of Skog in
northern Sweden.
(Antikvarisk-
Topografiska Arkivet,
Stockholm.)

end of the month. On or about 1 September his entire armada
sailed across the Pentland Firth to Duncansby Head, across the
Moray Firth to Kinnairds Head, and down the east coast of
Scotland to the Firth of Forth, making a landfall there on the
4th or 5th. It was probably here that the Scottish mercenaries
who were to serve in his army joined the fleet. With parts of the
Scottish mainland held by the Norwegians and a great fleet in
his coastal waters, Malcolm of Scotland could not afford to
offend Harald, yet at the same time dare not risk committing
himself openly to the Norwegian cause: if Harald was defeated
Malcolm could expect another English expedition against his
small kingdom. Therefore, Malcolm provided only sufficient
ships and men to ensure that if the invasion proved successful
his assistance would be remembered, but if it failed he could
disclaim both ships and crews as private adventurers.

The next day Harald's fleet continued southwards, and on
either the 7th or 8th arrived in the estuary of the Tyne, where
waited the last of the ships to be engaged in the invasion – those
of Tostig, carrying his English and Danish housecarls, Flemish
knights, and Flemish and Scottish mercenary spearmen.

Medieval sources are often accused (justifiably) of exaggerat-
ing the size of armies and navies. Three hundred warships
(together with perhaps a hundred transports and a hundred
lesser craft) and at least 10,000 men do seem excessive numbers,
yet all the evidence points to these figures being reasonably
accurate. The northern invasion has always been overshadowed
by the drama of Hastings, yet it is obvious that Harald
Hardrada's invasion forces were at least the equal of William's,
and constituted a much greater threat to England in the long
term.

The allied fleet continued southwards to Cleveland, between
the Tees and Esk, where a landing was made. No resistance was
encountered and the Norwegians were able to subjugate the
whole area, taking much plunder. It is likely that a force was left
here to hold the district for Harald. Continuing southwards, the
fleet next stopped at Scarborough, where the townspeople seem
to have been alerted, withdrew into the town, and refused to
yield. Harald sent men up on to the cliff which looms over the

town and had a huge pyre built there. Burning faggots were then hurled down into the town. 'One after another the houses caught fire, until the town was completely destroyed. The Norwegians killed a great number of the people there and seized all the booty they could lay their hands on. The English then had no choice, if they wanted to stay alive, but to submit to King Harald. In this way he subdued the country wherever he went.'*

Harald probably left another force to hold the port of Scarborough and the fertile vale of Pickering, then sailed farther south to make another landing at Holderness. Here for the first time he encountered some English troops, either select or great fyrd or both. There was a brief battle, the fyrd was crushed without trouble by the superior Norwegian forces, and the district of Holderness plundered and placed under Norwegian control. From here it was but a short trip to the estuary of the Humber, which the allied fleet probably entered on 18 September.

Many of the Norwegians would have traded at York in the past, and there would have been no shortage of pilots to guide the fleet up the great estuary and into the Ouse, which led into the very heart of northern England and to its capital, the third greatest city of the realm after London and Winchester, with a population of around 9,000. It was now mid-September, and the equinoctial gales had begun. Harald must have known when he sailed for England that he would have to spend the winter there, and to do this he needed a safe anchorage for his great fleet. The Humber and the Ouse provided this anchorage and at the same time would enable him to attack York from a nearby base, and separate the north of England from the south.

The first landing was made on the right bank, but this area was heavily forested and the next day the fleet moved on upstream, anchoring on the left bank close to the village of Riccall, where the country was more open. It was not possible to proceed farther upstream because the river became too narrow for the ships to turn round. The fleet was probably strung out over a distance of at least a mile, but Riccall itself was only some ten miles due south of York and about the same

*Snorri Sturluson, *Heimskringla*

Part of the Oseberg tapestry, one of the many rich treasures discovered in the 9th century Oseberg ship burial. It portrays warriors armed with spears and long shields, some with mail shirts, and one mounted. The other horses are all harnessed to four-wheeled wagons, which carry people as well as goods. (Universitetets Oldsaksamling, Oslo.)

distance south-east of Tadcaster, where the great Roman road from London to York crossed the Wharfe.

There is no evidence to support the story that a small English fleet fled up the Wharfe before Harald and anchored at Tadcaster, thus causing Harald to halt at Riccall in order to prevent them sailing down to cut off his retreat to the Humber. This whole story is based on one phrase in the Anglo-Saxon Chronicle, when Harold, marching north from London, reviews his lithsmen at Tadcaster – 'and thaer his lithe fylcade'. This mention of lithsmen has been erroneously interpreted to mean there were English ships at Tadcaster, but, as lithsmen might be warriors or seamen, their presence does not necessarily mean ships were also present.

Earl Morcar of Northumbria had now had about a week in which to muster his select fyrd and call out the great fyrd to deal with the emergency. It is not possible to arrive at definite figures for the strength of Morcar's army, but it must have included his own housecarls, the select fyrd – which included those tough thegns who had ousted Tostig and forced Edward to yield to their wishes – and thousands of poorly armed peasants. There had also been time for Edwin to join his brother in York, accompanied by his housecarls and a large contingent of the select fyrd of Mercia, while the Earl Waltheof had also arrived with men from the Huntingdon area. (Waltheof, younger son of Siward, was given the small earldom of Huntingdon by Edward the Confessor, and was about twenty years old in 1066.) A conservative estimate of the strength of the select fyrds of Mercia and Northumbria combined would be around 8,000 men. As some had already been engaged farther north, and Edwin did not take all his select fyrd to York, a figure of perhaps 4,000 select fyrd and a maximum of 750 housecarls might be feasible for the number of trained troops in York.

It is also possible that as many as 1,500 of the royal housecarls might have been in the York area. No details of the royal housecarls' movements are given for the summer of 1066, but at the start of that year they were deployed – as normal – at Wallingford and Slessvik. Harold may have concentrated them in the south to form his élite reserve, but it is equally possible he left the northern contingent at Slessvik to provide a stiffening for the northern forces, particularly as he had at least half the royal housecarls, his brothers' housecarls, and all the Danish mercenaries or lithsmen with him in the south.

Edwin and Morcar had undoubtedly gathered a mighty army at York, but it was still very much a provincial or earl's army, whereas it had to face a king's army which included a number of earls with their followers. Edwin was only about eighteen years old, Morcar even younger, and although they had experienced warriors to advise them, neither had fought in a major battle before. Harald had been fighting the Danes for almost as long as the two northern earls had lived, and had been fighting for Byzantium for a decade before that.

On the 20th, the day after anchoring the fleet at Riccall, Harald marched directly against York with at least 6,000 men, leaving the remainder of his army to guard the ships under the earls Paul and Erlend of Shetland and Orkney.

York was fortified, and although the fortifications needed repairing, they were sufficient to withstand attack by an army without siege equipment. Word of the invasion had been sent to London; the northern earls had only to sit tight and await the arrival of Harold with reinforcements. Perhaps they did not believe he would come to their assistance; perhaps their youthful confidence overruled the cautious advice of their elders; perhaps they recognized that in the event of a defeat by siege, York would be sacked and burnt, and it was therefore

149

The legendary battle of Bravellir (probably 6th century) portrayed by a composition based upon motifs from Gotland picture stones. Here may be seen two armies confronting each other, with archers in plenty and a considerable body of mounted warriors in action. At bottom left is what is probably intended to be merely a four-wheeled wagon, though it could be interpreted as some kind of war-chariot. (Reproduced from *Skalk* No 4, 1964, by kind permission of the artist R.W.H. and Dr. H. Andersen.)

better to risk defeat in the field, after which a peace might still be negotiated. Whatever their reasons, when they heard the Norwegian host was advancing on York, Edwin and Morcar led their army from the protection of that city's walls and marched against Harald, the Thunderbolt of the North. The two armies met two miles south of York, at a place named Fulford, in those days a village but now a suburb of the city.

Today there are two roads from Riccall to York, either of which might have been used by an army moving on York along the left bank of the Ouse. In 1066 there may have been one or two trackways, but in either case there was only one at Fulford itself, running along a low ridge, about half a mile wide, which sloped down to the Ouse to the west, and to a water-filled ditch and a dyke, with marshland beyond, to the east. That ridge therefore provided an excellent defensive position, from which Edwin and Morcar might have effectively blocked the road to York.

Harald Hardrada's army was approaching Fulford when the English came in sight. With years of experience behind him, Harald immediately saw what Edwin and Morcar did not, and ordered his army to deploy at once across the ridge. On the left flank, by the Ouse, Harald concentrated his main force under his own command, with his son Olaf and his loyal lieutenant Eystein Orri. His centre and right wing stretched comparatively thinly across the ridge and down to the dyke and ditch: this part of the army was commanded by Tostig and probably contained the English, Scots and Flemings, together with the contingents from the smaller Norwegian colonies. Edwin and Morcar now deployed into battle order and advanced slowly against this position, their forces in close formation. Edwin appears to have commanded the English right, Morcar the left.

The actual battle is mentioned but briefly in the Anglo-Saxon Chronicle, being overshadowed by later events, yet it was one of the few major battles of the age, involving more than 10,000 men. It is necessary therefore to turn to a Scandinavian source, Snorri Sturluson. Snorri tells the story as fully as anyone can with any accuracy, and his brief description is the basis for all later embroidery on the bare facts.

'The earls now advanced down the line of the dyke, and the Norwegian flank there gave way; the English went after them, thinking that the Norwegians would flee. Earl Morcar's banner was in the van.

'When King Harald saw that the English flank was advancing down the dyke and was now opposite them [i.e. his position], he sounded the attack and urged his men forward, with his banner, "Land-Waster", carried in front. The Norwegian onslaught was so fierce that everything gave way before it, and a great number of the English were killed. The English army quickly broke into flight, some fleeing up the river, and others down the river; but most of them fled into the swamp, where the dead piled up so thickly that the Norwegians could cross the swamp dry-shod.

'Earl Waltheof fled with the survivors towards the town of York, and there was great carnage there.'

It was a classic manoeuvre, executed by an experienced military commander who was 'quick to perceive an enemy's weakness and exploit any advantage'. First the English attacked his line at the weakest part, which he must have intended them to, and pushed it back. Harald himself held the left flank and eventually defeated the forces confronting him. When Morcar's men exposed their flank by pushing too far ahead on the east flank, Harald smashed through the weakened centre and swung part of his forces downhill into Morcar's flank, cutting off his retreat and pinning the English left flank against the dyke.

Horsemen in mail, brandishing spears, and armed with the round shields of Vikings or Anglo-Saxons, from an 11th century miniature. Note that those spearheads shown are winged, which has not prevented one from piercing shield and bearer, though this may merely be artistic licence.

151

Large iron stirrup with brass scrolls, found in the River Thames at Battersea. Probably Viking.

Unable to escape, Morcar's men died fighting, or tried to flee across the swamp, where they drowned. Meanwhile Edwin's men had broken, some managing to escape past Harald's force, the remainder pursued up-river to the gates of York, many of them being slain on the way.

The losses were exceedingly heavy on both sides. The Anglo-Saxon Chronicle states that the Northumbrians 'fought that host and made great slaughter of them; but a great number of the English were either slain or drowned or driven in flight, and the Norwegians had possession of the place of slaughter'. Harald Hardrada's losses were undoubtedly heavy, but nothing like so bad as those of Edwin and Morcar, whose effective forces in Northumbria were destroyed. The road to York and to complete dominance over the north of England lay open to Harald.

Snorri says that Morcar was killed in the battle, and quotes the court poet Stein Herdisarson:

> 'Many were lost in the water;
> The drowned sank to the bottom.
> Warriors lay thickly fallen
> Around the young Earl Morcar.'

After the battle of Fulford neither Edwin nor Morcar are mentioned again in the chronicles until December, when both are very much alive. In view of the fate of Morcar's forces it is quite possible he was captured, as may have been Edwin, and this would do much to explain the course of events after the battle and Snorri's remark, quoted above, 'Earl Waltheof fled with the survivors. . . .'

Harald's moves after the battle tell us much of the control he exercised over the allied forces under his command. Instead of advancing to sack and loot York, as might have been expected of a Viking host, he sent most of his army back to Riccall and proceeded unopposed and with only a small force into the city. 'After the battle King Harald of Norway and Earl Tostig entered York with as great a force as seemed to them necessary and received hostages (a hundred and fifty) from the borough, besides assistance in the way of provisions, and so retired thence

152

to their ships. They offered to conclude an abiding peace with the citizens provided that they all marched southwards with them to conquer this realm.'*

After Fulford Harald needed provisions for his great army and hostages to ensure the submission of the northern capital. He obviously received both without trouble. His magnanimous treatment of York and its citizens also shows that his aim was not just to conquer the north and hold it as a separate kingdom, but to secure an alliance with the northern lords in order to conquer the rest of England with their help. Tostig had promised him the support of the northern people, and no doubt Harald had believed him – as well he might. York itself had once been the capital of a Viking kingdom, most of the northern landowners had Danish blood, for their fathers had come to England with Knut, and until recently they had been ruled by Danes – the earls Siward and Leofric. The northern risings against Norman rule in 1069 and 1070 were largely inspired by Scandinavian sentiment – a preference for Sven of Denmark in place of William of Normandy – and the intensity of these revolts indicates the degree of Scandinavian influence in the north at this time.

Harald therefore spared York to encourage the north to come over to his cause; because he needed it as a winter base and a centre for the continuing supply of his army; and perhaps because it would eventually pass as a reward to Tostig. Whether the northern lords did in fact accept Harald's offer of an alliance against Harold and the south remains yet another of those mysteries which abound in 1066. Certainly such an alliance was offered to York, and the Northumbrians, now defenceless and possibly leaderless, may well have chosen to join Harald rather than see their lands, property, livestock and families ravaged and destroyed by the Viking horde. In the event, whatever their decision, it was not necessary for them to face Harald again in order to deliver it.

Harald and Tostig returned to Riccall, leaving the Northumbrians to reach their decision, or make the arrangements for an alliance. The submission of York was no guarantee of the surrender of the whole of Northumbria, and Harald had

Anglo-Saxon prick spur of iron, 11th or 12th century. This was the basic type of spur used throughout the 11th century. (Crown Copyright.)

*Anglo-Saxon Chronicle (C)

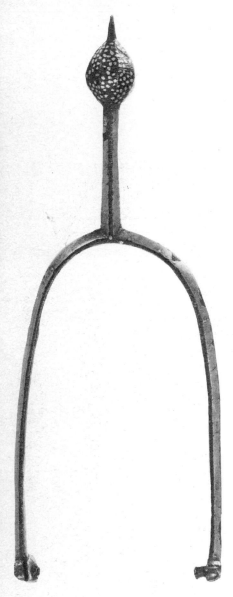

Anglo-Saxon prick spur of iron, embellished with gold and silver dots and sheeting. Early 11th century. (Crown Copyright.)

therefore demanded a further 500 hostages from all parts of the earldom. It would have taken several days for the Northumbrians to collect these hostages and procure further provisions for the Norwegian army, and there were probably hurried meetings of the leading lords and fierce debates. A second meeting with Harald had been agreed for the 25th at Stamford Bridge: here Harald would receive the hostages and provisions, conclude his alliance with York and possibly the whole of Northumbria, appoint his own officers to govern, and award lands to his leading supporters.

Stamford Bridge is eight miles north-east of York, at a crossing of the River Derwent, where four Roman roads met. It was an ideal spot to meet men from all over Northumbria, but it was in the opposite direction from York to Harald's fleet at Riccall, and why Harald chose to move so far away from his fleet at this time remains a mystery. Of course, scouts could warn the fleet of the approach of any English army arriving from the south, and the fleet could then move down-river to safety, but a large number of men had to be left to man the ships for such a manoeuvre, and more than anything else this one move of Harald's smacks of complete confidence in his position – he did not know Harold Godwine, and it seems he underestimated the measure of his next opponent. On the other hand, the move to north-east of York did place him in an ideal spot for communication with any holding forces left in Cleveland, Scarborough and Holderness, while remaining close to York, and provided his army with a fertile area rich in crops and so far untouched by his foragers.

On the 24th Harald marched two-thirds of his army along the valley of the Derwent to Stamford Bridge: the remaining third, about 2,500 men, stayed to guard the ships, under Eystein Orri, the earls Paul and Erlend and Harald's son Olaf. The weather was exceptionally fine, and rather than march some fifteen miles in armour, most of those men who owned armour left their mail shirts on board ship, going ashore armed only with helmet, shield, spear and sword: there were also a number of archers. That night the army, between 5,000 and 5,500 men, camped at Stamford Bridge to await the arrival the next day of the

154

spokesmen of the defeated Northumbrians, with the demanded hostages and supplies.

The Norwegian host had made its first raid on the English coast on or about 10 September: the northern earls must have been aware of the size and intent of the Norwegian fleet by the 13th at the latest. It is 198 miles from York to London, and even allowing for the fact that in 1066 there existed a Roman road all the way, a horseman was unlikely to achieve more than sixty miles a day. News of Harald Hardrada's invasion fleet could not have reached Harold in London until either the 16th or 17th: nine days later he was fighting the Norwegian forces.

In London Harold had only some of his royal housecarls, his Danish lithsmen, his brothers' housecarls, and that part of the select fyrd of Wessex (probably king's and earls' thegns) which had been with his reserve all summer. Messengers were immediately despatched back up the road to the north to summon the select fyrds of East Anglia, the east midlands, and at least some of the west midland shires. Harold may also have recalled his royal housecarls from the south coast, though he may have left them in position to harry and delay any landing by William, for *if* half the royal housecarls *had* been left at Slessvik, then Harold would have expected them to join him on his arrival in the north. The select fyrd of Wessex, now mostly dispersed, was left in the south, and it appears the select fyrd of London and the surrounding area also remained at home.

Harold had no more than three or possibly four days in which to gather troops to him in London, for on 20 September at the latest he left that city to march on York, gathering some of the midland and East Anglian fyrds to him *en route*. Because of this hurried departure he probably had no more than 2,000 men with him when he left London, although all were élite troops.

Harold's march north ranks with the greatest military movements in history: in distance, speed and the number of troops involved it was without parallel in his time. Travelling both by day and by night, with only brief stops along the way, his rapidly growing army covered the 190 miles to Tadcaster in

Anglo-Saxon scramasaxes or single-edged knives found in the Thames and dating from the 10th and 11th centuries. The blade lengths range from 18.5 to 28 cm.

155

five days, arriving at this village on the Wharfe on the evening of the 24th. Here Harold received the news of the dreadful defeat at Fulford from a number of survivors of the battle who had fled southwards, and heard that York had capitulated. If Harald Hardrada knew of Harold's approach, now would be the time that he would strike, before the English could recover from their march or be reinforced by stragglers. 'Then meanwhile came Harold, the king of the English, with all his levies on the Sunday to Tadcaster and there drew up his household [a poor choice of term] troops in battle order.'* This shows that Harold expected an attack from the direction of York.

The actual phrase used here is 'and thaer his lith fylcade'. This has been variously interpreted as drawing up his mercenaries for review, preparing for battle (as above), and a meeting with an English fleet in the north – the latter interpretation I have already dismissed as inaccurate. Fylcade is from the verb fylcian, meaning to array or to set in order. The Norske equivalent fylkja had the same meaning. It seems likely that Harold would have arrayed (i.e. drawn up in battle order) his troops at this point, firstly in case of attack from York, only nine miles away, and secondly to organize the confused conglomeration of shire levies, housecarls and lithsmen into some semblance of order, so as to be able to deploy quickly in the future. It would also have been an opportunity to count heads and make an inspiring speech. It is doubtful if Harold could muster more than 5,000 men, 6,000 at the most, and all exhausted by their march. They would have needed all the encouragement he could give them.

But the very swiftness of Harold's reaction and march north had given him the tactical advantage of complete surprise, and at dawn the next morning, the 25th, he advanced unopposed and undetected upon York. Almost as important was the fact that his speed was to result in the Norwegians being brought to battle only a few hours before an alliance was formed between them and York, or possibly the whole of the north: a few hours' delay in London or on the march could so easily have cost Harold the loyalty of the north, with incalculable effects on subsequent events.

Reconstruction of an Anglo-Saxon chieftain's shield from the Sutton Hoo ship burial, 7th century. (British Museum.)

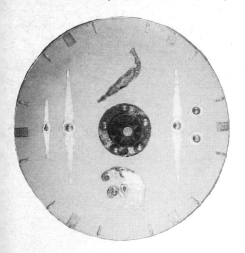

*Anglo-Saxon Chronicle (C)

Harald Hardrada had left no garrison in York – possibly he felt unable to trust his men in the city – and when Harold's forces arrived there early in the morning, their entry into the city must have been watched with mixed feelings. Harold obviously did not trust the citizens, and had all gates guarded to prevent word of his arrival being sent to the Norwegians. After a brief rest, during which time he obtained details of the Norwegian forces and their position, Harold marched his army out of the present Walmgate Bar and headed towards the village of Gate Helmsley.

It is eight miles from York to Stamford Bridge and it is doubtful if the English arrived there much before noon. Their advance would not have been visible to the Norwegians in the valley of the Derwent until they topped the ridge one mile west of Stamford Bridge, at the village of Gate Helmsley. Snorri says that at first all the Norwegians could see was the dust from the horses' hooves and the gleam of shields and mail. Obviously this was no humble deputation of citizens bringing hostages and provisions. Harald summoned Tostig to him and asked what this army could be. Tostig replied it might be a hostile force, although it was also possible that they were Northumbrians seeking mercy and protection from the Norwegian king in exchange for homage to him. Harald decided to wait until he could see more of this army: 'And the closer the army came, the greater it grew, and their glittering weapons sparkled like a field of broken ice.'*

It is incredible that at this late hour Harald still had no certain knowledge of the approach of the English army: he cannot have had any scouts or even outposts on duty. Such laxity from a military leader such as Harald Hardrada is hard to understand, yet all contemporary sources agree he was taken completely by surprise at Stamford Bridge. His overconfidence can only be explained by the assumption that he believed the south would not help the north; that Harold could not possibly arrive in the north so soon; or that Harold would not arrive at all, faced as he was by a Norman invasion of the south.

At last Harald concluded that the approaching army could only be that of the English king, unlikely as that must have

Viking shield from the Gokstad ship burial, late 9th century. Round shields, either plain as here or elaborately decorated as in the previous photograph, were still in use in the 11th century by the Norske warriors of Harald Hardrada and the Scandinavians in English service. (Universitetets Oldsaksamling, Oslo.)

*Snorri Sturluson, *Heimskringla*

Anglo-Saxon warriors with concave round shields as shown in 11th century manuscripts. The figures at the top are from a manuscript dated *circa* 1090. Note the form of headgear and the winged spearheads.

seemed to him. Tostig suggested they should retreat to Riccall and the fleet as quickly as possible. Harald rejected the idea as unworthy of a Viking warrior. It is also doubtful if all the Norwegians and their allies could have escaped a pursuit, for only a small number of them were mounted, whereas all the English were on horseback. Instead Harald decided to accept battle, and despatched three of his best men on the fastest horses available to summon Eystein Orri and the ship guard to Stamford Bridge. Then he ordered his banner to be raised and began issuing orders for a rather late deployment.

As with the battle of Fulford, the important battle of Stamford Bridge is passed over quickly by the contemporary chroniclers of the Anglo-Saxon Chronicle, and we must rely on Snorri's saga of King Harald for details of the battle. Snorri's account is not accepted by most English historians, but before entering into that matter, let us look at the known facts – the lie of the land and the preliminary skirmishing – about which there is no dispute.

The River Derwent is narrow until it enters the small valley where now stands the village of Stamford Bridge: here it broadens suddenly into shallows. The construction of a weir, and a lock a few miles downstream, have made the river deeper than it was in the 11th century, but nevertheless in 1066 it was a formidable obstacle, some 12 metres wide, with steep banks and a muddy bottom. There was no village here in 1066, only a wooden bridge, wide enough for two men to cross at a time, and resting on the stone pillars of its predecessors, probably built originally by the Romans for the Bridlington road, which follows the old Roman highway to the coast. This bridge was just below the modern weir, about 400 metres upstream from the present hump-backed road bridge. On either side of the river the land rises to a height of little more than 15 metres above the river. To the west of the river this slope is gradual, rising to the brow of the ridge whereon sits Gate Helmsley, a mile away. To the east the land rises more rapidly in a succession of hedged pastures which are now called Battle Flats. Despite the passage of time, the fields and river are much as they were in 1066.

158

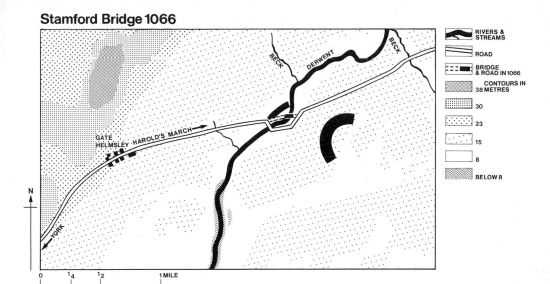

Stamford Bridge 1066

When the English army appeared at Gate Helmsley the Norwegians and their allies were scattered along the banks of the river, mostly on the east bank, but some on the west bank. Those on the west bank were ordered to hold the bridge and delay the English advance, while the main army formed up on the east bank to give battle.

There is little argument about the first phase of the battle, the defence of the bridge. Hopelessly outnumbered and with their backs to a river which could be crossed only via the bridge by two men at a time, the Norwegians on the west bank were in an unenviable position. Nor did the English show any signs of fatigue when they sighted their enemy in disarray and divided by the Derwent. It seems the men of the vanguard immediately spurred their horses and galloped down the gradual slope to the river, intent on seizing the bridge so as to isolate and despatch all the enemy on the west bank.

These unfortunate warriors can have had little time to organize themselves, but many would have been willing to give their lives to gain time for their more fortunate comrades. However, there was no point in senseless heroics; it would be a fighting withdrawal, not a last stand. Probably men began running across the bridge as soon as the horsemen were

Contour map of the Stamford Bridge area, showing the position of the Norwegian army and approximate position of the bridge and road from Gate Helmsley in 1066.

A Norman knight with kite shield slays a housecarl at the battle of Hastings. (From the Bayeux Tapestry.) The shape of the housecarl's shield is unusual, but may simply be a poor representation of a round shield. It is the only shield of this shape in the tapestry, though other round shields are all shown in profile. (French Government Tourist Office.)

identified as hostile, and a continuous stream of men must have crossed the bridge until the English seized it. Those Norwegians who stood fast to cover this withdrawal may have had time to form a crude semicircle before the bridge, their flanks resting on the river bank, but there could have been only a few minutes before the English were upon them.

The first English to arrive probably attacked from horseback, but as more arrived the later arrivals probably dismounted to get to close grips. The stranded Norwegians sold their lives dearly, but there was really little hope for those holding the line, and few of them could have been withdrawn to escape before the line was broken by the sheer weight of numbers and the fight deteriorated into small groups of struggling men. Some, pressed back to the river bank, jumped or fell into the Derwent and tried to swim to safety, but most were drowned and only the strongest of swimmers could have made it across to the east bank, without shield, helmet or weapons. The cluster by the bridge itself was suddenly reduced to one Norwegian – one of the few to wear a mail shirt that day – who held the English at bay for a while longer, wielding a two-handed axe which felled all his attackers, until he was finally and ignominiously despatched by a man floating downstream beneath the bridge in a small boat or swill tub, who stabbed the Norwegian from beneath with a spear.

Slowly the English began to file across the bridge, unopposed by the Norwegian army waiting some 200 metres back from the east bank, until they had formed line of battle on that bank. At first it may appear strange that Harald did not contest the crossing of the bridge from the east bank, but here were some 10,000 men mustered for battle; he would not have wanted to fight a minor skirmish for a bridge, but a swift and decisive battle which in one day would give him the whole of England: Stamford Bridge had to be another Fulford. If he allowed the English to cross the river, they would have to attack uphill, then he could counter-attack downhill, and it would be the turn of the English to fight with their backs to an unfordable river. Harold must also have recognized this, and accepted the challenge. The great battle of Stamford Bridge was fought for the control of all England.

A group of about twenty horsemen now rode forward from the English lines to offer Tostig the opportunity to return to his natural allegiance, when his brother the king would give him a third of the realm (possibly Wessex, or Edwin's and Morcar's earldoms). Tostig could not have hoped to gain more under Harald, but how could he possibly extract himself and his followers from the midst of the Norwegian army? He is reputed to have asked what terms would be given to his ally, the King of Norway, to which the legendary reply was 'seven feet of ground, or as much more as he is taller than other men'.* Tostig, whatever his inclination, had no choice but to stand firm with his allies, the English horsemen returned to their lines, and the main battle began.

The only account of the battle is in the *Heimskringla*, and it is quoted in full here, together with the description of the Norwegians' battle array, for it is the only primary source, upon which all later interpretations are based.

'King Harald now drew up his army, and formed a long and rather thin line; the wings were bent back until they met, thus forming a wide circle of even depth all the way round, with shields overlapping in front and above. The king himself was inside the circle with his standard and his own retinue of hand-picked men.

'Earl Tostig was also stationed inside the circle with his own company, and he had his own banner.

'The army was formed up in this way because King Harald knew that cavalry always attacked in small detachments and then wheeled away at once. The king said that his own retinue and Earl Tostig's company would make sorties to wherever the need was greatest: "Our archers are also to stay here with us. Those in the front rank are to set their spear-shafts into the ground and turn the points towards the riders' breasts when they charge us; and those immediately behind are to set their spears against the horses' chests."

'Now the battle began. The English made a cavalry charge on the Norwegians, who met it without flinching. It was no easy matter for the English to ride against the Norwegians because

*Snorri Sturluson, *Heimskringla*

of their arrows, so they rode around them in a circle. There was only skirmishing to begin with, so long as the Norwegians kept their formation. The English cavalry kept charging them and falling back at once when they could make no headway.

'The Norwegians observed this, and thought the enemy assaults rather half-hearted; so they launched an attack themselves on the retreating cavalry. But as soon as they had broken their shield-wall, the English rode down on them from all sides, showering spears and arrows on them.

'When King Harald Sigurdsson saw this, he led a charge into the thickest of the fighting. The battle soon became very fierce, and great numbers were killed on both sides. King Harald Sigurdsson now fell into such a fury of battle that he rushed forward ahead of his troops, fighting two-handed. Neither helmets nor coats of mail could withstand him, and everyone in his path gave way before him. It looked as if the English were on the point of being routed.

'But now King Harald Sigurdsson was struck in the throat by an arrow, and this was his death-wound. He fell, and with him fell all those who had advanced with him, except for those who retreated with the royal standard.

'The battle still raged fiercely, and Earl Tostig was now fighting under the royal standard. Both sides drew back to form up again, and there was a long lull in the fighting.

'Before the fighting was resumed, Harold Godwineson offered quarter to his brother Tostig and all the surviving Norwegians. But the Norwegians shouted back with one voice that every one of them would rather die than accept quarter from the English; they roared their war-cry, and the battle started again.'

Bearing in mind the conclusions drawn earlier concerning the ability of the English housecarls to fight from horseback in the Norman manner, this account of the battle seems quite straightforward, containing precisely the tactics one would expect from both commanders under the circumstances and at this date. Yet it has been almost universally disclaimed as fiction, written by a 13th-century Icelander who is accused of either describing the battle as it would have been fought in his own time – although his account of Stamford Bridge certainly does not resemble a 13th-century battle between knights and infantry; or of allowing his account to be highly coloured by the subsequent battle at Hastings, or even perhaps describing that battle and not Stamford Bridge at all. Of course, these two opinions confound each other, for if Snorri confused Stamford Bridge with Hastings, then he could not have been describing a 13th-century battle, or *vice-versa*.

The cavalrymen of the 11th century were little more than mounted missile men, who darted in to cast their spears then withdrew swiftly. Their aim was to weaken the shield-wall until such time as they could burst through the gaps created by themselves and the archers, when they could use their spears and other weapons to engage individuals – with the advantage of height which allowed them to stab or slash downwards, and the actual physical help of a large horse trained in war. It appears that this was the initial role of the mounted Englishmen at Stamford Bridge, though they probably dismounted to help those on foot after the Norwegian counter-attack failed, so that most of the battle was fought in the traditional manner between two forces of infantry armed with sword, axe and spear, Dane and Englishman against Norwegian and Englishman, Scot and Fleming. Both sides had archers, but the relatively minor role played by them suggests that neither side had very many.

The shield-wall adopted by Harald's army was the traditional defensive formation of Scandinavian, Anglo-Saxon and German warriors of the age, and was to remain in use for another hundred years after 1066. It was quite capable of withstanding cavalry attacks, which is why one rarely hears of cavalry actions unless cavalry fought cavalry. Cavalry against infantry was largely ineffective at this time, and this is confirmed by all five of the major battles of the Anglo-Norman period (Tinchebrai 1106, Brémule 1119, Bourg Théroulde 1124, the battle of the Standard or Northallerton 1138, and Lincoln 1141), at all of which almost all the English knights dismounted to fight on foot. Snorri's description of the hedge of spear points at Stamford Bridge reminds one of the Scottish schiltrons, Swiss pike columns, and English squares of later centuries, all of which were also capable of rendering cavalry ineffective on its own.

However, all depends on whether Snorri's account is acceptable or not, and perhaps the best argument for him is a brief summary of his quality as a historian. Snorri was born in Iceland in 1179 and murdered there in 1241. He was brought up at Oddi, the centre of Icelandic learning, and an ancestor of his had been Harald Hardrada's right-hand man in the Varangian Guard. He wrote his *Heimskringla*, or *History of the kings of Norway*, around 1230. The events of 1066 are described in Section III of this work, in King Harald's Saga, and it is important to realize that Snorri's biography of Harald is more complete and less openly prejudiced than any of the biographies of the other main characters of that year. It is admitted that his saga is inaccurate when describing English affairs, but the English chronicles contain similar errors when dealing with Scandinavian affairs and this is no way invalidates the rest of the chronicles: there is, therefore, no reason why Snorri's writings on Norwegian matters should be considered unreliable. On the other hand, his saga and the Anglo-Saxon Chronicle agree on a number of basic points – the date of Fulford, the capture of York, the events leading up to Stamford Bridge, that Harald was caught unprepared, and that most of the army had left its armour at Riccall.

Snorri based his *Heimskringla* on a considerable body of historical work, stretching back a hundred years to the works of Ari Thorgilsson (1067–1148), on whom Snorri relied considerably. Ari was a meticulous and scrupulous historian who rejected whatever he could not accept as fully accurate; he also obtained his facts from the men who had experienced the events, or from their sons.

Snorri is known to have used for King Harald's Saga three written sources which are still extant: *Agrip*, probably written before the end of the 12th century, and *Morkinskinna* and *Fagurskinna*, both written early in the 13th century. He also relied on the excellent contemporary evidence preserved in the court poetry of the skalds. A modern examination of these sources and a comparison with Snorri's text has revealed him to have been a careful and selective historian. But in the end it is the reader who must examine the facts and make up his own mind.

After Tostig had refused quarter – at this point he may have had good reason to hope that he might yet gain the crown in Harald's place – the battle entered its third phase, which Snorri describes thus:

'At this point Eystein Orri arrived from the ships with all the men he had; they were wearing coats of mail. Eystein took King Harald's banner, "Land-Waster", and the fighting began for the third time, more fiercely than ever. The English fell in great numbers, and once again were on the point of being routed. This stage of the fighting was called Orri's Battle.

'Eystein and his men had run all the way from the ships so hard that they were tired out and almost unable to fight before they arrived on the scene. But then they fell into such a battle fury that they did not bother to protect themselves as long as they could still stand on their feet. Eventually they threw off their coats of mail, and after that it was easy for the English to land blows on them; but some of the Norwegians collapsed from exhaustion and died unwounded. Nearly all the leading Norwegians were killed here.'

The Anglo-Saxon Chronicle describes the end of the battle in more detail: 'There were slain Harald Hardrada and Earl Tostig, and the remaining Norwegians were put to flight, while the English fiercely assailed their rear until some of them reached their ships: some were drowned, others burnt to death, and thus perished in various ways so that there were few survivors, and the English had possession of the place of slaughter. The king then gave quarter to Olaf, son of the King of the Norwegians, to their bishop, to the Earl of Orkney, and to all those who were left aboard the ships. They then went inland to our king, and swore oaths that they would ever maintain peace and friendship with this land; and the king let them sail home with twenty-four ships.'

Of Harald Hardrada's 10,000 men perhaps 1,000 may have

escaped by being stationed in Cleveland, Scarborough and Holderness, and at the very most it was another 1,000 that sailed from the Humber in those twenty-four ships. If, say, 1,000 had died at Fulford (approximately seventeen per cent casualty rate), then 7,000 Norwegians and their allies must have perished at Stamford Bridge and in the relentless pursuit which followed the battle. Harold could not afford further trouble from either the Norwegians or the Northumbrians, and he no doubt pressed the vicious pursuit to its limit to ensure the Norwegians would not return, and to show the northern lords that his victory was complete. And it was!

The English casualties are unknown, but although heavy cannot have been half those of the Norwegian army, which was so annihilated that it was to be an entire generation before a Norwegian king could undertake another foreign expedition.

Stamford Bridge was the most costly battle ever fought in England in terms of casualties. Such large-scale battles are rare in medieval history, yet Harald had been called upon to fight two such battles within five days. He was perhaps the greatest military leader in northern Europe at the time, and his forces had at first matched those of Harold in numbers. When Eystein's force arrived the Norwegians must have outnumbered the English, although the reinforcements were so fatigued by their rapid march that they were unable to fight in their mail shirts and their value cannot have been nearly so great as their numbers imply. Yet Harold had gained a stunning victory, incredible in its completeness: one wonders if it was beyond the mental and physical capabilities of any medieval army to endure two such large-scale battles within so short a time.

After negotiating the peace with the Norwegian survivors, Harold moved to York and began the complicated and delicate task of reorganizing the government of the north. There must have been many accusations and counter-accusations amongst the northern lords, and there was also the problem of the spoils of war to be resolved. Besides the Norwegian hostages and literally hundreds of ships, there was Harald's fabulous treasure, which he had brought with him to England, and much loot collected from the coastal areas of the north. Harold would have needed Harald's treasury to recoup his heavy expenses of the summer, and he needed ships to rebuild his damaged fleet, but it seems his much depleted force of housecarls and lithsmen was now grumbling for a share-out, in view of their exceptional services and the size of the captured treasure, while whoever was to govern the north would need financing to be able to get the earldom back on its feet after the ravages of the invaders.

Six days after Stamford bridge, on 1 October, Harold received news from the south which caused him to postpone dealing with all these problems until later: William of Normandy had landed on the south coast on 28 September.

Harold was almost 200 miles from the nerve centre of his realm; three times farther from London than William. Harald Hardrada's treasure and the other booty was placed in the care of the Archbishop of York, and Maerleswein, Sheriff of Lincoln, was appointed to govern Northumbria, as Harold hurriedly gathered his few élite warriors to him. Messengers were despatched immediately to the south, east and west of England, summoning those select fyrds which had not marched north, and Edwin and Morcar were charged with the gathering of what forces they could in the north, and to follow Harold south as soon as possible.

Early the next morning, 6 October, Harold left York, accompanied by the tired remnants of his royal housecarls, lithsmen, his brothers' housecarls, and those loyal thegns of Wessex who had accompanied him all summer, and marched south to act out the role which Harald Hardrada's men had just been forced to play, and to an everlasting place in history.

7
The Southern Invasion

On the night of 26–27 September, following the parading of the body of St Valéry around the Norman camp beside the Somme, the adverse winds miraculously died away and the wind began to blow from the south. As dawn broke on the 27th, the sun shone from a clear blue sky and the sea was calm. William could have been excused for showing caution at this moment, after his experience on the 12th and almost forty-five days of continuously contrary winds, but he knew his army was at the end of its tether; it had to be now or never. He gave the order to embark.

The Norman chroniclers tell us that, in their relief at release from the interminable wait, men raced each other to be first aboard their ships, some even forgetting their belongings in the frenzy to sail as soon as possible. Some equipment may already have been on board, but the loading of provisions, weapons, horses and men was an enormous task which had to be completed before 5.34 pm, the time the sun set that day. High tide was at 4.00 pm. The moon (six days old) set at about 9.15 pm, and it was therefore necessary for William to have his armada on the open sea by about 6.30 pm to avoid the perilous situation of having hundreds of ships crowded together in the vicinity of land in the darkness.

As each ship was ready, it moved downstream to the mouth of the Somme and anchored to await the others. By nightfall the task was accomplished and the fleet hove-to on the open sea, each ship bearing a light at the masthead to assist in keeping the fleet together. After waiting out part of the night thus, William ordered the sounding of trumpets, the prearranged signal to hoist sail, and the fleet began its brief but momentous voyage.

Wind and sea conditions appear to have been ideal and there is no mention in the chronicles of any mishap or losses at sea. It began to get light about 5.00 am, and the sun rose an hour later. As visibility increased at this crucial point in the crossing, William found that his flagship was alone in the Channel, having out-distanced the smaller warships and the heavily laden transports. He hove-to again and had breakfast, a charade which can have fooled few of those on board. If two or three ships of the English navy should appear now, the whole enterprise would come to nought. The moment highlights the vulnerability of any hostile fleet crossing the English Channel, and the hazardous nature of the Norman invasion: a sudden change of wind, a fleet of English warships descending on the wallowing transports, and suddenly chaos, destruction and ruin. William gambled everything he had, and for which he had fought these past twenty years, against the prize of the crown of England.

Eventually the lookout at the masthead sighted other Norman ships coming over the horizon and before long William's ship was surrounded by a forest of ships' masts. Miraculously, only two ships had been lost in the darkness, one of which, and possibly both, reached England safely but, separated from the rest of the fleet, the crew or crews met a speedy death at the hands of the local inhabitants. The voyage continued in daylight without further mishap and, according to Guy of Amiens, the fleet entered Pevensey haven and completed disembarkation by 9.00 am that morning.

At this point we run into difficulties, for while there is no doubt the fleet landed in the Pevensey area, the chroniclers' accounts of the landing and initial movements of the troops are

Anglo-Saxon socketed arrowheads. These are typical of the barbed and plain arrowheads used by Vikings, Normans and Anglo-Saxons alike.

Scandinavian warriors attacking a house, from the Frank's Casket of *circa* 700. This illustrates the use of the bow in war by the Vikings from at least the beginning of the 8th century. Note the concave round shields. (British Museum.)

obscure and conflicting. The problem is compounded by the fact that high water at Pevensey on the morning of the 28th was 4.35 am, and the tide was on the ebb until approximately 11.20 am. Either the landing was achieved against an ebb tide and took longer than is implied, with a subsequent shift farther inland as the tide came in again, or it was made earlier and over a wider area. To help come to a clear understanding, it is necessary to take a look at how the coastline was probably shaped in 1066.

Pevensey Levels is now a roughly semicircular area of mostly grazing land, about six miles in diameter, separated from the sea by a high bank of shingle. In the 11th century there were also large areas of cultivated land here, but there was no protection from the sea, and therefore at high tide these areas became islands in a large expanse of shallow water, while at low tide they were separated by mud flats and deep, winding water channels. The largest cultivated areas were probably joined by causeways. The saltings or sea marshes of Essex are a perfect example of this type of terrain today, and a study of any modern map of the English coastline between the Thames Estuary and Harwich will give a good impression of how the south-east coast must have appeared in the 11th century. Into this extensive tidal lagoon projected, from the western side, a peninsula about three miles long, on the point of which the Anglo-Saxons had built the market town and seaport of Pevensey, beside the Roman fortress of Anderida. Behind this peninsula lay a sheltered harbour, originally built by the Romans. The only direct communication with points to the west was by the old Roman road to Lewes, and from thence to

London. There was no major road to the east or north, although it is believed there may possibly have been a causeway which ran north-east from Pevensey via Wartling to Ninfield.

The chroniclers agree that William landed at Pevensey itself, and it is probable that some other ships entered the harbour and made use of its wharves to unload. The remainder of the fleet must have run ashore at various points along the coastline, probably to the east of the harbour, on the shingle beach exposed by the ebb tide. (Local tradition records that at least some of the Normans landed to the east of Pevensey, at Bulverhythe, near modern Bexhill, and elsewhere amongst the many little havens within the saltings.)

William must have had some knowledge of this part of the English coast, for the abbey of Fécamp had been granted Rye, Winchelsea and Steyning by Edward the Confessor, while the brother of William's steward and greatest friend, William fitz Osbern, held part of the lands of the great church at Bosham. Harold had seized these strategic points on the coast from the monks of Fécamp before Edward's death, but this would not have prevented them from describing the terrain to William in 1066, and it is known he consulted the abbot of Fécamp about the invasion. Yet William could not have known where he would be able to land, and once the fleet had landed it would have become obvious that he could not keep all his ships at Pevensey in safety.

Pevensey itself was too cramped to hold as a major base, while the surrounding salt marshes would restrict the movement of foragers and were tactically dangerous, permitting the local inhabitants – with their knowledge of the terrain and tides – to engage the invasion forces at a great disadvantage. The returning tide would also carry the ships farther inland (the alternative was to be constantly marooned by sea and mud alternately), scattering them amongst the multitude of channels, only to leave them high, dry and in some cases isolated at the next low tide. William could not effectively muster his troops for any action, either offensive or defensive, in such terrain, and one of his first actions after landing was to conduct a reconnaissance of the area immediately inland.

The martyrdom of St Edmund, king of East Anglia, by the Danes, illustrating Scandinavian bows. (From a drawing belonging to the Antiquaries of London.)

Norman archers during the battle of Hastings, as portrayed in the Bayeux Tapestry. Of all the Norman archers illustrated in the tapestry (28 in all) only one archer (shown here at bottom left) is wearing mail and an iron helmet.

Accompanied by not more than twenty-five knights, all mounted, William set off inland. The only tracks the party could find were so difficult to negotiate that the knights had to dismount, and when they returned they were carrying their hauberks, presumably because it was too exhausting to wear them when struggling across the rough countryside. William must have known of or found the road to Lewes, and the result of this reconnaissance suggests that he was looking for a route eastwards, where lay the bulk of his fleet, and where another, larger peninsula, on which stood the sea port of Hastings, offered a good defensive position.

Wace describes William's second act vividly: 'Then the carpenters landed. They had great axes in their hands, and planes and adzes hung at their sides. They took counsel together, seeking a good position to fortify. They had brought with them from Normandy the elements of three wooden forts, ready for putting together, and they now took enough material for one out of the ships. It was all shaped and pierced to take the pins they had brought cut and ready in large barrels. Before evening set in, they had completed a good fort on English soil, and there they placed their stores. Everyone then ate and drank well, right glad that they were ashore.'

This fort was almost certainly placed within the ruined walls of the Roman fortress, and the two together would have provided William with a secure base for his equipment and other vital stores, and a tower for a last ditch stand if necessary. But because of the limitations of Pevensey, 'The next day they marched along the coast to Hastings. Near that place William fortified a camp, setting up the two other wooden strongholds. The foragers, and those on the lookout for booty, seized all the clothing and provisions they could find in case their shipborne supplies should fail them. And the English could be seen fleeing before them, driving off cattle and quitting their houses. Many took shelter in burying places, and even there were in great alarm.'*

Their alarm was justified: the Bayeux Tapestry portrays the invaders burning a house of some note, capturing and killing livestock, and seizing other foodstuffs; at best many of the local

172

*Wace, Robert, *Roman du Rou*

Battle of Hastings

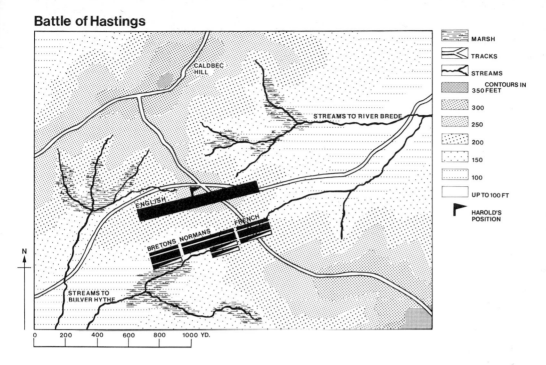

inhabitants could now expect death by starvation or exposure in the coming winter. The sheer numbers of the invaders must also have reduced even the burghers of an important port like Hastings to shocked impotence, particularly as most of the fighting men would have sailed to London with the English fleet.

Wace's account of a march along the coast to Hastings is most unlikely, simply because of the saltings and their innumerable channels, but there is no definite knowledge of how William did move his army from Pevensey Levels to Hastings. One theory is that the army marched some twenty-six miles overland via the peninsula from Pevensey to Polegate, north to Hailsham, then eastwards via Herstmonceux and Ninfield. Another theory depends on the presumed existence of a causeway leading north-east to Ninfield, the army thus being able to march to Hastings by a more direct overland route, a distance of some fifteen miles. A third theory is that William re-embarked the army (which some writers believe had

Contour map of the battle of Hastings, showing positions of the opposing forces. The double line of cavalry in the Norman centre is assumed, as it would have been impossible to deploy in a single line until the archers and infantry had advanced to attack the English position.

173

not all been disembarked on the 28th) and sailed it to Hastings. Neither of the first two theories explain why the army should march when the fleet would have to be moved to Hastings anyway, for it would hardly have been abandoned in the salt marshes.

We will never know what really happened, but it is interesting that the Domesday Book reveals there were two distinct tracks of devastation from Pevensey to Hastings, although these could have been made purely by foragers. A garrison would certainly have been left at the Pevensey fortress, with a small number of ships protected within the harbour there. It is reasonable to suppose that all mounted men were then sent to Hastings overland, by one or both of the routes outlined above, because it would not have been wise to try to re-embark the horses. The remainder of the army, and its equipment, could then have re-embarked without much trouble, sailed out of the saltings on the next high tide, and so arrived at Hastings during the 29th. Whatever did happen, William was as lucky as he had been during the sea crossing: had the Wessex select fyrd been mustered and in position, no Norman force trying to wend its way overland from Pevensey would have reached Hastings without some nasty surprises and possibly heavy casualties along the way.

Hastings was a much better site for a base, with a larger harbour and a more numerous and prosperous community, which was capable of yielding both booty and sustenance for the invaders. It could also be easily defended, for in the 11th century Hastings was located at the bottom corner of an isolated, inverted triangle of land approximately ten miles long by six miles wide. The wide and marshy valley of the River Brede cut across the north face of this triangle and was tidal right up to Sedlescombe. The tidal lagoon of the Bulverhythe River sealed off the triangle to the west. The valleys of both these rivers were impassable in 1066 and the distance between the ends of their tidal waters (between modern Sedlescombe and Crowhurst) was only about four miles. That gap was hilly and full of steep valleys. Only one road linked this peninsula to the hinterland, the old Roman road leading northwards

174

through the great forest of Andredsweald, which ran for some eighty miles from Petersfield in Hampshire to Ashford in Kent, and which was seldom less than fifteen miles deep throughout most of that length. This road led to Maidstone, where it joined the London–Dover road, and crossed the Brede at Sedlescombe, probably by ferry. A great army could not cross by a ferry and this meant the only way out of the Hastings peninsula was a prehistoric track, which followed the high ground between the Brede and the Bulverhythe, heading north-west to Caldbec Hill, on the northern outskirts of modern Battle. There the trackway forked, the right-hand branch passing round the source of the Brede to link up with the Maidstone road, while the left-hand branch led westwards to the Lewes–London road. It was just over sixty miles to London, whether following the Lewes road or joining the Dover road. William's army could lie safely at Hastings by simply denying that track to any attacking army, but, of course, the blocking of that same track by an English army would effectively isolate William's army in an area which could not feed it for long.

William's camp, centred upon the remaining two wooden fortifications with their palisaded ditches, was built on the height above Hastings, overlooking both town and harbour. Many of his ships were now drawn up on the beaches round Hastings for safety from the weather, their masts unstepped, yards, sails and oars stowed away, but a considerable fleet could remain safely moored in the harbour, sufficient to maintain his lines of communication with Normandy should an English fleet appear.

While the fortress at Hastings was being built, William held a council of war with his half-brothers Robert of Mortain and Odo of Bayeux. This much the Bayeux Tapestry tells us, and no more, but we can guess the questions in William's mind. Where was Harold? How strong was his army? And what were the Norwegians up to? If Harald Hardrada had invaded the north of England, Harold could be in the north now, and if he was defeated there, then William might end up fighting Harald Hardrada for the kingdom, or be forced to divide it, as it had been divided before.

London might be open to attack, but if William advanced from the Hastings peninsula he might lose contact with his fleet and risk battle on his enemy's terms, for the farther he advanced from his base the more the strength of his army would diminish due to stragglers and garrisons left to guard his lines of communication, for he must at all costs maintain a link with Normandy, and his hopes of winning a decisive battle must shrink in proportion to this decrease in strength. So long as he kept his army at Hastings he was safe; the peninsula could be defended against an attacking army and if the worst happened there was a sizeable fleet waiting in the harbour to effect a rapid withdrawal to Normandy.

Until he had some intelligence of the situation in England and the whereabouts of Harold's army, the only sensible course was therefore to remain in the Hastings area and let the enemy come to him. But to do this William needed enormous quantities of food for his army, and consequently his next action was to despatch foragers far and wide: as most of his army consisted of adventurers and mercenaries, this inevitably meant looting, murder, rape and burning.

William had everything to gain by an early confrontation, but at this stage he did not know of Harold's predicament and it is unlikely he ordered a deliberate harrying of the Hastings area to provoke an early attack on his position. William had some 10,000 men to feed, and it was a perfectly normal procedure for the age to seize the required provisions from the surrounding countryside by force. Ten thousand men needed a great deal of food, and twenty years later the Domesday Book recorded that the area had still not recovered from the devastation caused, the manors and villages being assessed at only twenty-five per cent of their former value, while some twenty villages appear to have been destroyed completely and were never rebuilt. Of course, such widespread destruction – for over ten miles to the north and north-east of Hastings, along precisely the route any hostile force must attack – also had the advantage of depriving of supplies any large hostile army which might enter the same area. At the same time it might provoke Harold into a hasty move, but primarily the devastation took place out of necessity, and because the foragers were in a hostile land. William had done well to prevent his freebooters inflicting similar damage round Dives and St Valéry, and they would have thought him mad if he had tried to restrain them in enemy territory.

The first reliable news to reach William of the situation in England appears to have come from Robert fitz Wimarc, a member of Edward the Confessor's household and an English landowner of Breton and Norman parentage. A messenger from Wimarc reached William's camp either on 30 September or very soon after and Wimarc's aim seems to have been to prevent bloodshed between the men of his own blood and those of his adopted country. But his messenger gave William precisely the information he needed: that Harold had marched north and overwhelmed a great Norwegian army, killing King Harald, Tostig and an immense number of their men. Wimarc warned William that the Normans could not stand a chance against an army which had just defeated the greatest warrior king in the north, and advised him to either withdraw from England or at least avoid open battle by remaining within his fortifications.

William now knew that it was Harold with whom he had to deal, and his actions until this time reflect William's own respect for the size and quality of the English army, and of Harold as a military leader. His reply to Wimarc was that he would fight Harold as soon as possible, yet he still made no attempt to advance from Hastings.

William's apparent inactivity during the two weeks prior to the battle of Hastings has been criticized in the past. He now knew that the king of England and his army were in the north, and he could have made a lightning advance to seize Winchester or London – or both – yet he did nothing. Some writers believe that William was merely being cautious, that he had a greater respect for the English army than many 20th-century historians: others that Harold had in fact left some forces in the south (most of the Wessex select fyrd and perhaps the bulk of the southern contingent of the royal housecarls) and it was the presence of these forces which made William remain in a position where he could not be outflanked or cut off from the sea. But William was only carrying out his favourite and intended strategy of wait and see, and once again exhibiting those qualities of patience, self-control and remarkable leadership which had already held the Norman army at Dives and St Valéry for two months, and won for him all his past victories. What use to fight a small battle against a local force, if such a force existed at this time: he needed to defeat Harold and the English army in a decisive battle, and he knew that once Harold could be persuaded to enter the Hastings peninsula, sheer weight of numbers would be cancelled by the narrowness of the watershed between the Brede and Bulverhythe, and quality would then count – the Norman mailed knight against the Anglo-Saxon housecarl, William's professional mercenaries against Harold's territorial reservists. In the event William was to achieve his double aim of fighting a single decisive battle *and* remaining close to his fleet and lifeline to Normandy. This in itself shows the quality of his leadership, and the accuracy of his assessment of Harold's character.

For William must have known that Harold was too proud and impetuous to allow a foreign army to spend the winter in Wessex, within two days' march of London, and this knowledge of his opponent is underlined by a series of provocative messages which now passed between William and Harold. Their content is not important in a military context, but the passage of these messengers between the two camps is, for there can be no doubt that these messengers were able to impart some intelligence to their commanders of the whereabouts and strengths of the opposing armies. However, they could not have told William what he needed to know most of all; whether Harold intended to rush south to Hastings and give battle at once, or seal off the peninsula and attempt to starve the Normans out.

Although William's landing had encountered no opposition, it had been observed, and only three days later his presence at Pevensey was reported to Harold at York: a well-organized post-riding system must therefore have existed between

London and the northern capital. Harold's reaction was immediate – he must return to London at once, and there are some who believe he may have started south before the news of the Norman landing reached him, arguing that he would not have spent six days in the north when he knew there remained a possibility of a Norman invasion. But six days seems a small amount of time to devote to recovering from such a major battle as Stamford Bridge, negotiating a peace with Harald's heir, and making sure the north was once more loyal, or its loyalty secured by faithful officers and a military presence. Harold would not have wanted to leave an open back door behind him when he marched south, and his presence in London was not vital for the summoning of the select fyrd – this could be organized by his officers.

If a messenger from the south coast could reach York in three days, then by 4 October messengers could have returned to London to order the mustering of the select fyrds of London and the surrounding shires. Other messengers would also have sped to east and west of the road south, summoning men from far and wide to muster at London. Harold himself left York on the 2nd, accompanied by perhaps 1,000 or 1,500 royal and earls' housecarls, Danish lithsmen, and king's and earls' thegns together with a number of select fyrd men. Any bodies of fyrd encountered on the way south – those from the west and east midlands and East Anglia who were too late to take part in the battle against the Norwegians – would have been turned about to march south with Harold, but few other forces would have accompanied him, as the fyrd to either side of the London–York road had already marched north with him and few of these men are believed to have been taken south by Harold.

Harold arrived in London on the evening of the 6th, he and his élite having averaged just forty miles a day for five days. At London he would have found the fyrd of London and surrounding shires already mustered. He could not expect the men from the west to begin to arrive for some days, but all over the south the select fyrds were gathering again, while the depleted forces of Mercia and Northumbria were also being mustered afresh by Edwin and Morcar and would soon be

179

moving south. His army must gain new blood and strength with each day that passed; meanwhile his tired élite would rest.

William had made no attempt to move out of the Hastings peninsula while Harold was in the north, nor was he likely to do so now the king was mustering an army in London, and this caution on the part of William must have led Harold to several conclusions: that William was not strong enough to launch an offensive against London or engage an English army in the open field, and/or that William wanted the English to attack him on the peninsula, where his rear and flanks were secure and an escape route waited behind him.

Harold must have been familiar with the terrain around Hastings (Crowhurst was one of his own manors) and foreseen all the advantages and disadvantages of William's position; there was only one solution. Once he had mustered sufficient men, he would make a forced march to within striking distance of William's army. If he achieved surprise it would help to cancel William's advantages in having an all-professional army, possibly more cavalry, and certainly a superiority in archers: if he failed to achieve surprise he could assume a defensive position and hold William on the peninsula until sufficient reinforcements arrived to enable him to drive the Normans into the sea. Therefore it was vital to hurry south as quickly as possible, so as to defeat or isolate William before he could learn details of Harold's strength and movements.

This strategy did not demand a vast army – though 5,000 men would have been considered a large army in the 11th century – and Harold needed only to wait long enough in London to gather sufficient men for his purpose: others could follow later. Of course, all the above is only this writer's interpretation of the situation, but the sheer speed of Harold's movements suggests this may well have been his design, for in the twelve short days between receiving news of William's landing and engaging him in battle, he marched 190 miles to London, assembled a new army, and marched another sixty miles to do battle. That he never intended a purely defensive stand, to starve William into defeat, is confirmed by his despatch of about seventy ships of the fleet on the evening of the 11th to prevent any attempt by the Normans to withdraw from Hastings. No 11th-century European ship was capable of imposing a long blockade, and the ships could only have been expected to cover, or merely threaten, William's rear for a few days.

In the late afternoon of 11 October, Harold also sent messengers to tell the assembled fyrds of the south-eastern shires that the army would concentrate on the 13th 'at the hoar apple-tree',* a well-known landmark at the junction of the Sussex Hundreds of Baldslow, Ninfield and Hailesaltede. This meeting place is generally identified as Caldbec Hill (renamed Mont-joie by the Normans) and was therefore well chosen, for this was the point at which the road from Hastings forked, one branch leading to the Lewes–London road, the other to the Maidstone–London road. If William wished to advance from the peninsula at any time, he must take one of these roads. Caldbec Hill was also situated amongst that confined and hilly country between the Brede and Bulverhythe, far from ideal country for cavalry, and gave a fair view of the country to the south. Hastings itself was only seven miles away, and the meeting place was therefore also a suitable position from which to pounce on an unsuspecting enemy, just as Harold had so recently pounced on Harald Hardrada from Tadcaster. But Caldbec Hill was considerably closer to Hastings than Tadcaster was to Stamford Bridge, and Harold seriously underestimated his opponent if he thought he might catch William as unprepared as he had caught the Norwegians: there was a deal of difference between the Norman warrior and the Viking raider. Yet he could not deploy farther north because of the dense mass of the Andredsweald, which pressed down to within a short distance of Caldbec Hill, and, in any case, if he failed to achieve surprise, then there was an ideal defensive position only half a mile to the south.

Harold may also have underestimated the strength and quality of William's army. It is quite possible he did not know of the approximately 2,400 war horses William had, or refused to accept reports of such numbers, dismissing them as gross exaggeration. No state in western Europe had tried to transport horses by sea at this date, and from his own experience at sea

*Anglo-Saxon Chronicle

181

Harold would have appreciated the grave dangers in attempting to ship thousands or even hundreds of horses across the Channel so late in the year. But even if he knew of William's strength in cavalry, there was no real need for him to fear defeat because of it. If he could achieve surprise from Caldbec Hill, then William's cavalry would lose much of its value; if he failed and had to take up a defensive position until reinforcements arrived, then his professional infantry was certainly a match for the Norman cavalry. In 1066 the age of the infantryman was far from over, and that the Norman cavalry was not the all-powerful force it has been made out to have been is confirmed by the Battle of Hastings itself. The best accounts of the battle are Norman, yet all frankly record the repeated failure of the Norman knights to break the English shield-wall. Similarly, the shield-wall was proof against arrows; Harold's army was to be defeated by its lack of discipline and by William's control of the battle and the discipline of his troops, rather than by the cavalry and archers of which Harold was well aware.

The chroniclers also record that at about this time Harold's brother Gyrth tried to dissuade Harold from leading the march on Hastings, on the grounds that England could stand the loss of an army but not the loss of its king at this crucial moment. Gyrth offered to lead the army in his place, the king to remain in London to organize the reinforcements and, should Gyrth be defeated, to lay waste the land between London and Hastings so that the Normans would starve during the winter. It was a sensible suggestion, but neither Harold's position nor his temperament would allow him to delegate this responsibility. It was his sworn duty as king to protect his people, and it was neither honourable nor politically wise at this time for the king to remain in London while an enemy held a strategic port and devastated one of the richest parts of England.

We do not know for certain when Harold left London, but he probably delayed his departure until the last possible moment for, with an all-mounted army, he could cover the sixty miles to the meeting place in two days and if he was to achieve surprise he needed to move south as quickly as possible. Therefore, he probably waited six days in London, the dribble of reinforce-

182

ments gradually increasing as each day passed, so that by about the 9th perhaps a thousand select men a day were arriving from the south-western and East Anglian shires. On the morning of 12 October at the latest he marched out of London. Neither Edwin nor Morcar, nor any of their important thegns, had yet arrived with reinforcements from the midlands and the north, but the king had sufficient men for his purpose and he may have had word that the earls were starting south very soon, for the brothers did arrive in London with their troops about a week after Harold left the city.

The English army marched south-east at first, via Crayford, through flat and open country, and was seldom far from the Thames. It crossed the Medway at Rochester and probably halted at that town for the night, though the vanguard may have pushed south as far as Maidstone. The next morning the whole army marched south along the Hastings road and a mile or so beyond Maidstone entered the Andredsweald, which was some twenty miles deep in this region. It must have been mid-afternoon before the van of the army reached Bodiam and a mile farther on crossed the Rother. About two miles south of the Rother, at Cripps' Corner, the army turned west, leaving the Roman road, and followed an ancient trackway in order to avoid the wide, tidal waters of the Brede at Sedlescombe. At Vinehall the army turned due south onto the trackway which led to the meeting place on Caldbec Hill. Shortly afterwards it forded the Brede and emerged from the great forest in the region of the modern village of Watchoak.

These trackways were hard going for the thousands of tired men and horses, and it was probably evening before the army's vanguard arrived at the hoar apple-tree, where waited the selectmen of Kent, Surrey and Sussex. William of Jumièges says the army rode all night: certainly it would have been strung out over several miles and made poor speed along the trackways after darkness fell. Weary men must have continued to arrive at the meeting place well into the small hours, and it is doubtful if Harold's army would have been capable of a lightning advance in the morning to surprise William.

There are no contemporary figures of any value upon which

to base an estimate of the strength of the English army gathered on Caldbec Hill by dawn on 14 October, and the strengths given in modern works are therefore normally arrived at by a study of the battlefield and the battle itself. As is well known, the battle was an exceptionally long and finely balanced one, and this suggests the forces may have been roughly equal, any inferiority in quality on the English side being compensated for by the terrain. This is borne out by contemporary sources, though it is believed the English may have been slightly more numerous than their enemies. We have seen that William probably brought around 10,000 men to England, of whom perhaps 8,000 at the most are believed to have taken part in the battle of Hastings (2,400 cavalry, perhaps 1,000 archers, the rest infantry). William would have wanted to take the maximum number possible of his 10,000 men to the single decisive battle with Harold. This gives a maximum figure of 8,000 to 8,500 for the English. Estimates based on the length of the English line give a similar figure, but of course these are entirely guesswork, for no matter how many men formed the front rank, we cannot arrive at a total without knowing with certainty the number of ranks behind this front one, while it is doubtful if the English fyrd would have formed continuous lines at all, rather it would have formed compact groups by shires, each under its sheriff.

The total number of housecarls in England in 1066 has been estimated earlier at 4,000. Harold must therefore have had between 1,500 and 2,000 at Hastings, even allowing for heavy losses at Stamford Bridge and the absence of the surviving housecarls of Edwin and Morcar. If Harold had perhaps 1,000 Danish lithsmen (the crews of say twenty-five to thirty ships) at the beginning of the northern campaign, then it is reasonable to assume he may have had perhaps as many as 700 lithsmen at Hastings. Therefore it does not seem over-optimistic to estimate that there were possibly 2,500 professional warriors – housecarls and lithsmen – at Hastings.

The remainder of the army, 6,000 men at the most, was almost certainly all select fyrd. We know that gathered at Caldbec Hill were select men from London, Kent, Surrey and Sussex; from the neighbouring shires of Bedford, Berkshire,

Essex and Buckingham; from Hampshire, Dorset, Somerset and Gloucester in the west; and from the East Anglian shires. There were also the men from Nottingham, Northampton and Lincoln, who had joined Harold on his way south, and some of the men from York and Lindsey, who had fought at Stamford Bridge. These areas should have been capable of producing 6,000 select men, particularly as few of the levies from the southern shires had gone north. The chroniclers state that Harold marched on Hastings before half his army was assembled: by the 12th he had all the men he could effectively use in the cramped terrain north of Hastings, and he is hardly likely to have used poorly armed peasants of the great fyrd when he could have had select men to spare.

That the fyrd men at Hastings were from the select fyrd and not the great fyrd is confirmed to some extent by the Bayeux Tapestry, which, contrary to common belief, shows very few English troops without armour. In the famous hillock scene six men are shown, all without hauberks or helmets. These are usually referred to as peasants of the great fyrd, but three have kite shields and could just as easily be select men. Four unarmoured figures are shown running away at the end of the battle: they have neither helmets nor shields, but these would have been abandoned during the flight in any case. The only other unarmoured figures, out of a total of almost sixty English soldiers portrayed in the main section of the tapestry, are the solitary archer and one man shown just prior to the death of Harold.

Of these 6,000 select men at least 500 must have been well-equipped king's and earls' thegns, men who were in effect professional warriors. It is quite likely, therefore, that on the 14th Harold could muster around 3,000 fully armoured professional fighting men, the match for any Norman knight, and 5,000 to 5,500 select fyrd, who would be well-armed and good fighting men, but not professional warriors, and not accustomed to fighting in large-scale battles.

William the Great of Normandy was not the type of man to be caught by surprise. He also knew, from first-hand experience, Harold's value as a military leader, and of his reputation for striking fast and hard. He had erected fortifications to defend his base in England and seems to have maintained a screen of foragers-cum-scouts as far as ten miles north of this base. It was these foragers or scouts who first saw the approach of the English army, and who rode posthaste to Hastings to warn William, arriving at his headquarters some time in the late afternoon. Nevertheless, Harold had achieved some measure of surprise, for William of Poitiers records that when William received this intelligence most of his army was out foraging and had to be hastily recalled. The entire army was then stood to arms all through the night, William apparently anticipating a surprise night attack. At first light William ordered an advance towards the English, and appears to have seized the initiative at this point, although Harold may still have achieved all he had ever hoped for – to reach a good position sufficiently far south along the Hastings road from which to bar William's only way out of the peninsula.

Sunrise on the 14th was about 6.30 am. By 6.00 am at the latest the van of the Norman army had commenced its advance, with the remainder of the army following in a column which must have been strung out over a distance of some three miles. Advancing along the narrow ridge which commences at Baldslow and runs north-west towards Battle, about 7.30 am the van arrived at the highest point on that ridge, marked 462 feet (46 metres) on the Ordnance Survey maps and nowadays known as Blackhorse Hill. This is thought to have been the Telham Hill of the chroniclers. Because of the very gradual downward slope from this high point and a bend in the track, which would have been flanked by trees, the two armies were not yet in sight of each other. Here William seems to have halted the head of the column to await intelligence from his scouts. These soon informed him that the English army was about two miles ahead and taking up a position on the ridge at Santlache, which ran almost at right angles to the ridge on which the Normans now stood and was separated from it by lower

186

ground, much of which was marshy. The order was passed for the men to don hauberks and helmets and prepare for battle.

William must have used this short delay to ride forward and view the situation for himself. About a mile from the crest of Telham Hill, where Glencorse School now stands, he would have had his first view of the English army, swarming all over the Santlache ridge to form a long line, which barred his advance. He must have made his decisions regarding deployment at this time, then ridden back to the waiting army to assemble its various divisions into the order in which they would be needed.

It must have been at least 8.00 am, therefore, when the van of the Norman army reached this spot and for the first time the two armies saw each other, separated by little more than 1,200 metres. At this point it is necessary for the terrain to be described in detail in order to appreciate the problems that faced William in deploying his troops, and to understand fully the course of the crucial battle which was now about to commence.

The position selected by Harold was an ideal one for infantry to hold against an enemy strong in cavalry and archers, the perfect defensive position for an army famous throughout western Europe for its steadfast foot soldiers. From the meeting place at Caldbec Hill a narrow neck of land (on which the High Street of Battle now stands) runs southwards. In 1066 the land to either side of this neck sloped away steeply, furrowed by gullies cut by rainwater and choked with undergrowth. Just south of Battle Abbey this narrow ridge dips suddenly from approximately 85 metres to 65 metres, forming a low saddle with a valley beginning to either side of it. Two streams, rising about 200 metres apart, flow in opposite directions down these two valleys, which must have been very marshy in the 11th century. At the point where the ridge from Caldbec Hill begins to dip, a fairly level cross-ridge extends for some 1,500 metres: it was on this cross-ridge, where four trackways met, that Harold decided to make his stand.

The cross-ridge runs from east to south-west and at its highest level is about 800 metres long and 150 metres deep. It is between 60 and 77 metres above sea level, and at its highest point, just east of centre, the crest rises to 85 metres. It was probably bare of trees in 1066 and would have been mostly rough grassland, dotted with bracken, gorse and brambles, although there is some indication the southern slopes were cultivated.

At the centre of the south side, facing the Normans, the slope to the top of the cross-ridge was 1 in 15, sufficient to reduce considerably the effectiveness of both cavalry and archers. At the eastern end the slope was 1 in 22, and at the western end only 1 in 33. However, the flanks were protected to some extent by the two streams already mentioned. Nor could the position be outflanked because, on the northern face of the cross-ridge, there rose six or more other streams which ran in steep hollows to east and west, effectively barring any movement round the flanks. The ground in front of the western flank was particularly wet and marshy, and here also rises a small hillock, which was probably wooded in 1066 as it is today, and around which the ground was boggy and treacherous.

The narrow ridge to Caldbec Hill, with its inaccessible side slopes, prevented any attack from the rear, as did the steepness of the northern face of the cross-ridge; 1 in 6 to the north-west, 1 in 4 to the north-east. These same features meant that retreat was not really feasible for the English, but at the same time the neck would hinder any pursuit in the event of a defeat. Not much more than a mile north of the cross-ridge began the Andredsweald, into which no pursuer would be able to enter without extreme caution.

The land extending southwards from the cross-ridge was called Santlache. The meaning of the word is doubtful, perhaps 'sandy area'. The Normans changed the name to Sanguelac and Senlac, meaning 'blood-lake', either by accident of pronunciation or by design, but the name Senlac was not used for the battle fought here until the 12th century, and the Domesday Book calls it simply the battle of Hastings.

The English troops were deployed along the highest part of the cross-ridge, on a front of perhaps 800 metres, and about 50 metres in front of the ridge's crest. It is most unlikely that the flanks were refused at all, as some writers suggest, as this would have meant placing some men on lower ground and sacrificing the advantage of high ground. In any case, the flanks were secured from cavalry attack by the very nature of the terrain. Nor would any artificial obstacles – such as stakes or pitfalls – have been created on the southern face in front of the English line; there simply was not the time to do so. Harold was probably still on Caldbec Hill when he first received news of William's advance, for he was deploying his men on the cross-ridge when the Normans passed Telham Hill at about 8.oo am. William's early advance 'came upon him unexpectedly before his army was set in order'.*

From the descriptions given by the chroniclers, the English army seems to have been deployed in a solid phalanx, which from the estimated strength of the army must have been ten or twelve ranks deep. The chroniclers make it quite clear that the English were very tightly packed, so that the dead could not fall down, nor the wounded withdraw. Of course, the length and depth of the cross-ridge limited the number of men that could be deployed upon it and, according to Florence of Worcester, many deserted because there was insufficient room. The horses were almost certainly left on Caldbec Hill.

Harold's position on the ridge can be positively identified, since by William's orders the high altar of Battle Abbey church was built on the exact spot, and this was revealed by excavations in the 19th century. Harold naturally chose the highest point, just east of centre, from where he could see over the heads of his men and watch the movements of the enemy. Here he raised his two standards, the dragon of Wessex and his personal standard of the fighting man.

A strong contingent of royal housecarls would have guarded the king on his slightly elevated position, and it would have been in keeping with normal practice for his brothers Gyrth and Leofwine to retain at least some of their own housecarls around themselves, standing slightly back from the front ranks. The remainder of the housecarls, lithsmen and those select men with hauberks would probably have been sufficient to form the two front ranks, each man occupying a space of about 62 cm. When under missile attack these two ranks would have closed up to

*Anglo-Saxon Chronicle (D)

present a wall of shields. When an attack was launched after the missile barrage the first rank would have stepped forward to gain the space needed to swing its weapons, but the second rank would have supported them by thrusting its spears through the gaps between the men. The archers were probably deployed behind the first two or three ranks.

There is considerable controversy over the number of English archers present at Hastings, and why they were inferior in numbers to the Norman archers. It is not really worth entering into the controversy, as there is no evidence on which to base any accurate numerical estimate. The real crux of the matter is that the English army still used archers in the Scandinavian manner – relatively few in number and useful only in the opening phase of a battle, battles normally lasting between two and three hours at the most. On the other hand, William had recruited a considerable body of archers and organized them as a distinct arm; they were not merely an appendage as in the English army. Obviously, William had far more archers than Harold: that is all that mattered then, and now.

When William rode ahead of his army to study the English position, he must have seen at once the natural strength of that ridge and the great difficulties he would have to face in deploying to attack it. At this time he must have decided not only how to deploy for the attack, but also how that attack was to be made, and he plotted tactics which were most sophisticated for the age.

The ridge along which the Norman army was still advancing when it first saw the English position was too narrow to allow deployment, yet at the foot of its decline, at the Santlache saddle, the two streams and their marshy areas reduced the front to a mere 200 metres in width; it was out of the question to attempt an attack on a narrow front through that gap. Therefore William was faced with two hazardous alternatives: to deploy from column into line before he reached the saddle, in which case his two wings would have to pick their way across the broken and marshy ground and ford the streams, a manoeuvre which would throw into confusion the formations necessary for the success of his plan; or to advance through that narrow gap in column and deploy into line beyond the streams but within less than 200 metres of the enemy.

Judging that Harold would not abandon such a strong position to attack him during deployment, William decided to deploy on the far side of the streams. He had already organized his army into three divisions, but there is some dispute over which of the three divisions formed the vanguard of the army. It seems reasonable to assume it would have been that which was to form the right or east wing of the army, the Franco-Flemish division commanded by Roger of Montgomery, as this division had to make only a small swing off the trackway to its right to assume its position. This wheel would have presented the men's shielded side to the enemy, could have been quickly accomplished, and once in position the division could cover to some degree the deployment of the other divisions. Under Montgomery's command were the mercenaries from many lands, including Flanders, France, Picardie, and Boulogne, as well as a Norman contingent under Roger of Beaumont. Its strength has been estimated at about 1,500 men.

As the central division would block the trackway once in position, the second division to deploy was that on the left wing under Alan of Brittany, containing men from Maine, Anjou and Poitou, as well as from Brittany, to a total of about 2,000. This division had to perform an extremely dangerous manoeuvre, marching across much of the front of the English line, with their unshielded side towards it, in order to take up position on the left or west flank, in front of the hillock which was only some 150 metres away from the enemy. Their deployment was covered to some extent by the advance of the main body, the Norman division, into the centre. This division was stronger than the other two put together, possibly 4,000 men, and was commanded by William and his two half-brothers.

Why Harold allowed William to deploy his army at such close range will never be known. The English could have charged down upon their enemies while they were still only half deployed, with the remainder piled up along the narrow trackway to the rear, but they chose to stand firm on their ridge, as they were to do throughout that long day. It is likely that

Harold, having seen the Norman cavalry and archers in action, realized that the only sure way of defeating them with an army outnumbered possibly two to one in both archers and cavalry, was to cancel out the Normans' superiority in these arms by remaining firmly on the defensive, behind an impenetrable shield-wall. He had an excellent position, and sufficient men to hold it. William had to attack, uphill and across bad ground, or admit defeat. But by assuming a purely passive role, Harold did surrender the initiative, enabling William to dictate the course of the battle and employ his mobility and firepower to their best advantage.

As each division formed itself into line, three distinct factions emerged: a front rank of archers, a second rank of infantry, and a third rank of cavalry. The third rank, and possibly the second, was also subdivided into groups of knights under their lords, so that William's whole army was divided into manageable units of three distinct arms, and in three divisions. It is fairly certain from this initial deployment that William's plan was to soften up the English line with archery, create gaps with an infantry assault, then exploit those gaps with the cavalry, which would also conduct the pursuit. The organization of the Norman army at this moment revealed the degree of control that William was able to exercise over his troops, and is in marked contrast to the English army which, although theoretically divided into an élite and the select men in shire groups, was, because of the cramped position, in fact little more than a homogenous mass, incapable of any tactical manoeuvre: here they would stand, and die.

The battle was begun at about 9.30 am or 10.0 am by the Norman archers, who advanced to within effective bow range, about 100 metres, and began to shoot. Because they were shooting uphill, those arrows with a flat trajectory were stopped by the English shield-wall, while those with a high trajectory must have passed over the heads of the defenders. The barrage seems to have had little effect on the English, but the Norman archers suffered casualties because of their exposed position and they were withdrawn fairly soon so that the second wave, the heavy infantry, might make its attack.

As the infantry drew near the shield-wall it was met by a

murderous storm of missiles of all sorts. Despite heavy losses, the infantry closed with the English line, only to receive even heavier losses from the housecarls and lithsmen, the two-handed axes in particular wreaking havoc, for there was no defence strong enough to withstand them. Seeing the infantry's plight, William now committed his third line, and it is quite clear from William of Poitiers' account that the cavalry was sent in at this early stage because the infantry needed assistance. (The accounts of the battle as given by William of Poitiers and depicted in the Bayeux Tapestry should be studied in detail as the main and most reliable sources; too many modern writers depend on the unreliable but more stirring and detailed 12th-century account by Wace.)

But the cavalry proved no more successful than the infantry, the English being helped by their superior position on higher ground, by the fact that they were on the defensive and so did not have to move to attack, and by the ease with which their axes sheared through their opponents' shields and hauberks. (The impression this frightful weapon made on the Normans comes over vividly in the contemporary accounts, and it is significant that the battle-axe was to become one of the favourite weapons of the Anglo-Norman knights when fighting on foot – as they almost invariably did.) Then on the west flank the Breton knights and infantry began to give way, and the movement turned into a rout, with the English charging down in pursuit. The Normans in the centre began to give way also as their flank was exposed, and this in turn caused the east flank to give ground, until the whole line was in retreat, and even the baggage guards began to run away. The Norman chroniclers admit it was a débâcle, and the episode is fully illustrated as such in the Bayeux Tapestry. Amidst the confusion the rumour inevitably spread that William had been killed. Striking and threatening those he could reach, William lifted his helmet so that his face might be seen and, according to William of Poitiers, shouted: 'Look at me. I am living and with God's help I shall be victor! What madness leads you to flight?' He probably also reminded them there was nowhere to run to; only the sea lay behind them.

William succeeded in rallying at least part of the Norman cavalry and was thus able to strike into the flank of the English who had rushed down the western slope in pursuit of the Breton division. The result was disaster for the English, and salvation for William.

The Bayeux Tapestry shows the death of Gyrth and Leofwine about this time, and it is quite possible that the so-called undisciplined rush of 'ill-armed peasants' after the Bretons was in fact a deliberate counter-attack led by Harold's brothers. The moment to counter-attack is when the enemy has made his attacks and is at the point of failure. If the pursuit down the western slope was deliberate, then it was well timed, but why did not the centre and east flank advance in support? Possibly Harold did not wish to risk all on that one counter-stroke, and was seeking a small victory, one which would win him a few days during which his losses could be made good, while William could only grow weaker. He probably realized also that infantry pursuing cavalry could not succeed, except perhaps on the marshy ground before the west flank. The first two ranks on this flank do not seem to have been involved in the pursuit, standing aside to allow the fresh select men through, and this tends to confirm that Harold was reluctant to relinquish any part of the line held by the shield-wall, even temporarily.

The select men inflicted considerable casualties on the Breton cavalry and infantry, who were trapped in the morass round the hillock to their rear (the Bayeux Tapestry shows their horses tumbling on their heads), but as they tried to return to the protection of the shield-wall they were cut down almost to a man by William's Norman knights. Some made a stand on the hillock, but could not have held out for long in isolation.

So far the battle had lasted about the length of time most battles of the period could be expected to last, perhaps one and a half or two hours. Those who had been fighting would need a breather, and both sides must have needed to reorganize their lines and rearm, the English darting down the slope a short way to retrieve their missiles. There is no mention in the chronicles of a lull at this point, but it is most likely that there was one.

After a while William resumed his attack. It is unlikely he

194

allowed his defeated troops to rest and ponder for too long, and that he now launched an attack with the cavalry is significant; either the infantry was too badly cut up to be effective on its own, or he felt he needed to show the infantrymen that the knights at least were not yet beaten.

This phase of the battle seems to have consisted entirely of repeated attempts by the cavalry, possibly supported by the infantry and/or dismounted knights, to break the English shield-wall; a continual ebb-and-flow movement which would have kept the élite in the English front ranks constantly engaged, yet enabled the Normans to take turn and turn about, so that they were always more rested than their opponents. The stories of feigned flights, undisciplined English pursuits, and repeats of William's triumph of the morning cannot be taken seriously. Feigned retreat by entire armies could be and was used in medieval warfare, but only by careful planning before the battle: it was simply not possible to conduct a spontaneous feigned retreat of an entire army in the medieval period without it turning into a genuine rout. It is far more likely, though the Norman chroniclers would not have admitted it, that, like the Bretons, the Norman and other cavalry also broke from time to time at particular points and retreated from the battle temporarily. They may or may not have been pursued. It is also possible that feigned retreats *were* staged to lure out impetuous Englishmen, but that these were conducted by small groups of knights, such as a baron and his *familia*. The knights in such groups were professional warriors, accustomed to fighting alongside each other, and could easily have feigned retreats, only to turn and catch the pursuing English infantry out in the open.

Whatever happened, William maintained a relentless series of mounted assaults against the English line for several hours so that slowly, imperceptibly, yet inevitably, the English house-carls died and the shield-wall therefore either shortened or became weakened by the insertion of select men who did not have hauberks and who were no substitutes for veteran housecarls wielding two-handed axes.

By mid-afternoon, perhaps about 3.30 pm, the fog of war

descends on the chronicles as much as it must have done on the weary combatants. The battle had already lasted twice as long as any great battle of the time – both sides were exhausted, yet there was no sign of a decision. The English shield-wall was weakening, perhaps shorter now and leaving small parts of the ridge undefended on the extreme flanks for the first time. Yet the Normans had suffered severe casualties too, including the loss of many of the precious horses, and William knew he would not be able to fight another day, when Harold would most likely have been reinforced. It had to be today, or never.

In a final bid for victory William now ordered a general attack by all three arms: no matter that all were weakened, together they might now achieve what they had failed to achieve in the first hours of the battle.

The vital point about the final assault is not that the archers for the first time used trajectory shooting – it is most unlikely they had never done this before – but that William now used all three arms simultaneously, whereas in the morning they had been used successively. Therefore, the archers had now to shoot *all* their arrows on a high trajectory. No matter that William used all three arms together only because each was too weak to attack on its own, the result was the same whatever his reason. For the first time the Normans were also able to obtain a foothold on the top of the ridge at the western end, where they were at last able to engage the English on equal terms and, outflanking the shield-wall, soon began to carve a way into the English right flank. The same situation soon developed on the opposite flank, but dusk was approaching now and the English had only to hold to win: no matter what the cost, so long as they could stand firm the Normans could not win in the long run.

But at last the Norman knight was coming into his own, using the advantage of height and the weight of his horse to force the English line back. The shield-wall was breaking up into isolated stretches and small circles, which could be dealt with one by one. Round the king and his standards, on the highest point, the royal housecarls remained firm, but they were under attack from both flanks as well as the front, and after about two hours of savage slaughter on the ridge a band of

196

twenty-five mounted knights was at last able to break down that last line of defence, although at tremendous cost to themselves. Harold fell dead, struck down by the four survivors – Guy of Ponthieu, Walter Giffard, Hugh of Montfort and Eustace of Boulogne. The dragon of Wessex and the fighting man of the house of Godwine tumbled to the bloody ground. The battle of Hastings was over.

It was now dusk. The fyrd men were in total rout, racing for their horses and the safety of the gloomy Andredsweald. But the housecarls fought on, many dying around their lord and king, others retreating slowly. The Normans must have been near total exhaustion, but William wanted a complete victory, with every last scrap of resistance crushed, just as Harold had annihilated the fleeing Norwegians only nineteen days earlier. He sent Eustace of Boulogne in pursuit with a considerable force of knights. Against his better judgement Eustace, on William's insistence, pressed the pursuit right up to the forest's edge and here, about a mile from the battlefield, in almost complete darkness, many of the Norman knights rode unsuspectingly into a deep ravine, which was completely concealed by bushes and brambles. Those men and horses that survived the sudden headlong plunge found themselves assailed by missiles, as a band of select men who had rallied nearby aimed a hail of spears and stones upon them, slaying every survivor in a last frenzy of revenge. Eustace and some fifty knights turned back, only to be halted by William. Here Eustace was wounded by a blow between the shoulders from an unseen hand, but William led the men forward once more to beat off this last stand.

The incident was an apt end to a battle which had been fought with such savage bravery by both sides, and should have taught William much about the Anglo-Saxon character. That it did not was to be a tragedy for both Norman and Anglo-Saxon, and to prolong the conquest of England for another three and a half years.

8
The
Conquest of
Southern England

The Normans spent the entire day after the battle of Hastings burying their dead and treating their wounded: the English dead, apart from Harold and possibly his two brothers, were left where they had fallen, and Orderic reported seeing heaps of bones on the battlefield when he visited it seventy years later.

On the following day William withdrew to his fortified base at Hastings. The Anglo-Saxon Chronicle says of this move: 'Duke William returned to Hastings, and waited there to see if there would be any surrender. . . .' There was none, nor could William have seriously expected any. Harold and his two brothers had died on the field of Hastings, and with them had died almost all the housecarls. Three of the five great earldoms of the kingdom were without earls, but William knew he had defeated only a part of the military forces available to the realm, and neither of the two northern earls had been at Hastings. There was also the aethling Edgar. Even now a new leader might be emerging to provide a focal point for a new army to concentrate upon, and William's battered and depleted army was in no condition to fight another major battle.

William's losses on the 14th have been estimated by

Lieutenant-Colonel Lemmon at about thirty per cent, including both the dead and those incapacitated by their wounds. In view of the length and bloodiness of the battle, this seems a more than reasonable estimate. He could not use his sailors and non-combatants in land battles, and in any case needed the former to man part of the fleet, but he no doubt pressed into service for garrison duty at the Hastings and Pevensey forts all those who were capable of wielding spear or sword. Nevertheless, of the 8,000 men with whom William had begun the battle of Hastings, it is doubtful if he had more than 5,300 available for any further fighting. Bearing in mind the losses in horses – William himself had three cut from under him – it is likely that no more than twenty-five per cent of that total, say 1,300 or 1,350, could be mounted. This was hardly sufficient to occupy or conquer a kingdom the size of England – unless the English could be caught off balance immediately after their defeat at Hastings and the loss of their king.

We know William stayed for five nights at Hastings after the battle. In the circumstances he is hardly likely to have wasted five days, except by necessity. His army had been severely mauled, suffering heavy losses in an exceptionally prolonged battle. According to the history of the half-English Eadmer, who was born in 1060 and who questioned men who had fought at Hastings, the Norman losses were so heavy that the survivors concluded that their victory was 'without doubt entirely due to a miracle of God'. It is far more likely that William withdrew to his fortified base so that his battle-weary army could rest and recover, meanwhile despatching ships to Normandy with news of his initial triumph and to bring back urgently needed reinforcements, while at the same time foragers were sent out to meet the ever-present need for supplies. He may have needed the five days for reinforcements to reach him, though not many could have been raised in such a short period, so he is unlikely to have received any reinforcements so soon; or it may have taken his army five days to recover from the effects of the battle. This latter view would tend to confirm that Harald Hardrada was defeated at Stamford Bridge partly because his army simply could not endure two great battles within the space of only five days. It must be remembered that mail could not prevent severe bruising or broken bones, and it was normal for many survivors of a battle to have minor wounds, which, although not actually rendering them useless, would certainly have affected their performance for a week or two.

William must have recognized the need for speed after Hastings, not only because a second army might be assembling to oppose him again, but also because his army needed winter quarters and a great deal of food: he could not remain in the ravaged Hastings district much longer, for his army had now been living off this restricted area for nineteen days. The Anglo-Saxon Chronicle passage quoted at the beginning of this chapter continues: '. . . but when he realised that none were willing to come to him, he marched inland with what was left of his host, together with reinforcements lately come from oversea, and harried that part of the country through which he advanced until he came to Berkhamsted.'

Having defeated a major army in the field, the normal follow-up would be to seize the capital, the centre of government and power. However, in 1066 there were two main centres of power in England; the old capital of Winchester, which was still the seat of the Treasury, and London, the chief commercial city of the realm, which Harold had used as his capital and where his *Witena gemot* still waited. London was also an assembly point for the fleet, only a part of which had sailed round the south-east coast to 'blockade' Hastings, and was the most likely centre of any future resistance. But any movement by William from the Hastings peninsula was hindered by the terrain, which had made it such a safe place for his initial base. Movement to the immediate west was rendered difficult by the Sussex marshes, while to the north lay the Andredsweald, some twenty miles deep and eighty miles in length, reaching almost to Winchester. Only a single road pierced this forest in the direction of London, and any advance directly on London by that route would obviously be extremely hazardous. The only other route from Hastings was a circuitous minor road to the important fortified port of Dover, where, William had been warned, a great many English were gathering. Not far from Dover was

Canterbury, the ecclesiastical capital of the realm, and from Canterbury there was a major road to London which would take William round the eastern end of the Andredsweald and enable him to approach London via the flat and open country just south of the Thames. On 20 October William marched his army out of the Hastings peninsula, heading northwards to circle Rye Bay before turning east.

The chroniclers' accounts from this point until William's coronation in London are so sparse that there is insufficient evidence to trace William's movements with any accuracy. Fortunately, this gap has been meticulously researched and filled by the works of the Hon. F. H. Baring and Dr. G. H. Fowler. Baring noticed that in south-eastern England the value of manors as recorded for 1067–68 was in many cases more than twenty per cent lower than the value recorded at the time of King Edward's death. He plotted 217 of these manors and found that they occurred along the possible lines of march taken by William's army. It also emerged that the spoliated manors, except in the area north of London, were in clusters, at intervals of approximately twenty-five miles, and from this it was concluded that the usual length of a day's march was around twenty-five miles, with the following day spent in foraging. (It is possible that a combined infantry–cavalry force, or all-infantry force, might have marched twenty-five miles in two days, halting to forage on the third day, as it could have carried sufficient supplies to make one overnight stop without foraging.) Fowler made a closer study of the despoliation in Bedfordshire and neighbouring counties, plotting William's line of march from Wallingford to Berkhamsted.

By following the lines of despoliation thus revealed, Baring and Fowler were able to reconstruct with a fair degree of certainty the manoeuvres carried out by William after Hastings, which resulted in the collapse of all further resistance in the south-east. The following description of William's movements is therefore based on the works of these two writers.

The despoliation has been referred to by some writers as devastation, a deliberate policy of terror to induce a swift surrender, but in fact Dr. Fowler has shown that the pillaging

William's movements between 20 October and 10 December, 1066. The coastline between Hastings and Pevensey is approximately as it would have appeared in 1066.

along William's line of march was consistent only with that necessary to feed an army marching through enemy territory, and was not nearly so widespread or damaging as the pillaging carried out by the northern rebels in 1065! William and his magnates wished to possess a rich and prosperous land, not a devastated one, and when William *did* wish to subdue the English by devastation of the land, as in the north after the revolts of 1069, he did this so thoroughly that some areas remained barren and uninhabited even after his death eighteen years later.

William's first halt after leaving his base at Hastings was Northiam, and as this is such a short distance from Hastings it is probable that he sent parties out from Hastings to forage, then concentrated the army at Northiam for the march. From Northiam he continued northwards, detaching a small force at Tenterden to burn Romney, where it is believed one or both of the Norman ships lost in the crossing had landed and the crews been slain. (William of Poitiers says only that 'He took what vengeance he would for the slaughter of his men,' and it is possible the men of Romney had attacked some of William's foragers.) This was William's only deliberate harrying and was no worse than the inhabitants might have expected from their own lord if they had angered him. The army was then able to march eastwards, and made its next stop at Folkestone, where it may have erected a motte and bailey castle, as the damage around the town indicates a garrison was left here. From there William marched on Dover and deployed his army across the road to Canterbury, effectively isolating the fortified town and port.

A crowd of frightened refugees seems to have gathered at Dover, seeking safety rather than concentrating to oppose the Normans, and the demoralized garrison surrendered before any move could be made against it. William spent a week improving the defences of the port and whilst here his army was hit by an epidemic of either dysentery or gastro-enteritis. William could not afford to wait indefinitely in Dover for his men to recover, and when he marched up the Roman road towards Canterbury on or about 31 October, he left behind a third of his army,

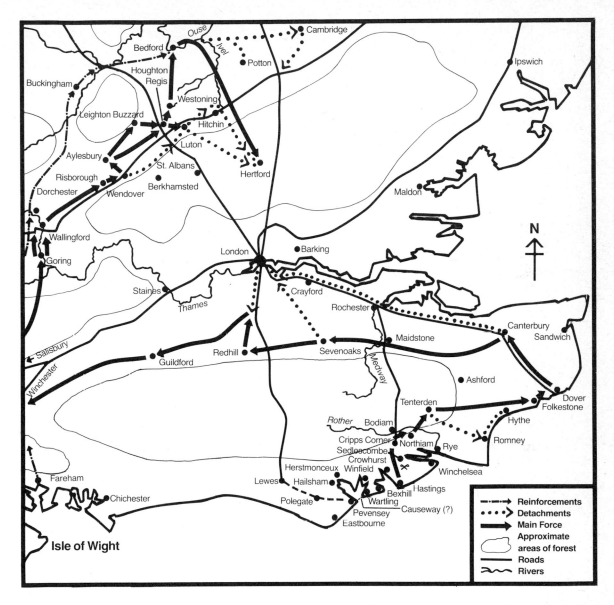

Reinforcements
Detachments
Main Force
Approximate
areas of forest
Roads
Rivers

mostly because of illness, though some fit men must have remained to garrison this important fortress.

Before turning inland, William had therefore secured a line of fortified posts along the English coast; at Pevensey, Hastings,

Folkestone and Dover. Possession of these ports deprived the English fleet of its bases on the south-east coast, and at the same time provided harbours at which reinforcements from Normandy could arrive safely. It is also important to remember that the function of a Norman motte and bailey castle was to provide a centre of power, from which the garrison could ride out to maintain control over the surrounding countryside, or 'hole-up' until reinforced if the enemy's army arrived in the area. William was to follow the same pattern of conquest and fortification wherever he went.

Canterbury surrendered to William before he arrived at the city, and here the men of Kent came in to submit 'like flies settling on a wound', as Guy of Amiens put it. William had secured his rear and lines of communication with Normandy, occupied the chief ecclesiastical city of the realm, and the way to London now lay open before him. But London was on the north bank of the Thames and William could neither attack nor besiege it from the south, except by way of a single bridge linking the city to the suburb of Southwark on the south bank. Therefore he despatched 500 cavalry, with about the same number of infantry following in support, on a lightning attack on Southwark in the hope of seizing the southern end of the bridge and bringing about a surrender by this demonstration of force. At the same time the remainder of the army marched due west, heading for Nutfield in Surrey (near Redhill): from this position it would be ideally situated for an advance to the north of London, or westwards to Winchester. William fell sick *en route* and stopped at 'the Broken Tower', a place which has never been identified, but which may have been Sevenoaks. William could not afford to waste a day at this crucial moment, and must have been back in the saddle as soon as humanly possible.

The cavalry attack on London defeated a force of Londoners on the south bank and burnt Southwark, but failed to secure either London Bridge or the surrender of the city. William must also have learnt about this time that the *Witena gemot* in London had elected Edgar the Aethling as king. The Anglo-Saxon Chronicle is in fact rather vague on this subject: 'Archbishop

Ealdred and the citizens of London wished to have Prince Edgar for king, as was indeed his right by birth, and Edwin and Morcar promised that they would fight for him, but always when some initiative should have been shewn, there was delay from day to day until matters went from bad to worse, as everything did in the end.'

There is no greater condemnation of Harold's refusal to accept Gyrth's advice than this bleak statement. London was crowded with frightened and hungry refugees, no way to begin a determined attempt to withstand a siege. The *Witena gemot* was not a king with a single voice and was accustomed only to advising, not ruling: it was, in any case, beset by fears and jealousies, real and imaginary. Edgar may well have been elected as the next king, but he was only fourteen years old and perhaps not yet speaking English well; what could he do, or inspire?

Edwin and Morcar had arrived in London with the only substantial organized force left in the kingdom, but they were teenagers, virtually unknown to the people of the south. The only other surviving earl was Waltheof, himself only twenty, a minor figure at this stage, and again from a northern family, the house of Siward. Harold's three sons had no official rank, were also teenagers, and it is doubtful if they would have been in London at this time. The Archbishops Stigand and Ealdred, and the Bishops Wulfstan and Walter of Hereford, were present in the *Witena gemot* and had strong voices there, but they were old and were not men of action. There was no one else, no one to step forward to grasp the country by the scruff of the neck and shake it into resistance, and lacking a leader the English frittered away the valuable days after Hastings. Only Ansgar, Sheriff of London and Middlesex, who had been badly wounded at Hastings and was now carried about in a litter, seemed capable of arousing any martial spirit, and he set about the difficult task of defending London itself.

Some 400 to 450 knights had landed at Fareham at the end of October to reinforce William's army and on or about 6 November William resumed his advance, not towards London but towards the old capital of Winchester. The reinforcements moved up to the region round Andover, thus sealing Winchester off from any support from the west or north. William halted about five miles from the city, and here representatives from Winchester formally submitted to him. Harold's sister Edith, Edward the Confessor's queen, was now in William's protection, and he had seized not only the ancient seat of power of the West Saxon kings but also the English treasury. There can be little doubt that the capture of both the religious and political centres of the kingdom signalled the end of any potential resistance in many parts of southern England, and individual lords, both lay and ecclesiastical, began to submit to William in the hope of retaining their lands and property under him.

After spending four nights in the Winchester area, William began his advance against London. The infantry followed the ancient West Ridgeway and crossed the Thames at Goring, but William and the cavalry followed the Icknield Way to cross at Wallingford. The force of cavalry formerly at Andover may have continued to cover William's flank, reaching the Thames farther upstream, for there was considerable despoliation in the Sutton Courtney area. It is believed William had a motte and bailey castle built at Crowmarsh, on the north bank of the river and within the existing ramparts of an Anglo-Saxon burh. That Wallingford was an important crossing place on the Thames – the vital link in the route between Winchester and London – is confirmed by the presence of the barracks of the royal housecarls here, occupying an area of fifteen acres.

While William fortified Wallingford, probably during the third week of November at the latest, Archbishop Stigand arrived to submit to William and swear fealty, at the same time denying Edgar. It is strange that it should have been Stigand of all people who approached William at this time. Morale in London would have been low once it was known the Normans had crossed the Thames: an attack on London could be expected shortly and an embassy might well have been sent to negotiate with William. Both William of Poitiers and Guy of Amiens hint that Stigand may have represented a large body of opinion in London; other writers have suggested Stigand sought only to secure his own future, and certainly William allowed him to remain archbishop for almost five more years, and even consecrate a Norman bishop, despite the Pope's displeasure and the objections of the Norman ecclesiastics. Perhaps Stigand came as an envoy but yielded to William's offer to respect his office. Stigand would not have been above retaining power at the expense of the other English magnates, nor would William have hesitated to offer such a bribe if it would make the chief ecclesiastical magnate of the realm his man and thus ease his path to the throne.

William's movements after the halt at Crowmarsh appear to be rather aimless, but Dr. Fowler has shown that William had three main objectives during this period and achieved all three: to seize as many royal manors as possible, for these were centres of English feeling and also the source of his future personal revenue; to seize as many of the Anglo-Saxon burhs as possible to use as fortresses; and to isolate London in particular and the south-east in general from any support from the rest of England.

At the beginning of the fourth week in November William commenced this phase of his campaign, the main body of the army marching along the Icknield Way on the north-west slope of the Chiltern Hills, which guarded the left flank of the column, to Harold's manor of Risborough and the royal manor of Wendover. Here the army split into three columns, the baggage in the centre continuing along the Icknield Way to Luton, the right wing (consisting mostly of infantry and moving only short distances each day) providing cover to the south of this route, and the main body on the left striking first northwards, to secure the royal manor of Aylesbury, then eastwards in two divisions to the valuable group of royal manors at Leighton Buzzard, Houghton Regis and Luton. This movement also cut the Watling Street and sealed London off from reinforcements from the north-west.

From Luton the baggage marched towards Hertford, which was the next concentration point for the army. The right wing wheeled east to cross a tributary of the Ivel at Langford, and shortly afterwards turned south to rejoin the centre at Hertford, sending a detachment to secure Harold's manor at Hitchin. The left wing again turned north, heading for Bedford and seizing Harold's manor of Westoning on the way. From Bedford the main body proceeded along the high ground on the west bank of the Ouse, crossed that river at one of the many fording places, and wheeled south towards Hertford. However, a detachment of cavalry was first sent eastwards from Bedford to cut the Ermine Street, and it also seized Earl Waltheof's manor of Potton. It then proceeded to Cambridge before turning south to head for Hertford.

It is possible that at the beginning of the advance from Crowmarsh a strong detachment of cavalry was despatched to secure Buckingham and to guard the left flank of the army. Riding eastwards, this detachment could have established a post on the Watling Street, then linked up with the left wing of the army for that column's advance on Bedford and Cambridge.

All columns eventually concentrated in the vicinity of Hertford, where the army was spread out over a wide area. A series of posts to the east now barred passage along the Ermine Street, while to the south-west a garrison at St Albans commanded the Watling Street. The string of garrisons left at the burhs and manors taken *en route* also ringed London to the north and west, and the city was thus cut off from the only areas from which any reinforcements might be expected.

We have no definite dates for this series of manoeuvres to isolate London, but Dr. Fowler estimates that the force which had the greatest distance to cover, that which seized Buckingham and later moved through Bedford and Cambridge with the left wing, covered some 150 miles at the most after leaving Crowmarsh. Even at only ten miles a day, allowing time to forage and establish garrisons and outposts at the places taken *en route*, the army could therefore have been concentrated round Hertford by the end of the first week of December; say 10 December at the latest.

William's army was now poised within a day's march of London. At this date the city had a population of between 15,000 and 20,000 and was still contained within the Roman walls, that is within the square mile known today as the City, although there may have been small suburbs outside these walls at Bishopsgate, Ludgate and Cripplegate. Westminster was highly vulnerable, being separated from the city by two miles of open country, but it is difficult to see how William could have invested London with his small army. However, at about the time William concentrated his army at Hertford, the English leaders in London seem to have decided that any further resistance would now be futile, and around mid-December all or most of them journeyed from London to Berkhamsted to submit to William. 'There he was met by Bishop Ealdred, Prince Edgar, Earl Edwin, Earl Morcar, and all the best men from London, who submitted from force of circumstances, but only when the depredation was complete. It was great folly that they had not done so sooner when God would not remedy matters because of our sins. They gave him hostages and swore oaths of fealty, and he promised to be a gracious lord to them. Nevertheless, in the meantime, they harried everywhere they came.'* Other chroniclers include the names of Wulfstan, Bishop of Worcester, and Walter, Bishop of Hereford, among the emissaries.

There is no mention of kingship in this passage, but William of Poitiers says that William was urged by these English leaders to take the crown, the emissaries advising him that they were accustomed to serving a king and wished to have one as soon as possible. This would have amounted to an election by the *Witena gemot* but, again according to his chaplain, William hesitated to accept so soon, preferring to wait until the situation was less confused and he could be sure there would be no rebellions before accepting the crown. However, he allowed himself to be persuaded by 'the unanimous desire of his army', and a march on London was ordered.

English chroniclers take the view that the occupation of London followed the surrender at Berkhamsted inevitably and without incident, but French chroniclers indicate that some form of resistance continued. William of Poitiers says that the city did not submit until the Norman army was in sight of London itself; Guy of Amiens gives a long account of preparations for a siege and negotiations between William and

*Anglo-Saxon Chronicle (D)

the Sheriff Ansgar; and William of Jumièges refers to a skirmish when the city was entered, the skirmish taking place either within or immediately without the city walls.

Most of those leaders who did not agree with the embassy to Berkhamsted would have fled before the Normans reached London: for example, the Norfolk thegn Eadric, who was probably in command of the English fleet, fled to Denmark, possibly with the survivors of the lithsmen. One of those who did not run was the wounded Sheriff Ansgar, and it is perhaps significant that William had him imprisoned, sent to Normandy, and kept a prisoner there until his death. It is impossible to tell what happened, but it does seem likely that there was some attempt at resistance by the people of London, possibly led by Ansgar. It could not have lasted long, and common sense would have soon ensured that there was no further resistance. All the leaders had submitted, fled or been imprisoned, and hostages were now held by the Normans.

William himself did not enter London at this time, but halted at Barking and sent a strong body of troops into the city to build a castle within the south-east corner of the Roman walls, where the great White Tower of London was later to rise. Meanwhile preparations were put in hand for the coronation in the great new church at Westminster, which at the beginning of that same year had witnessed first the funeral of its founder and, immediately afterwards, the coronation of Harold.

The ceremony took place on Christmas Day, performed by Ealdred, Archbishop of York, Stigand being barred because he was still unrecognized by Rome. William could not afford to let anything mar the absolute legitimacy of his coronation. However, Stigand assisted, in his capacity as Bishop of Winchester, as did the Norman Geoffrey of Mowbray, Bishop of Coutances.

The ancient rites as used for the English kings were followed, and William swore 'that he would govern this nation according to the best practice of his predecessors if they would be loyal to him.'* However, there was one departure from the accustomed order, imported from France, whereby the king-elect was presented to the assembled people for formal

*Anglo-Saxon Chronicle (D)

acceptance as their lord. The question was put to the English in their own language by the Archbishop of York, and in French to the Normans by the Bishop of Coutances. The representatives of both peoples replied, as was required of them, with loud cries of acclamation.

William could not be sure that London was his, nor that his coronation in Edward the Confessor's church would not provoke some form of rising. Therefore, Westminster was filled with Norman troops on 25 December, and the minster itself was ringed by Norman guards. These guards, mistaking the shouting in English and French within the minster for a riot, promptly set fire to the surrounding wooden buildings. Their intention seems to have been to break up any planned attack by flushing out the populace, but the result was utter confusion as the owners of the fired buildings rushed out and tried to save their property, while most of those in the minster rushed out in panic when they saw flames rising round them, and heard the cries of fear. Ordericus describes the scene vividly. William alone before the altar, deserted by all except the archbishops and bishops, and trembling violently. William had never shown physical fear before, and it is unlikely that he trembled thus through fear of an armed uprising. It is far more likely that he was seized by a superstitious dread, for at the very moment when the Grace of God should have come upon him and made him a king, there was a great tumult, the windows of the church lit up with fire, and all the people fled from about him. Momentarily at least he must have thought that God, whom he had used as he used everyone in his ambitious scheming, had turned against him.

After a moment the priests continued with the ceremony, to the central point of consecration, then coronation and enthronement, whilst smoke and the smell of burning drifted into the minster, together with cries of fear, anguish and anger. It was to prove a remarkable portent of what was to follow all too soon in an England under the Normans.

9 The Conquest of Northern England

The defeat of the English army at Hastings need not have signalled the end of all resistance to the Norman invaders, yet it did. Harold and his brothers were dead, and with them most of the élite housecarls, but half the potential military strength of the realm had not yet been called upon to fight the Normans, and the men of the south-west, much of East Anglia and the whole of England north of the Ouse had yet to see a Norman. However, all the surviving magnates had now submitted to William, either before his coronation or just after it, no leader remained to organize a co-ordinated resistance and the heavily populated south-east of England had been cowed by the apparent ease with which the invaders had for seven weeks marched at will through the land, taking the chief ports and ecclesiastical and political centres of the realm without a blow being struck in their defence. Not one community through which the Normans had passed during this period had offered even token resistance: Dover, with its new fortifications, had surrendered when summoned; and even London, with its strong walls and concentration of troops and men of high rank, had submitted with only a minor skirmish at most. Of course,

England lacked 'modern' fortifications, into which troops could retire to wear out the invader in prolonged sieges, but medieval warfare was not purely battles and sieges. Throughout the summer and autumn the men of England had been guarding their coasts when they should have been busy on their land. In September the Norwegians had arrived to harry large areas of the north, and for two months after that the Normans had pillaged their way through south-east England: the destruction of property and the means by which life was maintained, particularly at this time of the year, had crushed the ability of the people to fight, and men throughout the land were now too busy struggling to survive the winter to think of armed resistance.

It is usually accepted that at first William intended to establish a genuine Anglo-Norman state in which everything would continue to function as it had under his kinsman Edward the Confessor. He would have been prepared for some opposition, and expected to make some changes in order to secure his rule, but in the main it seems certain that he tried to govern his new realm through the existing civil and ecclesiastical hierarchy. In return he would have expected the traditional rights and revenues of an English king, but at this date it is doubtful if he envisaged any drastic changes to the English way of life. This was much the way he had acted when he secured the annexation of Maine.

His success depended to a large degree on gaining the loyalty of the English nobility, and his patronage of and patience with the aethling Edgar, who was granted large estates, and the earls Edwin, Morcar and Waltheof are proof of his good intentions in the first two years of his reign. Tostig's former lieutenant, Copsi, was made Earl of Northumbria in a mistaken attempt to rule the northerners with an English lord. Copsi was murdered by the Northumbrians after only five weeks, but was replaced in the autumn of 1067 by Cospatric of the Bernician house, who bought the earldom from William. Similarly, English sheriffs and other king's officials were maintained in their positions.

William also brought to a country now overrun by mercenaries and adventurers the strict peace and order exercised in his own duchy. His followers were told to conduct themselves as Christians in a Christian land: women were not to be molested, while brothels, excessive drinking and brawling were prohibited, as was all violence and looting. Brigandage was also forbidden, and all roads were made safe so that honest men could journey throughout the land without fear.

Yet simultaneously with this attempt to maintain the *status quo* came inevitably the first Norman settlement on the land and consequently the introduction of Norman feudalism. William had all the great estates of Harold as king and Earl of Wessex, and he now confiscated all the lands of those who had fought against him and fallen at Hastings, and of those who had not yet submitted to him. These lands, apart from those kept by William himself, were now given to his most loyal and faithful followers as reward for their services, honouring the pledges he had made before the invasion. This redistribution of land was conducted in an orderly fashion and William was careful not to antagonize the English unnecessarily. No Norman received any land that had been taken unjustly from an Englishman, while all those Englishmen who submitted to him were allowed to retain their lands in return for a large fee and taking the oaths of homage and fealty. Thus the pattern of William's progress to absolute power in Normandy began to be repeated in England from the very first weeks of his reign, for the bulk of the confiscated lands were awarded to his magnates, and all land, whether given to Norman or Englishman, was now held in *fiefs de haubert*, with the military service of knights as well as fealty owed in return for its holding.

As soon as possible William also carried out a tour of East Anglia, which because of its long, exposed coastline and Scandinavian sympathies was particularly susceptible to a Danish invasion. No opposition was encountered, only submissions, but nevertheless William established a series of castles here, and allotted them large garrisons of infantry and cavalry. His closest friend William fitz Osbern was left at a new castle at Norwich to watch over the east coast, and Odo was established at Dover to guard the south-east.

By the spring of 1067 William believed he had re-established peace and order in the realm under a joint Anglo-Norman aristocracy which had sworn loyalty to him. In March he went back to Pevensey, where he took ship for a triumphant return to Normandy. With him went the aethling Edgar, the earls Edwin, Morcar and Waltheof, Archbishop Stigand, and many other Englishmen of note: they went as guests, trophies and hostages.

William seriously underestimated the dogged character of the Anglo-Saxons when he assumed their external peacefulness signalled their subjugation. Nor did he appreciate fully how meaningful were the words of the English leaders when they submitted at Berkhamsted: the English did indeed need a king, and would perhaps have accepted William's authority in that role, but they would not or could not accept the heavy-handed local lords he left in place of the Anglo-Saxon earls and thegns. Before he departed for Normandy William instructed his lieutenants to show tolerance and goodwill to the English, but in his absence his subordinates soon began to oppress the people: 'Bishop Odo and Earl William [fitz Osbern] were left behind here, and they built castles far and wide throughout the land, oppressing the unhappy people, and things went ever from bad to worse.'*

Sullen resentment against a foreign tyranny soon flared into open rebellion in the absence of a king. In the west Edric the Wild, a Herefordshire thegn, formed an alliance with Welsh princes and devastated Herefordshire as far as the River Lugg. In Kent there was an attempt to seize Dover castle, and in the south-west the towns were uniting in opposition to Norman rule, with the centre of resistance at Exeter, where Harold's mother had fled with his three sons.

William returned to England on 6 December and, after spending Christmas at London, marched to Devonshire with an army containing Englishmen as well as Normans and other Frenchmen: the Englishmen may have been select fyrd, mercenaries, or landowners and their retinues giving their first feudal service. When the people of Exeter refused to submit, promising only to render to him the dues which they were accustomed to yielding to an English king, William laid siege to

*Anglo-Saxon Chronicle (D)   215

the city and after eighteen days caused it to surrender by undermining the walls. A castle was built in the city, then William returned to Winchester for Easter. The commander of the castle at Exeter later led an expedition into Cornwall and soon the whole of the south-west was under Norman lordship and control, with Exeter now a Norman stronghold.

Harold's sons raised a force of mercenaries in Ireland, like their father and grandfather before them, and descended on Bristol later that summer, but they were beaten off by the townsmen. They sailed on to Somerset, where they defeated the fyrd, but these were merely local raids in the traditional Viking style, and were never a serious threat to William. In fact, similar raids the following summer served only to force the English into closer support for their new overlords against a common enemy, and these last representatives of the house of Godwine never achieved any importance.

Mathilde had arrived from Normandy in time to spend Easter with William at Winchester, and by Whitsun William felt confident enough to crown her Queen of England at Westminster. But William's problems in England had only just begun. The aethling Edgar had already fled to Scotland, and soon afterwards Edwin and Morcar also fled northwards, where they found ready support from Cospatric in Northumbria and particularly at York, and allied themselves with their Welsh nephew Bleddyn, son of Gruffydd and their sister Edith.

William now launched his first campaign against the north. Advancing to Warwick, he threw up a mound and erected a wooden tower there, then continued northwards, probably along the Fosse Way, to Nottingham, where he repeated the process. The building of these castles as advanced centres of Norman power so overawed the rebels that William was able to enter York without a battle. He built a castle in that city and received the submission of many northern magnates, including Edwin and Morcar: Cospatric fled to Scotland. Whilst at York William also negotiated a treaty with the king of the Scots, and thus averted a Scottish invasion. He then returned to the south, building further castles at Lincoln, Huntingdon and Cambridge as he did so.

216

However, in January 1069 the north rose again, killing William's recently appointed Norman earl of Northumbria, Robert of Comines, and all his 1,000 soldiers in Durham. York quickly surrendered to the insurgents, but the castle held out and by a rapid march William was able to relieve the garrison and retake the city. He built a second castle on the bank of the Ouse before returning south.

Until this point William seems to have persevered in his efforts to rule England as a king and not as a military conqueror. He repeatedly attempted to maintain English magnates in their positions of authority and had not dispossessed the English landowners on a large scale. No important abbey had come under Norman rule, English clerks were still employed and despatched writs in English to reeves who were for the most part English, and in more than two-thirds of England his authority was still represented by earls of English birth. The rebellions of 1069 put an end to all this and provoked a dramatic shift in William's policy. It was now obvious that he could never be sure of his kingdom until he had complete Norman settlement on the land, and to achieve this he needed full military control. This meant the building of castles at all points of strategic importance; at all important towns and ports, and at all the road junctions and river crossings which linked them. Until such time as all land was given as fiefs to Normans, in return for military service, he had to employ mercenaries to provide large garrisons for these castles, and these could only be paid by taxes levied on the people. From the beginning of 1069, therefore, his rule became increasingly harsh and oppressive, and essentially military in character, for he was now engaged in the conquest of a realm which had never really been united under the English kings, and which had never really submitted to rule by Normans. As each district was brought under control, so the lands passed to loyal Normans, who built castles in which they and their troops lived, safe and aloof from the English people around them, yet dominating the surrounding countryside. It was a path familiar to William from his youth in Normandy, and he pursued it in England as relentlessly as he had done there.

217

In these circumstances William considered it wise to send his queen back to Normandy, and it was not long before the reaction he had now come to expect from the English occurred. In the autumn a great Danish fleet of between 240 and 300 ships, commanded by Sven's three sons and his brother, appeared off the English coast. It came at the invitation of the English rebels, who hoped the King of Denmark might now press his claim to the throne. Most of the English leaders were half Danish, and the people too would be content under a Danish king, particularly in the north and in East Anglia.

Following the traditional pattern of Danish attacks, the fleet raided Dover, Sandwich, Ipswich and Norwich before sailing into the Humber, where the Danes landed to join the men of Northumbria under Cospatric, the aethling Edgar, Earl Waltheof and the sheriff Maerleswein. The Norman garrisons at York rashly left their castles to engage these forces and were annihilated in the worst defeat ever suffered by the Normans in England. Other spontaneous but unco-ordinated risings also occurred in Devon and Cornwall, Somerset and Dorset, and – the most serious of all after the Northumbrian rising – in Cheshire and Staffordshire under Edric the Wild.

Leaving these other risings to be dealt with by his lieutenants in the various regions, William marched on York. The Danes fled before him and the deserted English rebels were forced to withdraw. William left part of his army under Robert of Mortain to watch the Danes on the Humber, then crossed the Pennines to deal with the Mercian rising in Staffordshire, which he is reported to have crushed without trouble. In William's absence the Danes returned and York was retaken, but on his return William bought the Danes off by allowing them to pass the winter in the Humber and to keep all the plunder they had taken so far. The English rebels were again forced to retreat.

William held Christmas at York, then set his army to systematically devastating Yorkshire so that no rebellion could ever take place in the north again. 'In the fullness of his wrath he ordered the corn and cattle, with the implements of husbandry and every sort of provisions, to be collected in heaps and set on fire until the whole was consumed, and thus destroyed at once all that could serve for the support of life in the whole country lying beyond the Humber', wrote Ordericus. Famine and pestilence followed and so appalling was the loss of life that even William's admirers spoke against him. 'Often I have seen fit to praise William according to his merits, but I cannot applaud him for an act which reduced both the bad and the good to common ruin through overwhelming famine ... such barbarous homicide ought not to go unpunished.'*

Early in the new year Waltheof and Cospatric again submitted to William and received back their earldoms. Neither Edwin nor Morcar had joined this revolt, but William no longer trusted them and they had taken up arms in self-defence. Now Edwin was killed as he fled to Scotland, and Morcar eventually found refuge on the Isle of Ely.

Although it was mid-winter William now marched westwards again to crush the men of Cheshire and the Welsh who were attacking Shrewsbury. This winter march over the Pennines caused near mutiny amongst his mercenaries, but William succeeded in bullying them through, subdued the region and built castles at Stafford and Chester. The systematic devastation in Yorkshire was repeated in parts of Derbyshire, Staffordshire, Shropshire and Cheshire. William then turned south and at Salisbury, confident that the English were at last crushed, he paid off the mercenary portion of his army.

Thus by the spring of 1070 William had established his authority over the entire realm by military conquest: thereafter he was troubled by only one minor rising, that of Morcar and Hereward in the fastness of the Isle of Ely, which he reduced by siege between 1070 and 1071.

By the end of this three-year period of revolt and oppression (1067–1070) the great Anglo-Saxon earldoms had ceased to exist and the redistribution of land had created such a sweeping change of lordship that England could never be the same again. The Old English aristocracy had been replaced by a Norman one, which in turn appointed Norman sheriffs and other officials. Some of the English nobles fled to Scotland, others to Scandinavia, Flanders, or even Byzantium, where they took service in the Varangian Guard and fought the Normans once

*Ordericus Vitalis, *Historia Ecclesiastica*

more, this time from southern Italy, and in the last decades of the 11th century Europe was full of English exiles. Those who stayed in England were gradually suppressed, either by the new feudal laws of the Normans, under which there was no longer any absolute right of inheritance, or by having Norman lords placed above them. Thus Edwin's son, as sub-tenant of Walter de Lacy, held only two manors in Herefordshire, where his father had held seventeen.

In the Church the same loss of authority prevailed. The Archbishop of York died in 1069, and in 1070 Stigand was at last deposed. Both vacancies were filled by Normans and thereafter Norman bishops and abbots were appointed as each major ecclesiastical office fell vacant. By the time of the Domesday Survey in 1086 there were only two English abbots of any importance and one English bishop (Wulfstan of Worcester), while only eight per cent of the land remained in the hands of Englishmen.

Such drastic changes could not be accomplished without creating a legacy of bitterness, which was not eased by the way the new aristocracy dominated the land from their castles, thus isolating themselves from the people in a way no English lord in his hall had ever done. The rift was widened by the suppression and dispersion of the English nobility, for the new lords had no English social equals and as a result everything French came to represent gentility, while the English language and customs were regarded as barbarous and the mark of social inferiors. Consequently, although the hatred of everything Norman lasted at least into the second generation after the conquest, it was not long before those who wished to rise in the world began to imitate their new lords, and Norman names, fashions and customs were adopted.

The Domesday Survey also shows that William was able to establish in England a form of feudalism which was superior even to that which he founded in Normandy. As conqueror William claimed all England, so that all the land of the realm was in his gift. He retained about one-fifth of the arable land for himself, and granted the remainder as fiefs, all held directly from him and therefore all owing the military service of knights to the king alone. This gave him a centralized authority and strength denied him in Normandy as a vassal of the King of France, and no other European king was to achieve such a great degree of control over his state for several centuries.

Almost all the major estates were granted as fiefs by 1070, with their military quotas definitely established to provide the military resources William needed urgently during the 1067–70 period, and it is estimated that by the end of the English rebellions he could muster between 5,000 and 6,000 knights from these fiefs. More significantly, so far as his power as king was concerned, was the way the fiefs were allocated. England before the conquest had been divided into several thousand estates: under William these were grouped into large lordships administered by fewer than 200 tenants-in-chief. Of this number twenty, together with twelve of the richest prelates, controlled some forty per cent (by value) of the land, while almost a quarter of England was held by just eleven of these magnates, all of whom were either relatives or close friends of William, and most of whom were known to each other and often closely related.

Most of these magnates held a similar position in Normandy, and because many of their sub-tenants had accompanied them for the invasion of England, these sub-tenants now became tenants and vassals of their lords in England. Thus England became a reflection of Normandy, another part of the duchy over the sea, and it is noticeable that many of the magnates – William included – preferred to spend as much of their time as possible in Normandy, returning to England only when their affairs there compelled them to. The number of Normans estimated to have come to England is in itself significant; perhaps 10,000 at the most in a country with a population of 1,500,000. As in Normandy 150 years before, the Normans established a small and exclusive warrior-aristocracy over the native peasantry and townspeople, using the land for their own purposes and gain, without a thought of nationhood, although they had unity under a king. With a French aristocracy using the French language to govern in the French feudal manner, according to mostly French laws and customs, and with Anglo-

Saxon literature and art replaced by those of France, England had become a mere appendage of Normandy – and William's bottomless coffer for his activities in Europe.

Until 1066 England might almost have been regarded as part of the Scandinavian world. Many of the people were part Danish because of Scandinavian settlement over the past two centuries, and at one time England had been part of Knut the Great's Scandinavian 'empire'. The Norman conquest, by changing the ruling dynasty and importing a new French aristocracy, wrested England from Scandinavian domination and the older associations with Germany and the Rhineland, and brought the country into a direct relationship with western Europe and the Latin culture of the Mediterranean.

The end of Norwegian dominance had been marked by the defeat of Harald Hardrada, for Stamford Bridge broke the power of the Norwegian kings for several decades, and Harald's son Olaf, spared by King Harold, became known as Olaf Kyrre – the peaceable. The stronger Danish connection did not last much longer. Sven joined his sons' fleet in the Humber in the spring of 1070 and, uniting with the English rebels on the Isle of Ely, raided parts of the east midlands, but by now the Normans had the kingdom so tightly under control that Sven realized there was no longer any hope of pressing his claim to the crown successfully and in the summer he signed a peace with William and sailed his fleet home to Denmark.

It cannot be truly said that the events of 1066–70 caused the Viking Age to end, for events had been bringing about that end for twenty years. (The fortified trading centre of Jomsborg had been destroyed in the early 1040s; Denmark's greatest trading centre at Hedeby was pillaged and burnt around 1050; the Norwegian kingdom of Dublin was lost in 1052; the death of Yaroslav in 1054 had marked the end of Norwegian power in the kingdom of Kiev; and the death of Thorfinn, greatest of the Orkney earls, in 1065 had been another severe blow.) But the defeat and death of Harald Hardrada in 1066, and the network of military garrisons established all over England by the Normans during the years 1067–70, were the final blows which, together with the spread of Christianity, sealed the fate of the

222

Vikings. By the summer of 1070 all effective Scandinavian interference in English affairs had come to an end, and the changes of 1066–70 signalled the end of Scandinavian dominance as surely as they signalled the end of the Anglo-Saxon way of life. From now on England was a part of Europe, involved in the mainstream of European political, ecclesiastical and cultural developments.

The unification of Normandy, Maine, Brittany and now England under one ruler was of immense importance to Europe, and no power could afford to ignore this new group of states in the north. For the rest of his life William was to be engaged in defending his possessions, and it is ironical that these attacks on him were co-ordinated after 1072 by Philip I of France, from whom William had offered to hold the crown of England as a vassal, and who throughout his long reign (1060–1108) strove to break the Anglo-Norman connection.

On William's death in 1087 Philip achieved this aim, for Normandy passed to the eldest son Robert, while William's next son, William Rufus, became King of England. Encouraged by Philip, the brothers were at war with each other from 1091 to 1096, when Robert went on crusade, pledging his duchy to his richer brother in return for a loan. On his return he was unable to prevent the succession of his younger brother Henry to the English throne on the death of Rufus in 1100.

By 1106 Henry I of England was strong enough to invade Normandy, and by his victory over Robert at Tinchebrai he reunited England and Normandy under one ruler. The relative importance of the two countries was now reversed, however, for Henry introduced the stronger English systems of government, formulated by William the Conqueror, into Normandy, and by c. 1135 the weaker and poorer duchy had been taken over by the richer and more efficiently organized kingdom, so that Normandy now appeared to have been conquered by England.

For nearly 450 years the Norman and Angevin kings of England and their successors were to wage intermittent war with their suzerains the kings of France, invading France time and time again in a vain attempt to retain their homeland. By the reign of Henry VIII all except Calais had been lost, but the long wars had forged a nation, sharply distinguished in social structure and personal temperament from the French, and it was Henry VIII's abortive invasions of France in 1522 and 1523, and the French landings on the English coast in 1545 and 1546, which finally led England into true nationhood and greatness, for as a result of these last cross-Channel expeditions Henry launched an extensive naval construction programme, the foundation upon which the great maritime British Empire was built.

The Norman invasion of England in 1066 is acknowledged as a watershed in European history, for it signalled the end of the barbarian invasions of Europe that had begun with the fall of the Roman Empire in the 5th century AD. It also marked the beginning of the English nation, which was to produce one of the greatest empires the world has seen.

Bibliography

Primary sources have been used as much as possible in the writing of this book because, despite the doubt cast upon their accuracy over the centuries, they remain our only real contact with the events. Their information has been backed up where possible by reference to other surviving artifacts of the period; tapestries, weapons, armour, equipment and ships.

PRIMARY SOURCES

Anglo-Saxon Chronicle, trans, G. N. Garmonsway, London 1953 and corrected 1960. The Anglo-Saxon Chronicle in fact consists of a number of chronicles covering the same events, notably: the A version, compiled at Winchester; B and C versions known as the Abingdon Chronicles; D version or Worcester Chronicle; E version or The Laud (Peterborough) Chronicle, copied in the 12th century from the Kentish Chronicle now lost; and F version, a bilingual (English and Latin) summary made at Canterbury after the Conquest.

Bayeux Tapestry, see book by F. M. Stenton and others, London 1965, which gives the complete tapestry in black and white photographs and has an excellent text; and the National Geographic Magazine, August 1966, which gives the complete tapestry in colour. The Bayeux Tapestry was commissioned by Bishop Odo soon after the conquest and would have taken about two years to complete: it was for display in the cathedral of Bayeux, consecrated in 1077. The tapestry is a great aid to historians studying the events of 1066, but is in fact based to some extent on contemporary written sources – especially William of Poitiers and a version of the Anglo-Saxon Chronicle – and on oral traditions derived from the Anglo-Norman court, notably from Odo himself and his entourage.

Chronicle of Battle Abbey, trans. M. A. Lower, London 1851. Written by the monks some time between 1150 and 1176, this chronicle is often unreliable but is useful for its knowledge of the local district.

Domesday Book, ed. Dr. J. Morris, Chichester 1975–   . This is still being reprinted at the time of writing by Phillimore & Co. Ltd. Seventeen volumes are currently available.

Eadmer, *Historia Novorum in Anglia*, trans. G. Bosanquet in *History of Recent Events in England*, London 1964. Eadmer was a monk of Canterbury, born 1060, and wrote his history about 1095.

Florence of Worcester, *Chronicon ex Chronicis*, ed. B. Thorpe, London 1848–49, 2 vols. Written before 1118, this is a balanced revision of several chronicles, some of which are now lost.

Guy of Amiens, *Carmen de Hastingae Proelio*, in *Scriptores Rerum Gestarum Willelmi Conquestoris*, ed. J. A. Giles, London 1845. Written *c.* 1067 and certainly before 1070, this work is usually attributed to Guy of Amiens, who was a Frenchman, not a Norman; the work was not popular at the time. It was lost twenty to thirty years later and the later chronicles were therefore based on the only surviving contemporary account by William of Poitiers, who probably used the *Carmen* as a source book. A copy of *Carmen* was not found until 1826. The work is often unreliable, but has some parts of great value.

Henry of Huntingdon, *Historia Anglorum*, ed. T. Arnold, London 1879. Written before 1154 and of limited value.

Ordericus Vitalis, *Historia Ecclesiastica*, ed. A. Le Prévost, Paris 1838–55, 5 vols. Written before 1138 by a Norman monk born in England. Ordericus met many veterans of the conquest and gives a more balanced account of the events than most Normans.

Snorri Sturluson, *Heimskringla*, trans. M. Magnusson and H. Palsson, Harmondsworth 1966 (King Harald's Saga only), and ed. P. Foote, London 1961 (complete work). For assessment of Snorri's value see Chapter 6.

Vita Edwardi Regis, ed. F. Barlow, London 1962. See Chapter I for comment on value.

Vita Wulfstani, ed. R. R. Darlington, London, 1928. The writer is somewhat prejudiced in favour of his subject.

Wace, Robert, *Roman du Rou*, ed. H. Andresen, Heilbronn, 1877–79. The most elaborate Norman account, written *c.* 1160 by a poet-historian born in Jersey, but not always factual.

William of Jumièges, *Gesta Normannorum Ducum*, ed. J. Marx, Rouen 1914. Written *c.* 1070 by a contemporary of William, but very brief.

William of Malmesbury, *Gesta Regum Anglorum*, ed. W. Stubbs, London 1877–79, 2 vols. Written *c.* 1120 and a comprehensive history.

William of Poitiers, *Histoire de Guillaume le Conquérant*, ed. and trans. with parallel Latin-French texts by R. Foreville, Paris 1952. Written *c.* 1072–74 by William's Norman chaplain and prejudiced in favour of the Duke. However, William of Poitiers had been a soldier before becoming a monk, and because he was familiar with military matters his account is one of the more reliable sources.

The following modern authors have produced parts of the contemporary accounts in a readily available form:

Douglas, D. C., *English Historical Documents*, Vol. 2 (1042–1189), London 1953. Contains extracts from the Anglo-Saxon Chronicle, William of Jumièges, William of Poitiers, Ordericus Vitalis, William of Malmesbury and Henry of Huntingdon.

Stubbs, W., *Select Charters*, ed. H. W. C. Davis, London 1929 (9th edition). Includes the *Laws of Knut* 1016–35 and *Rectitudines Singularum Personarum* 960–1060.

Whitelock, D., *English Historical Documents*, Vol. 1 (500–1042), London 1955. The introductions to this volume provide a good summary of the historical setting, and some of the laws are relevant.

SECONDARY SOURCES

Baring, F. H. *Notes on the Battle of Hastings*, Hastings 1906.

Barlow, F. The Effects of the Norman Conquest, in *The Norman Conquest: Its Setting and Impact*, D. Whitelock *et al.*, London 1966.

Beeler, J. H. *Warfare in England, 1066–1189*, New York 1966.

Beeler, J. H. *Warfare in Feudal Europe, 730–1200*, New York 1971.

Brown, R. A. *The Normans and the Norman*

Conquest, London 1969.

Chambers, R. W. *England before the Norman Conquest*, London 1926.

Clapham, J. H. *The Horsing of the Danes*, in *English Historical Review*, XXV, 1910.

Douglas, D. C. *Edward the Confessor, Duke William of Normandy and the English Succession*, in *English Historical Review*, LXVIII, 1953.

Douglas, D. C. William the Conqueror: Duke and King, in *The Norman Conquest: Its Setting and Impact*, D. Whitelock *et al.*, London 1966.

Foote, P. G., & Wilson, D. M. *The Viking Achievement*, London 1970.

Fowler, G. H. *The Devastation of Bedfordshire and neighbouring counties in 1065 and 1066*, in *Archaeologia*, LXXII, 1922.

Glover, R. *English Warfare in 1066*, in *English Historical Review*, LXVII, 1952.

Grierson, P. *Visit of Earl Harold to Flanders in 1056, in English Historical Review*, LI, 1936.

Haskins, C. H. *Normandy under William the Conqueror*, in *American Historical Review* XIV, April 1909.

Haskins, C. H. *The Normans in European History*, New York 1966.

Hollister, C. W. *Anglo-Saxon Military Institutions on the eve of the Norman Conquest*, Oxford 1962.

Lemmon, C. H. The Campaign of 1066, in *The Norman Conquest: Its Setting and Impact*, by D. Whitelock *et al.*, London 1966.

Lloyd, A. *The Year of the Conqueror*, London 1966.

Oleson, T. J. *Edward the Confessor's Promise of the throne to Duke William of Normandy*, in *English Historical Review*, LXXII, 1957.

Rudkin, E. H. *Where did William land?* in *Sussex County Magazine*, Vol. 11, 1928.

Sawyer, P. H. *The Density of the Danish Settlement in England*, in *University of Birmingham Historical Journal*, Vol. VI, 1957.

Stenton, F. M. *Anglo-Saxon England*, Oxford 1950.

Turner, G. T. *William the Conqueror's march to London*, in *English Historical Review*, XXVII, 1912.

Whitelock, D. *The Anglo-Saxon Achievement*, in *The Norman Conquest: Its Setting and Impact*, D. Whitelock *et al.*, London 1966.

Wilkinson, B. *Northumbrian Separatism in 1065 and 1066*, in *Bulletin of the John Rylands Library*, XXIII, 1939.

FURTHER READING

The following books were also studied but either have limited relevance to the exclusively military aspect of 1066, or do not concentrate entirely on that one year, but cover a much wider span of history. They are nevertheless valuable in obtaining a knowledge of the background to the events of 1066, and do have some passages of relevance. Those books which deal exclusively with 1066 include too many uncertain theories to be relied upon without weighing their every word against other authorities. However, some of their theories are worth considering, and these authors contribute much by making the reader take a fresh look at what has become a somewhat hackneyed subject.

Adam, R. J. *A Conquest of England*, London 1965.

Almgren, B. *et al. The Viking*, Gothenburg 1966.

Arbman, H. *The Vikings*, London 1961.

Brøgger, A. W., & Shetelig, H. *The Viking ships, ancestry and evolution*, Oslo 1951.

Brønsted, J. *The Vikings*, Harmondsworth 1960.

Brooks, F. W. *The Battle of Stamford Bridge*, in *East Yorkshire Local History Society*, 1963.

Butler, D. *1066: The Story of a Year*, London 1966.

Douglas, D. C. *The Norman Achievement*, London 1969.

Freeman, E. A. *History of the Norman Conquest*, London 1867–79.

Furneaux, R. *Conquest 1066*, London 1966.

Haskins, C. H. *Norman Institutions*, New York 1960.

Hollister, C. W. *The Military Organisation of Norman England*, Oxford 1965.

Howarth, D. *1066 The Year of Conquest*, London 1977.

Humble, R. *The Fall of Saxon England*, London 1975.

Jones, G. *A History of the Vikings*, London 1968.

Korner, S. *Battle of Hastings, England and Europe 1035–1066*, in *Bibliotheca Historica Lundensis*, Lund 1964.

Loyn, H. R. *The Norman Conquest*, London 1965.

Loyn, H. R. *The Vikings in Britain*, London 1977.

Matthew, D. J. A. *The Norman Conquest*, London 1966.

Norman, A. V. B. *The Medieval Soldier*, London 1971.

Sawyer, P. H. *The Age of the Vikings*, London 1962.

Seymour, W. *Battles in Britain*, Vol. 1 (1066–1547), London 1975.

Shetelig, H. *Viking Antiquities in Great Britain and Ireland*, Vols. 1–4, Oslo 1940–54.

Slocombe, G. *William the Conqueror*, London 1959.

Spaulding, O. L. *et al. Warfare, a study*, London 1925.

Stenton, F. M. *William the Conqueror*, London 1925.

Wilson, D. *The Anglo-Saxons*, Harmondsworth 1971.

Index